DATE DUE

DATE	ISSUED TO
OCT 27 1999	
FEB 28 2000	
MAY 13 2000	
DEC 11 2000	
OCT 24 2002	

DEMCO 32-209

FM 407 (1

WILDLIFE EXTINCTION

WILDLIFE

Drawings by Bob Hines
Wildlife Illustrator

Distributed by the Charles Tuttle Co.
P.O. Box 410, Rutland, Vermont 05701

EXTINCTION

Text and photographs by
Charles L. Cadieux

Stone Wall Press, Inc.
1241 30th Street, N.W.
Washington, D.C. 20007

Published March 1991

Library of Congress Catalogue Card No. 90-71599
Cadieux, Charles L.
    Wildlife Extinction
Wash., D.C.: Stone Wall Press, Inc.

ISBN 0-913276-59-6

Credits

Dust Jacket Photography by Charles Cadieux

Chapter
1   Cartoon courtesy of J.N. "Ding" Darling Foundation
     Photo by Charles Cadieux
2   Photo courtesy Oregon State Office, Bureau of Land Management
3   Drawing by Bob Hines
     Photo by Charles Cadieux
5   Photos courtesy of Wyoming Game and Fish Department—
     LuRay Parker
6   Drawing by Bob Hines
7   Drawings by Bob Hines
8   Drawing by Bob Hines
9   Drawing by Bob Hines
10   Drawing by Bob Hines
12   Drawing by Bob Hines
     Photo courtesy of Florida Game and Fresh Water Fish
     Commission—Jim Reed
15   Drawing by Bob Hines
21   Drawing by Bob Hines
27   Photos by Charles Cadieux
32   Photo courtesy of Florida Game and Fresh Water Fish
     Commission
35   Photo courtesy of Zoological Society of San Diego—Ron Garrison

Acknowledgements

Thousands of people have helped me put together this plea for endangered wildlife. Hundreds of people have contributed directly by furnishing data, by giving me facts, or by pointing me to answers I sought in vain when working alone. At the risk of omitting many who have helped me, I'd like to acknowledge the important help given me by the following:

Phil Million, Tom Smylie, Megan Durham, Norma Upgrand, Roy Tomlinson and Dr. Jim Lewis of the U.S. Fish and Wildlife Service; John Viser III, Executive Director of the Berry B. Brooks Foundation; Lonnie Williamson of the Wildlife Management Institute; Jack Lorenz of the Izaak Walton League; Ted Williams and George Laycock and Les Line of the *Audubon Magazine*; Chris Wille, Audubon's man in Costa Rica; Bill Turner of the Denver Zoological Park; Harry Tennison of *GAME COIN INTERNATIONAL*; the many wildlife professionals in seven African nations who patiently answered hundreds of questions, especially John Ledger of the Endangered Wildlife Trust in Johannesburg; LuRay Parker of the Wyoming Game and Fish Department; and last, but certainly not least, my wife of 45 years, Elida, who put up with extended field trips, with my long hours at the word processor, and with a husband whose thoughts were all too often on the words of this book rather than on the happenings of the day.

WILDLIFE EXTINCTION is dedicated to the
Berry B. Brooks Foundation of Memphis, Tennessee—
honoring the memory of a sportsman-hunter-Conservationist
by working for the best interests of wildlife worldwide.

Table of Contents

Preface

As wild species after wild species is pushed to the brink of extinction, with some disappearing forever each day, what should our role be in this intriguing soap opera of evolution?

"Chuck" Cadieux's work on endangered wildlife says every bit as much about *homo sapiens* as it does about wild creatures. His book is a fascinating look at what we humans are doing to the world around us, using the fish and wildlife we share the planet with us as so many "canaries in the mine."

Cadieux's book, one of many he has given us about the natural world he understands so well, is often as alarming as it is enlightening, educational, and entertaining. It is also controversial and saddening. Controversial because Cadieux doesn't mince words when it comes to the subject of human population growth and its impact on the quality of life for all species inhabiting the planet. Though the author most eloquently describes several highly encouraging case histories of wildlife species being brought back from the precipice of extinction, he does not hold out much hope for the future—given the course we humans are following today.

I've always thought that if any American writer were the personification of "Mark Trail," the conscience of our newspaper comic section, it would have to be "Chuck" Cadieux. Like Trail, Cadieux tells wildlife stories in a way that immediately involves the reader in the trials and tribulations of the critters featured in that day's adventure.

It is this "Trailistic" style that makes Cadieux so readable. He brings us the whole picture of the plight of endangered wildlife in a series of fascinating snapshots of the battles being waged for the integrity of wild ecosystems. Some fights, such as the one being waged over the old growth forests of the Pacific Northwest—with the Northern Spotted Owl as the species on center stage make front page news today. Others, such as the now nearly legendary success stories of the return of the whooping crane and bald eagle, while not as topical, are nevertheless still front page news when it comes to our ability to save the most critically threatened of the world's wild animals.

The story of the dusky seaside sparrow, while tragic, offers us important lessons in what to do before it is too late and emphasizes the painstaking steps that are absolutely vital if we are to prevent the disappearance of a species.

Cadieux's story of a male red wolf raising a litter of pups after its mate was devoured by an alligator is another reason Chuck's writing is so special. By relating that real life experience, the author brings us into the realm of the animals themselves and helps us understand both the natural and man-made trials they face in their struggle for survival.

In *Wildlife Extinction*, Cadieux takes the reader around the world and gives us an estimate of the numbers of animals left for each species discussed and a look at what is being done worldwide to halt the loss of the planet's threatened and endangered wildlife. He also shows us how over-protection can sometimes do more harm than good and discusses the thorny question of whose right it is to determine the value of one species over the other.

Cadieux also provides us with a hard look at the question of zoos and wild-life parks and takes a tough and, to some, what will be a surprising stand on the question of caging remnant populations of endangered animals.

Another thorny question—that of waterfowl hunting at a time when duck populations are at near record lows—is also a part of Cadieux's bold and extremely broad look at the impacts of humans on wildlife of all types. Some of his conclusions will be hotly debated among hunters and other wildlife conservationists, and that is exactly what should come from a thorough reading of this book. Cadieux doesn't ignore the tough issues or refrain from advising us and that is to our benefit and that of the world's increasingly threatened wildlife populations.

—Jack Lorenz
Executive Director,
The Izaak Walton League of America

1

Must They Disappear?

Thousand of species of wildlife have disappeared into the mists of extinction; more thousands are on their way to extinction. This is not a phenomenon of North America, nor is it only a sign of modern times. All over the world, species are becoming extinct. What is so dreadful is that they are now becoming extinct through our fault. As members of the human race, we must say *"Mea culpa, mea culpa, mea maxima culpa"* in the cases where wildlife species are lost through our fault. Some extinctions, obviously, are not laid at our doorstep. But we are worried about the constant day-by-day loss of wildlife species. **MUST** this happen? Is it within man's power to stop this remorseless march into oblivion? Can mankind stem the tide?

Must they disappear?

My personal answer is "Yes, they will continue to disappear, the rate of loss perhaps even accelerating—as long as mankind continues to crowd them out of existence." The first enemy of wildlife is the fertile womb of human females, the begetting of more humans than there is room for on this small planet. Obviously, the female womb cannot be filled without the cooperation of the human male—both sexes are guilty. There is plenty of blame to go around.

Obviously, there can be no wildlife species if mankind becomes so numerous that there is no longer room for humans to stand or habitat for animals to dwell. You accept that, of course, but you say that we need not dread that *reductio ad absurdum* scenario. But let us forget emotion and skepticism and look only at mathematics.

1

The world's population now is estimated at 4.2 billion. One fourth of that staggering total is Chinese. 800 million of our numbers are in India, and the Indian experts predict that their population will be bigger than China's population in a few years. As evidence they point to the obvious—India is adding new people at the rate of 16 million per year. India is alarmed. Saroj Kharpade, India's minister for Health and Family Welfare, puts it this way, "We are approaching a situation where there will be no houses, no water, no schools, no health facilities in adequate measure to take care of the increasing numbers." If the Minister's fears come true, will a billion Indians, unable to feed or house themselves, permit land to be set aside to save a tiger, or an Asian lion, or any one of the hundreds of species now endangered in India?

But that's in far off Asia, right? It can't hurt us. Wrong. Let's look a little closer to home. Mexico had a population of 79 million in 1985, according to best estimates. If the present trend continues, Mexico will have a population of 197 million in the year 2100. In 1990, we are receiving a veritable host of illegal immigrants from Mexico and from the countries to the south of Mexico where political conditions are much worse than in Mexico. We brag about our GROWTH in population. The Chamber of Commerce hails GROWTH in my home town of Albuquerque, New Mexico, where the population has risen from 45,000 in 1946 to half a million today. Growth is not progress.

But maybe this trend won't continue? India reports, in 1990, that they are sorely disappointed in the results of their efforts to limit human population growth—despite a farsighted educational program. Indian families continue to bring forth babies that they cannot care for, cannot feed, cannot house properly.

China has embarked on a strict program of limiting population growth, a program which includes forced abortion and compulsory contraception. In the cities a married couple is allowed one child, in the country there is supposed to be a two child limit, but this is not enforced because of the Chinese agriculture which is so labor-intensive that a family claims it needs more children to produce crops. China claims to be approaching zero growth reproduction—but that claim is not believed anywhere. Japan, perhaps, comes closest to achieving zero growth.

If the United States of America was managed to provide optimum conditions for both wildlife and humankind, our population should not be allowed to exceed 150 million—yet we are already past 250 million. *Legal* immigration is well above three quarters of a million persons per year, so that even if we had NO live births in the next twenty years (which is obviously impossible) our population would continue to grow by leaps and bounds. Illegal immigration probably adds more people than does legal immigration.

Our crowded world is already showing signs of substituting logic for high sounding principles when it comes to allowing immigration from over-crowded nations. The British have started sending Vietnamese refuges in Hong Kong back to Viet Nam. Reason? There is no room for them on that crowded rock. At the same time, no modern country has increased their quota to allow more Vietnamese to come to their shores.

Political unrest and dictatorships which oppress the people have swelled the flow of immigrants and would-be immigrants going to other nations. But the fundamental reason, underlying all other reasons, is that people come out of the country of their birth, because there is no room for them in the country of their birth. They are being crowded out, directly and indi-rectly, and there is no sign of a change from this condition.

Where do immigrants come from—immigrants that come legally to the United States? In order of importance, they are Mexico, the Philippines, Korea, Cuba, India, China, Dominican Republic, Vietnam, Jamaica and Iran. This is according to offical reports of the Immigration and Naturaliza-tion Service. With the possible exception of Iran, which has been ruled by a religious fanatic for a decade, and which has suffered unbelievable military casualties, all of these countries have one thing in common. All are over-crowded.

Every year for the past decade, African nations have suffered starvation caused by not having enough food to feed their growing populations. It is hard to say, but it is true that when American famine relief foodstuffs save the lives of five million women of child-bearing age, that action ensures that there will be ten million more people to face starvation in another decade. All attempts at making developing countries self-sustaining in food are doomed to failure if the population growth is not checked, and there is no sign of population control in any of the African nations. Nigeria has about 95 million people. The World Bank (hardly a radical organization) esti-mates that there will be 169 million in eleven more years. What chance is there to manage wildlife, to safeguard elephants, in a country where it will soon be impossible to feed people enough to keep them alive?

Thomas Malthus, English economist, died in 1834. But during his life-time he formulated the theory that bears his name and which states that the human population increases faster than the food supply, unless checked by war or pestilence. But "technocrats" have argued that the food supply can be greatly increased by such developments as better grain species, faster maturing crops and animals, and other technological wonders. If we are logical, we see that improving the food supply merely slows, but does not eliminate, the inevitable result that Malthus predicted.

According to the scientist, "We can take care of a doubling of human populations with improved food supplies."

"How about if the human population doubles again?"

With less certainty in his voice, the scientist answers, "We can handle that".

3

The Race with the Stork

And if it doubles again? The logic is inescapable.

In late 1989, the United Nations agency known as UNICEF predicted that one million children would starve to death in the next decade.

Africa today has an estimated total human population of 560 million. Its population is expected to reach 903 million by the year 2000 and this takes into account war, pestilence and famine. In the past ten years, Africa's elephant population has dropped from 1,700,000 to about 600,000. Do you not see any connection in those facts? Can you see any logical way out, except to reduce human population growth?

The simple, inescapable truth is that there are far too many people on this earth today. This overpopulation is crowding wildlife out of existence. If we cannot save ourselves from our own population runaway growth, how can we hope to save a species of wildlife?

Crowd them out of existence? I believe that is the most accurate way to describe the pressures against wildlife species.

Why do I say that? Come along and we'll take a look at the plight of some species.

The Delmarva Peninsula of Maryland, Delaware and Virginia has long been one of the greatest wintering grounds for migratory waterfowl. Fifteen years ago, it wintered as many as half a million Canada geese. Yes, they were hunted during legal season, but the hunting was intelligently managed and the number of birds returning each fall remained about the same. But the beautiful countryside of the Delmarva is very attractive to the burgeoning multitudes of humans who want to live in the nearby megalopolis —the area within 100 miles of Washington, D.C. and Philadelphia and Norfolk. The rich farmlands of the Delmarva are being sold for "development." The acres which fed geese during the long winter are now being covered up by shopping malls, condominiums and residental subdivisions. Fewer and fewer geese can find wintering quarters in the area any longer, and fewer and fewer geese winter there. Crowded out? Absolutely.

The Florida manatee, otherwise named sea cow—is the harmless half ton of blubber which feeds placidly on underwater vegetation, and harms no man. Recreational boating has invaded their waters to the extent that almost every one of the slow moving manatees bears the scars of the propellers of recreational boats. The environment belongs to the manatee. He was there first, and his need are few. He cannot tolerate sudden drops in water temperature, so he cannot move away. Mankind could move away, but mankind is not apt to turn Florida back to the manatee and the 'gator. The slow-moving manatee, peaceful denizen of the peaceful, slow-moving waters of Florida, is being crowded out of his environment by speedboats and slicing propellers. More about the manatee in chapter twelve.

The spotted owl, *cause célèbre* on the extinction front as these words are being written, requires "old growth" forest within which to hunt and to reproduce. Mankind is crowding them out of existence by cutting down the fully developed forests of the Northwest at an alarming rate. Americans do not need to cut those forests now—but the Japanese are willing to pay great sums of money for the great trees, and a very large percentage of mature forest produce goes directly to Japan, where it provides jobs for Japanese manufacture. If the big logs were cut only when America needed them, the milling and fabricating jobs would stay here in America. Today, an emotional struggle is going on—because lumbering towns have no other jobs to offer. Cutting the big trees extends the economic viability of those towns for a few months. When all of the tall timber is gone—the spotted owl is gone too. It will be a case of greed and short-term economics "crowding out" both the forest and the spotted owl which occupies that forest. But mankind is not apt to favor the owl in this popularity contest, nor can the spotted owl afford good lawyers. Unemployed voters do not reelect the representatives that caused them to lose their jobs. Unfortunately, the spotted owl has few people on its side, and owls do not vote. Mankind has crowded into the tall forests, crowding the spotted owl out—and out of existence. More about the spotted owl in chapter four.

Ducks are not listed as endangered species as of 1990—but they should be! Every indicator of duck populations points to a steady, inevitable, terrifying downward slide in numbers. Wintering duck censuses are taken, spring breeding population counts are taken by aircraft and land census teams, counts are made of breeding ponds, records are kept of hunter kill figures, by species. Graph these indicators and they point to one thing— complete extermination by mankind—using the method of legal hunting, sanctioned by supposedly intelligent management of hunting pressures measured against continental populations. A century ago the ducks could withstand these pressures, because there was half a continent to nest in, another half a continent to winter in, and only half as many people who wanted to hunt them. Today, mankind's agricultural practices have crowded them out by draining their sloughs in the most productive duck factory the world has ever known—the prairie potholes and sloughs areas of Iowa, North and South Dakota, along with southern Alberta, Manitoba and Saskatchewan. Mankind drains those sloughs so that mankind can produce more grain—for which there is no market—so that mankind's city dwellers can pay taxes to provide farm subsides, to store unwanted grain. Final irony is that subsidized production of wheat forced us to subsidize Communism in China and Russia—because we had to sell wheat at reduced prices. After all, we have to get rid of it so that we will have room to store another bumper crop—not needed by Americans. I grew up in what was the nation's best duck factory, the potholes of central and northern North Dakota. Now those productive areas have disappeared—crowding out the ducks to produce unwanted wheat. More about duck management later— with a chapter on why ducks are disappearing while most goose populations are flourishing.

6

The list of endangered species is very long—in North America we list such disparate species as the tiny Kirtland Warbler and the huge condor, the American crocodile and the majestic whooping crane, the arrow-swift peregrine falcon and the tiny blind salamander which never leaves its Texas cave.

In one of the most disgraceful episodes in man-caused extinction, the great African Elephant is now endangered! Growing hordes of humanity produced a tremendous market for ivory. Growing hordes of starving humanity in Africa produced a terrible need for money with which to feed growing hordes of children. Hunger and greed influenced thousands of Africans to ignore the laws of their countries and illegally kill the magnificent elephant for his ivory tusks. Elephant numbers have shrunk from nearly two million elephants a decade ago to less than 700,000 today. Synthetic materials which resemble ivory can be used for every legitimate need for the elephant's teeth. There is no cogent argument in favor of killing elephants —yet the slaughter goes on, motivated by the hordes of people in Japan and other orientals who want ivory curios, motivated by unthinking Americans who buy ivory curios, motivated by starving, poverty-stricken hordes of people trying to survive in Africa. Obviously, it is true that "only elephants should wear ivory." But crowds of humans want to buy ivory, and the future is mighty bleak for the largest of all land mammals.

In New Zealand—which Kipling described as that part of the British Empire "last, loneliest, loveliest apart"—dozens of species of beautiful birds are in danger of disappearing. They developed without humans until the last thousand years. They seemed to live in harmony with the first humans that invaded *Ao-te-roa* the "Land of the Long White Cloud". Incoming hordes of humans have changed the environment to the point where mankind is crowding out many forms of bird life.

In Asia, where one billion Chinese and half a billion Indians compete for the earth's fruits, the mighty Bengal Tiger, one of the most beautiful of all mammals, is in a precarious situation, valiantly protected by the Indian Government, even though the tiger kills hundreds of Indians every year. The Bengal tiger has been crowded into "tiger reserves" but there seems to be no chance that it can be restored to its former abundance—there is no room in India for more tigers. Other sub-species have almost disappeared in China, Sumatra and Indonesia, crowded out of existence.

South America, the world's richest repository of bird species, has seen the disappearance of entire genera, and the sad depletion of its avian wealth. Biggest enemy has been the senseless destruction of the world's largest rain forest. To make room for its millions of land-less people, Brazil has opened the entire drainage of the mighty Amazon for settlement. Slash and burn cultivation is eliminating the rain forest and caused the disappearance of species. Thin tropical soils, deprived of the forest cover, quickly erode and blow away and the "land-less" crowd of hungry *Brazilenos* moves

7

Volunteer Bob Tavernia cleans and applies glue to the Columbia mammoth tusk found in a stream bank in the Prineville District (Oregon)

deeper into the tropical jungle to despoil even more acreage. Is there a future for the brilliantly colored birds of the rain forest, facing the hungry crowds of land-less humans?

But as impressive as our lists of endangered species are, they are very incomplete when viewed on the long time scale during which evolution has changed so many species. It is irritating to true students of extinction to read where some pseudo-scientist estimates that X number of species becomes extinct every year. Most of the species which have disappeared were never even known to man, so how could anyone ever come up with a figure of species exterminated? We have to at least make their acquaintance before we can know that they have disappeared.

Paleontologists are discovering extinct species on a day by day basis. These species may have become extinct before man appeared on the scene. They may have flourished, unseen, along with mankind and are now becoming extinct for reasons not even guessed at. It is useless for us to mourn the passing of the giant lemur which disappeared from Madagascar when humans first came there, about 1500 years ago. We are not really sorry that we don't have to dodge *Tyrannosaurus rex* on our way down the freeway to

8

the office. This huge dinosaur probably was exterminated more than 70 million years ago.

Can we stop the disappearance of entire species? Do we want to?

First of all, we'd better take a look at the historic exterminations that have occured. There have been times when perhaps ten thousand species became extinct in a single year—because of climatic changes. There have been times when entire genera of fauna have disappeared at a single stroke. Man could do nothing about that—often it occurred before mankind came onto the world scene. In the next chapter, let's take a look at some of the great exterminations of the past.

2

Theories
of
Ancient Extinctions

Compared to the length of time that life has existed on earth, man is a comparative newcomer. If the history of the world was represented by a 24 hour clock, mankind has put in an appearance at about three minutes to midnight—at the end of history's clock.

Although man has done much to accelerate the rate of *known* extinctions, our effect has been miniscule when viewed over the millennia of geologic time. Consider . . .

Archaeologists tell us that several hundred species of very large animals lived on the North American continent before the coming of man. Then the earth grew much colder, as one of many Ice Ages caused the world to shiver. Polar ice caps piled up so much snow and ice—keeping it from year to year because summer didn't get warm enough to melt the glaciers—that a large portion of the planet's water was tied up in glacial ice. This lowered the sea levels and dried up the ocean between Asia and Alaska, allowing nomadic hunters to walk across from Asia into North America.

These nomads found a paradise for big game hunters. Giant animals, usually called *megafauna*, were roaming the continent south of the glacial ice. Camel-like animals, predecessors of the modern horse, antelope of several sizes and species, hairy mammoths, elephantine creatures of many descriptions—their numbers probably rivaled the big game herds of East Africa when the Europeans first described them.

According to fossil evidence, almost all of these huge animals became extinct in a short period of time. Short, that is, geologically speaking. It might have taken two years for them to perish, or it might have occurred over two thousand years. Viewed against the backdrop of geologic time, it makes no difference. Most of the large species disappeared; some of the smaller ones survived. An example is the distinctively North American species, the pronghorn antelope. The large ones became extinct, the smaller ones lived and we enjoy their speed and grace on the western plains today.

What caused the extinction of the megafauna? A theory that finds many supporters in this so-called enlightened age is that the human hunters found the megafauna completely without fear. It was possible to walk up next to the animal of choice and stick a lethal spear into that animal. According to this theory, the few hunters who were able to walk across the dry seabed of the Bering Strait between Asia and America—using primitive weapons, were able to exterminate these millions of large animals by killing them for food! We are asked to believe that hand-held weapons destroyed the mastodon and the tapir and the camel-like animals before these animals developed a wariness.

To my mind, this assumption poses very many more questions than it answers. Primitive weapons have never eliminated a species of wildlife—on any continent—in any age—to the best of my knowledge.

Consider the fact that the human population of Africa, assuredly more numerous than the glacial age nomads of North America, were not able to even make a dent in the big game populations of Africa before the coming of modern weapons. Arguably, African natives had more efficient, more deadly weapons than did the nomads of North America. Why did not this same extermination take place in Africa, or Asia?

Another theory holds that the megafauna of North America had not developed the ability to regulate their own body temperature. Products of a constant period of evolution, they had not experienced any reason to develop this valuable ability. Climates were sufficiently mild to allow survival at ambient temperatures. The same glacial age that dried the sea crossing from Siberia to Alaska cooled the great expanse which is now called Alaska to Florida. Unable to keep warm, the megafauna died by the countless millions. Across Siberia and into Alaska mankind has found mastodons buried in the permafrost, kept in the freezer for millennia, untouched except for a monumental case of "freezer burn"! Some species, more mobile than their larger companions, scurried southward ahead of the advancing ice and survived. Bolstering this theory of southward migration as a species-saving strategy is the survival of the smaller pronghorn and the demise of the large ones.

It is my personal belief that North America's megafauna perished by freezing, not by the spears and arrows of a handful of nomadic hunters. But we probably will never know the exact reasons with any degree of certainty.

There have been many cataclysmic extinctions over the millennia. Some of the more spectacular have probably been caused by cosmic collisions

11

which sent a heavenly body of great size crashing into the Earth. The impact sent up a huge cloud of dust, smoke and debris so dense that it blocked out the sun. Deprived of solar rays, Earth chilled rapidly and literally thousands of species froze to death. Other species found themselves deprived of plant food, for the absence of sunlight had stopped photosynthesis and plants froze solid.

The ejecta from the impact-caused explosion would have carried great amounts of nitrogen compounds high into the stratosphere. Here, normal chemical reactions would have produced acid rain—to a degree far greater than that which now imperils mature forests of Germany and trout lakes of our own Appalachians. This acid rain seems to have been lethal in the shallow seas, destroying *formaninfera* and zooplankton which were the building blocks in the food chain. With the demise of these minute organisms, plankton-eating species died. Sea mammals or salt water dinosaurs which might have eaten fish, found food scarcer.

Slowly, over a period of months or years or centuries, the dust settled out and the sun shone again. Collisions with meteorites are surely nothing rare in the cosmic world. Astronomers estimate that 200 million meteorites enter the earth's atmosphere every day. In fact, the flood of meteorites probably adds 900 metric tons to the planet's weight every day.

We have ample evidence that there were past collisions between our planet and some pretty sizable meteors. Fifty million years ago, a big one slammed into what is now Arizona. It blasted out a crater more than 570 feet deep and almost a mile across. Today it's a National Monument, administered by the National Park Service. In Oregon, the Willamete meteor was found in 1902. It weighed more than 14 tons, after burning up most of its mass in the fiery heat of friction attendant upon entering the earth's atmosphere. The Tungaska meteorite slammed into Siberia in 1908. Its weight was estimated at 200 tons and it scorched an area 20 miles wide.

Now think big! Think of a collision with a visitor from outer space weighing a thousand times as much. Can you imagine what might happen? Luis and Walter Alvarez of the University of Chicago postulated the idea in 1980 that a really big one had hit about 65 million years ago. That would put it at the end of the Cretaceous period—the end of the dinosaurs' tenure on earth.

Looking for geologic evidence that this happened, Edward Anders of the University of Chicago found levels of carbon in these geologic layers that were 10,000 times greater than the carbon deposits in layers under them and above them. Obviously, something burned at that time. Anders found evidence that this soot-like layer of prehistoric carbon was worldwide, appearing at the same geologic age level in Spain, Denmark and New Zealand. This surely hints at a huge fire, maybe one which covered the entire earth?

Studying this evidence of the greatest fire that ever was, scientists theo-

12

rized that the huge meteorite slammed to earth near the Bering Sea, or maybe in it. They found that such an impact would generate temperatures as high as 3,000 degrees Fahrenheit! The forests of North America and Siberia would have been set on fire, with heat-generated winds spreading the fire around the world! This collosal impact, estimated at 100 million megatons, sent soot, dust, dirt and iridium flying into the atmosphere to such an extent that it created a protonuclear winter, during which temperatures fell as much as 60 degrees in one week. Larger animals died. Smaller animals may have hibernated and lived through the darkness of this winter, which may have lasted as long as three years! Soot, thrown up by the explosive impact, absorbed sunlight to a far greater extent than does dust. Photosynthesis was completely stopped as the sunlight couldn't penetrate that filthy atmosphere. Without photosynthesis, all plant life died. Starved to death, the dinosaurs perished. Geologists can easily demonstrate the presence of the layer of iridium formed by this settling out of the dust.

Iridium is a chemical element which is quite rare in Earth's natural occurrence. However, it evidently was a very important component of the heavenly body which slammed into the earth. Geologic strata show a fascinating story of species extinction. Below a discernible layer of iridium, many species existed. Above that layer of iridium, those same species are no longer found. Using the simple logic of *Post hoc, ergo propter hoc* we must agree that the extinction was caused by whatever laid down that layer of iridium. Did a prehistoric collision between our planet and another voyager of the limitless cosmos cause the extinction of the *Brontosaurus?* Did a sudden deep freeze eliminate all dinosaurs, which were cold-blooded and huge, and leave the smaller mammals, which had learned how to regulate their body temperature?

In geologic formations near Gubbio, Italy, there is a fine example of what we are talking about. The rock is about 65 million years old. Above the iridium layer, there are no dinosaur fossils. Below the iridium layer, dinosaur fossils are common.

This tremendous extinction occured about 65–70 million years ago, at the end of the Cretaceous period. Before this cataclysmic collision, dinosaurs ruled the world. After this extinction, dinosaurs—for all intents and purposes—were gone. My belief that climatic changes caused the demise of the dinosaurs (they couldn't function in extreme cold) is stretched nearly to the breaking point when I remember that the crocodilians—also cold-blooded animals without the ability to regulate their body temperatures—survived this extinction and are with us seventy million years later. Is it possible that the crocodiles were saved by the insulating character of the water they lived in? It takes longer to cool down water than it does to chill air. Perhaps the margin of difference enabled the crocodiles to survive.

There is a growing feeling among students of the dinosaur age—a feeling that perhaps the dinosaurs were not cold-blooded, but had evolved the ability to regulate their own body temperatures. If this new theory turns out to be true, then we would have to rethink the entire matter of climate causing extinction of the dinosaurs. Perhaps, as Dr. Kenneth J. Hsu, eminent geologist-thinker, has suggested, "survival of the fittest might have been survival of the luckiest."

Quite apart from the possibility of cataclysmic extinctions, the disappearance of species is a constant, ongoing part of evolution. It helps to consider the evolution of species as if it were a slow-moving river, flowing steadily toward the future. Nature constantly experiments, always producing newer—not necessarily better—life forms. Some of them are successful and they endure. Others do not seem to work, and they disappear. The great Charles Darwin wrote. "What a book a devil's chaplain might write on the clumsy, wasteful, blundering, low and horribly cruel works of Nature?"

Contemporaneous with Darwin, some people theorized that species became extinct because the species itself—not the individuals composing that species—became senile. Sort of a situation where the species ran out of gas and gave up, with the analogy being drawn to the fact that human civilizations aged and became decadent—and disappeared. For example, the Roman Empire ran its course, weakened internally, and died. Could this have happened to species? While I feel that this theory is ridiculous, it is a sobering thought to realize that the average life span of a mammalian species is about a million years. Mankind, of course, has not existed that long in unchanged form. However, some sharks have been around much longer, and the lowly opossum has survived almost unchanged since the Mezozoic Age. How about the cockroach? Surely, it would have to be classed as a very great exception to the one million year life span theory. Some marine invertebrates, as shown by deep sea bottom formations, have survived relatively unchanged for 600 million years. Even the great extinction of 65 million years ago did not eliminate them.

Another theory held by those who felt that God created the world in perfect form and that no changes were needed was proposed with British arrogance. That British thinker said that God had created humans in perfect form. By this he meant the Englishman who was the perfect specimen. Retrogression—a steady deterioration of qualities scaled down the perfect (British) man into lower forms of life, such as the African, the Australian aborigine, and even the Mediterranean races which he deemed slightly inferior to the British. Throwing the theory of retrogression into the arena —ridiculous as it was from a scientific point of view—served to illustrate the fact that evolution does not necessarily produce "better" life forms, only "different" life forms.

The development of a new species does not necessarily kill off the old species which produced its genes, at times the new and the old species go their separate ways, and both are successful life forms.

14

There are countless side pockets and eddies in this flowing river of evolution. Species evolve to fit narrowly circumscribed niches. If the niche is too narrow, chances for survival over time are very limited. The Dusky Seaside Sparrow evolved to fit into a very distinct ecological niche along the banks of brackish or salt water marshes. Its very existence depended upon the permanence of this particular habitat. When man's "progress" erased that particular habitat niche, or at least squeezed it out of existence, the sparrow became extinct. This seems to be an obvious case of a "man-caused" extinction. Or was it just the result of a failed experimental eddy along the main stream of evolution? More about that sparrow in chapter five.

Another example will serve to illustrate this point even more clearly. In the eternal darkness of some caves in Texas, a blind salamander evolved. It was nature's attempt to develop a species suited to the absence of light. Untouched by the hand of man, this Texas blind salamander lived without sight, without even the concept of sight—for vision presupposes light. Removed from its protective darkness, the blind salamander would have two chances—slim and none. Unable to avoid any predators, it would be quickly exterminated. We can only consider the blind salamander as an interesting by-product of evolution, but a dead end which can hardly evolve into a higher life form.

Obviously, there have been many exterminations of species in which man played no part at all. It is certain that more individual species became extinct before man came onto the scene than after man came onto the scene. Perhaps there will be other cataclysmic occurrences which eliminate thousands of species once again. Perhaps *Homo sapiens* will be one of those eliminated.

The most likely threat to our continued survival lies in the probable coming of another glacial ice age. Evolutionary theorist Robert Ardrey feels that man is unlucky, because he came along in an "interstadial" period, doomed to evolve to the present state and higher, then perish after playing out our brief moment on the cosmic stage. Not to worry, though, be happy —for it won't happen in our lifetime.

But there are other extinctions which will happen in our lifetime, some of them caused by our actions, or inactions. They are of concern to us. If we can prevent even one extinction—we must. Whenever one species becomes extinct, we are the poorer. Wildlife serves in part as a "miner's canary." When the canary died, the air was unsafe for the miner to breathe and it was time to get out of the mine. When any species of wildlife becomes extinct, the world is less safe for mankind—and we cannot "get out of the mine." This fragile planet is our only home—if we cannot survive here, we become another extinct species.

"Ask not for whom the bell tolls. . . ."

3

We Can
Prevent Extinction:
Witness the Whooper

The least likely to succeed candidate for resurrection from almost extinction, the whooping crane, stands nearly six feet tall, cannot hide because of its bright white, black and red coloration, has to fly a dangerous 2,000 miles from its wintering grounds to its breeding grounds, usually only raises one chick per year, and does not attain sexual maturity until it is five years old. Talk about two strikes against it!

In 1941, there were only 21 whooping cranes in the entire world. Realistic odds on survival of this slow-reproducing species must have been about 100 to 1 against. Fossil remains show that the whoopers once were found from the Northwest Territories of Canada all the way down to Louisiana and even to Florida. They definitely were eaten by primitive man occupying this continent before the arrival of Columbus sounded the danger signal for so many species.

What caused their drastic drop in numbers?

Intensely territorial, the whoopers stake out their territory and defend it from all comers. As the plow broke the central plains, the whooper was forced to retreat, ever northwards, to find undisturbed locales for nesting purposes. The farther north, the shorter the "growing season." For the big whoopers the growing season was the short period between ice-out and the date when his single offspring could fly well enough to head south on the fall migration. Because the youngsters hadn't developed the strong flight muscles, the migrating birds had to stop very often on their southward trip which crossed Saskatchewan, my native land in the Dakotas, Nebraska,

Oklahoma and Kansas on their way down to their wintering grounds on the Texas shores of the Gulf of Mexico. That was a long and perilous flight, and fewer and fewer birds made it each year.

Things began to look up when the Aransas National Wildlife Refuge was created in 1937. Almost simultaneously, the Audubon Society sent Robert Allen to work fulltime with the remnant flock of whoopers. Perhaps more than any other person, Allen awakened the ecological conscience of the American people by his outpouring of writings about the whoopers. He can take at least partial credit for the wave of public opinion which coerced the U.S. Air Force into stopping flash bombing on a gunnery range near the refuge.

Slowly, painfully slowly, whooping crane numbers began to grow. Then in 1954, the long search for the nesting grounds of the whooping crane paid results and the world was told that the solitary big birds hatched their young in Wood Buffalo Park, well away from mankind in Canada's great expanses. Research into the breeding problems of the whooper quickly showed that they usually only brought one chick safely down the long journey. The reason was that the whooper lays two eggs, but begins incubation when the first one is laid. Thus one chick hatches out one or even three days before the other chick. Sometimes the parents merely accepted the hatching of the first chick and left the nest where the other egg chilled and the chick died. Even if both eggs hatched, the bigger sibling got all the food, and sometimes killed its smaller twin by stepping on it. Whatever the reason, only half of the eggs produced chicks. This turned out to be very important.

Numbers grew slowly from 21 in 1941 to 48 wild birds in 1968, 59 in 1971, then a disastrous drop to 49 in 1973. But the population base in 1973 must have been healthy, with lots of breeding age birds, for the trend turned sharply upward. In the fall of 1979, 119 whoopers made the trip down the length of the mid-continent to Aransas. At the same time, another flock was being created right along with the growth of the wild flock.

Noting that only one egg was usually hatched, biologists stole one egg from each of six Wood Buffalo nests in 1967, and "egg-napping" became an important tool in the whoopers struggle to avoid extinction. The egg-napping continued and the captive flock grew to 21. The wild flock brought MORE chicks south than they had before the egg stealing started!

The Patuxent Wildlife Research Center played tricks on the captive adults, using artificial lighting to create the 22 hours of daylight which the cranes would have known in northern Canada. Artificial insemination was resorted to when the cranes failed to pair off as they would have done in the wild. In 1978, two female whoopers produced a total of 19 fertile eggs.

Fortified by the knowledge that the "egg-napping" was not hurting reproduction in the wild flock, the U.S. Fish and Wildlife Service decided to create another wild flock—so as not to have all their whooping cranes in

18

one basket. Eggs from Wood Buffalo Park, and later from Patuxent, were inserted in the nests of Greater Sandhill Cranes nesting on Grays Lake National Wildlife Refuge in Idaho. The GREATER sandhill cranes hatched the whooper chicks and took them along on their much shorter flight down to the Bosque del Apache National Wildlife Refuge in New Mexico. That New Mexico flock has grown to number 34 individuals, but then something happened and the population is now down to 13. There seems to be a problem. Many of these birds have reached the age of sexual maturity, but show no signs of pairing off.

1980 was a good time to census the whooping crane. 76 cranes went north from Aransas toward Wood Buffalo park in Canada, 15 went north in the Bosque del Apache-Grays Lake flock and there were a total of 28 whoopers in captivity, most of them in the Patuxent Endangered Species Center. The world-wide population in 1980 was up to 121, a great improvement from the 21 birds in existence in 1941, but still not out of danger by a long shot.

But there were many dark clouds on this horizon. The Bosque wintering flock has failed completely as far as reproduction is concerned. That Bosque flock which numbered 15 way back in 1980, had now dropped to 13 individuals—and most importantly—no pairs! For the foreseeable future, the program of introducing whooper eggs into Grays Lake Greater Sandhills has been stopped.

Even the Aransas flock, which numbered 131 when they headed north in 1989, faced a serious problem. A three year old female of this flock died in 1989 of avian tuberculosis. The specter of disease has accelerated the search for a place to start a third flock.

Florida once boasted a non-migratory flock of whooping cranes, which disappeared centuries ago. Now the U.S. Fish and Wildlife Service is working with the State of Florida to set up a new population of whoopers, hopefully one that would not migrate.

Whooping cranes have captured the imagination of all conservationists, and of all bird watchers. Two events stand out in my relationship with the cranes which a Texas outdoor writer once called "a few loud-mouthed birds." The first happened up near the North Dakota-Saskatchewan border. We knew that a certain town drunk had killed and eaten an adult whooping crane. We had a box with his name on it, rescued from the town dump, which contained the feathers and lower leg bones of the whooper. We had heard a verbal description of "My daddy brought in a big white bird. When he held its head up over his head, the feet touched the ground." But we were not allowed to search the man's house, because the judge ruled that we did not have "sufficient cause" to suspect that he had killed the crane. The reason for the judge's decision was that the verbal description was spoken by the violator's daughter, and she was only nine years of age. The judge said that her testimony would be ruled inadmissible and that without

19

A white whooping crane stands among sandhill cranes on Bosque del Apache NWR in New Mexico

her testimony we would have no chance for a conviction. Forty years later, that decision still rankles.

The other event was on the Aransas National Wildlife Refuge in Texas. I was seated in a photo blind while 34 wild whoopers paraded past—in a driving rain! I didn't get any pictures, but I did gain an indelible memory. Each pair of whoopers kept one young chick between them as they foraged in the rain. About then, I began to hope for survival of the whooping crane.

We have seen the wild flock of whoopers grow from 15 in 1941 to more than 160 in the fall of 1989. Each year as the magnificent birds circle over Aransas and Bosque in farewell and then head north, we hold our breath (figuratively) until the next fall when they come back down the more than 2,000 mile migration path. We have cause for optimism in that the total population is growing. We have cause for hope in that there will soon be, we hope, a non-migratory flock. We have hope in that the scientists are learning much about the biology of the whooping crane and *should* be better able to see to the birds needs.

But, most importantly, public opinion has been aroused in two nations, and there is a tremendous drive to save the whooping crane from extinction. And I remind myself: If we can save the whooper, we should be able to save any species, even *Homo sapiens*, for the whooper was a most unlikely candidate for survival.

Tom Smylie, Information Officer for the U.S. Fish and Wildlife Service, has been very interested in the whoopers fight for survival for more than 18 years. I asked him for an up to the minute update in late summer of 1989. Here's what he had to say:

"When one hundred and thirty-one cranes migrated north from the Texas Gulf Coast in April and May, two stayed behind. The same two birds summered on the refuge in 1988. One, a three year old female, was found and recovered by Aransas National Wildlife Refuge biologists on April 21. She was placed in the care of the veterinarian at San Antonio Zoological Gardens in Texas where she was diagnosed as having avian tuberculosis. There is no known cure for the disease and she died on July 13.

"Another whooper was lost this winter on the Gulf Coast when a waterfowl hunter killed a four year old female crane on January 3, 1989. Her loss was exceptionally tragic because last fall she was successful in bringing her first chick to Aransas NWR. She was the first whooper known to have been illegally killed by a hunter since January 4 of 1968. The hunter first tried to hide the dead crane, then voluntarily turned himself in to authorities. He was fined $15,000 on federal charges, and the state of Texas has requested an additional $11,000 in restitution for damage to wildlife.

"On the positive side, it appears that the whoopers are having good success on the nesting grounds in Canada. Canadian Wildlife Service biologist

21

Ernie Kuyt reported finding 30 whooper nests in Wood Buffalo National Park in May. By late June, 21 to 26 chicks were seen. Fifteen eggs were transferred to the Patuxent Wildlife Research Center in Maryland where six eggs hatched. At the Patuxent Center eight experienced captive breeders laid nineteen eggs. Fourteen were fertile and nine hatched, making this the best production season for whoopers at Patuxent since 1984 when five females produced 31 eggs.

"Since 1975, whooping crane eggs have been transferred annually to Grays Lake in Idaho, from the whooping crane nesting ground in Canada and the captive flock at Patuxent Wildlife Research Center. The eggs were substituted for (greater) sandhill crane eggs and the sandhills became foster parents for the whooping cranes. The purpose of this experiment was to start a second wild, self-sustaining, flock of whooping cranes. 288 eggs have been transported; 210 have hatched, and 85 survived to flight age since the project began in 1975. The population peaked at 34 individuals in 1984–1985, but has declined to 13 in the spring of 1989.

"This spring, Dr. Jim Lewis, National Whooping Crane Coordinator in Albuquerque, announced that whooping crane eggs would not be placed under sandhill cranes at Grays Lake in Idaho due to continuing drought conditions. Lewis reported, 'in the past three summers, 39 eggs were transferred, but only six chicks survived to flight stage.' He added, 'with only 15 percent of the eggs resulting in 80 day old chicks, a transfer of eggs in 1989 cannot be justified.'

"No eggs have been produced by individuals cross-fostered in the 15 year old project. Dr. Lewis and Dr. Rod Drewein, Foster Parent Project Leader from the University of Idaho, do not know the reason for the absence of breeding, but suspected reasons are the small numbers of sexually mature birds, their wide distribution, and possible improper sexual behavior resulting from being raised by sandhill cranes.

"On May 5, the first evidence of mating in the cross fostering experiment occurred when a six year old female whooping crane was shipped from Patuxent to Grays Lake, Idaho. The hand-reared female of breeding age was placed in an enclosure within the territory of a wild, foster-reared male whooping crane. The purpose of the release was to see if the cross-fostered male would exhibit normal breeding behavior. The male exhibited interest in the female whooping crane and after a week, she was released. The two birds then began behaving as a pair and were observed copulating but did not construct a nest. In June the male began his feather molt and moved into the center of the marsh. The female was then joined by another male but no mating was observed.

"For those directly working with the whooping crane, each year offers new challenges and insights into the behavior and ultimate survival of this world-renowned species that once stood on the very precipice of extinction. In Robert Allan's 1952 report entitled, *The Whooping Crane*, he stated, 'we have a strong conviction that the whooping crane will keep his part of the bargain and will fight for survival every inch of the way. What are we doing to help? At the time of his report in 1952, there were only 33 wild whoopers—now there are 145 adults plus the 21–26 young of this year. The governments and the people of the United States and Canada have responded to Allan's challenge and the future of the regal birds is brighter now than at any time in this century.' "

As we go to press with this book, the total number of whooping cranes in the entire world is:

Wood Buffalo flock: 146 adults and about 24 young, total of 170 whoopers. There are 13 in the Grays Lake flock, for a wild population total of 183. The population at Patuxent now consists of 47 captive birds, which includes 5 breeding pairs. The captive breeding flock has produced 219 eggs, which have been used to produce young whoopers both at Grays Lake and at Patuxent. The ability to increase the size of the captive flock gives us even more hope for the future. There are two whoopers at the International Crane Foundation in Baraboo, Wisconsin, injured birds being cared for. This gives us a total world-wide population of 232. This is cause for rejoicing, but the whooper has a long way to go.

Food for thought: Would the whooper be extinct if it hadn't been for the selfless devotion to their cause of Robert Allen and the National Audubon Society? Would the wild flock have prospered if it hadn't been for the daring and insight of the biologists who thought of stealing one egg from each nest in Canada? Would the whooper still exist if it hadn't been for the establishment of the Aransas National Wildlife Refuge in Texas, where they winter every year?

Prognosis: the whooper is going to make it.

4

Spotted Owls
and
Timber Dollars

Animals evolve to fill particular niches in the environment. Mature forests, especially mature forests of slow-growing species, constitute a particular environment. There are many more species using a mixed age forest than there are in a mature forest. Browsers which feed on tender leaves and twigs find no food in the mature forest, and usually avoid it. Because little sunlight filters through the overhead canopy to reach the ground, there is very little understory brush growing between the trunks of the huge trees. If the mature forest is a rain forest—as it is in our Pacific Northwest, moss grows in the shadowy depths of the forest, and ferns prosper there, but there is little browse. Some specialized birds nest in the mature forest, making use of the "over-mature" trees which usually contain woodpecker holes. Specialized rodents live in the mature forest—field mice and voles.

Because there are prey species in the mature forest, there must be a predator species or two to feed on them, in accordance with the immutable law of nature which states that "for every meal, there is a diner." Over the millennia, the spotted owl has evolved to take its place at the dinner table in the mature forest.

The spotted owl is highly specialized in its habitat requirements. It NEEDS mature forest in which to hunt and in which to nest. The spotted owl is so genetically programmed that it can exist only in the mature forest. If that mature forest is cut down and replaced by green stuff in the second growth—other species will prosper, species such as deer and elk, turkeys, hares and rabbits—but not spotted owls.

24

Big mature trees are like bank accounts in that each tree is worth many hundreds of dollars. The industry cutting down these mature trees can be likened to the mining industry in that it exhausts its stock in trade and is self terminating. As a placer gold lode is mined out, the miners move away and the environment takes a century or more to recover from the effect of placer mining. When the mature forest is "mined," the lumbering industry moves on, looking for new forests to conquer, and it takes more than one hundred years for these majestic trees to rebound to their present state.

To oversimplify, perhaps, we can note that the profit motive rules the situation here, not national interest. America does not need the wood in the mature forests of the Pacific Northwest—our needs can be satisfied by using forests of quicker maturing species, providing wood with silviculture which can be operated as a self-sustaining forest. But there is a lot of money represented in a mature Douglas Fir stading in a mature forest. Never mind that it will take more than a century to re-grow that tree, it represents profits and profits make the world go around.

While it is true that America does not need that particular mature timber now, it is very true that Japan—the world's industrial leader—will pay great sums of money for this lumber. Japan is an advanced culture and Japan reveres its own mature forests and cultivates them just as they cultivate ornamental gardens. We do not.

If America's mature forests were selectively harvested, to supply America's needs, there would be no problem. With today's system, where American raw materials (wood) are exported to Japan for processing—short term profit comes to American workers, but long term secure employment goes to Japan. If we harvested our mature trees only as they were needed here in America, higher paying milling and cabinet making jobs would remain in America. This could have a beneficial effect on our balance of trade.

The northern spotted owl, *Stix occidentalis caurina* was proposed for listing as "endangered" in 1987. The U.S. Fish and Wildlife Service decided not to list it as threatened, much less endangered, at that time. There was raised a huge hue and cry as environmentalists rallied to the support of the spotted owl.

Then the Fish and Wildlife Service began a long and comprehensive study of the status of the northern spotted owl. In the middle of 1989, the F&WS revised its position and listed the northern spotted owl as "threatened." On April 26, 1989, the Fish and Wildlife Service announced that the northern spotted owl warrants protection because of significant modifications and loss of its forest habitat. In other words, the spotted owl was seeing its habitat destroyed by timbering. To justify its complete switch in position, the Service now claims that there is more hard, factual information available on the northern spotted owl today than on any other species suggested for listing.

The population of this threatened subspecies is now estimated at least

1,500 breeding pairs and an undetermined number of unpaired birds in Washington, Oregon and California, with perhaps another 50 breeding pairs in British Columbia. As this is written, the listing as threatened is only tentative, and the Service must decide within twelve months whether or not to make the listing final.

Remember now that untold millions of dollars of quick profits are endangered by any listing that the spotted owl is endangered. Under existing law, agencies of the federal government would have to ensure that their activities (for which read "timber sales") would not jeopardize existing populations of the northern spotted owl. About 90% of the old growth timber in the Pacific Northwest is administered by the Forest Service, by the Bureau of Land Management, or by the National Park Service.

The actions of the National Park Service over the past two decades show clearly that they will prefer to let old growth timber "go to waste" as far as human wants are concerned. The NPS feels, and I agree wholeheartedly, that the natural scene should be left unchanged by man whenever possible. If trees grow old and die, and come crashing to earth, the fallen tree fulfills a requirement in the natural order of things and thus, its "waste" is beneficial.

But the Forest Service and BLM are entirely different. Both cater to lumbering industries. The Forest Service routinely sells our trees at a loss, because their management of the trees, and their construction of roads, are expenses which outweigh revenues from the sales. The Forest Service proclaims that its forests are "Lands of Many Uses." This is a laudable thought, but the *primary use* is for sale of lumber and that is acknowledged by almost all foresters.

If the spotted owl listing becomes permanent, the Forest Service and the BLM will have to enter into what are known as Section 7 consultations with the Fish and Wildlife Service before they can offer for sale those lands occupied by the threatened species, the northern spotted owl. This quite naturally scares the timbering industry which knows that such consultations would almost certainly result in a decision to stop logging to protect owls.

Impartial thinkers point out that tourism brings far more money to Oregon than does logging of mature forests, over the long haul. Tourism is a self-perpetuating industry, logging is often a "one quick profit" industry which pays only one jackpot.

While the future of the owl hangs in the balance, its worth is being hotly discussed across all of Douglas Fir country. In Oregon's Willamette Valley, an enterprising man has sold thousands of T-shirts with the legend, "*SAVE A LOGGER, EAT AN OWL.*" Another shop sells caps with the legend, "*I love spotted owls. Fried they taste like chicken.*" While the battle rages, record amounts of raw timber grown on private and state land are being shipped for premium prices to Japan, China and Korea without ever seeing the inside of an American mill. The Mayr Brother mill in Hoquiam, Washington, now estimates its future supply in months instead of years or centuries as in decades past. American milling industry is being starved out by lumber companies which grab the quick and easy profit by shipping their logs to high paying markets in the Orient.

The shortage of timber for the American milling industry is not something new, nor can it be blamed on the northern spotted owl. In 1976, Oregon State University professor John Beuter reported that very little mature timber was left on private land and that the industry would have to depend upon the national forests if it was to continue to prosper. He pointed out that trees planted before World War II would become available in the year 2,000, but not before.

Historically, the U.S. Forest Service has "been in bed" with the timber industry, and has managed their timber sales for the benefit of industry profits, not for the best interests of the American public. Now, the Forest Service is being dragged into the modern world and forced to realize that other values—such as water and wildlife—**MUST** be considered before trees are felled.

One of the Forest Services' own, Jeff DeBonis is a timber sales planner on the Willamette National Forest. Accusing his own Service of "being in bed" with the timber industry, DeBonis asks the question "Why should the national forests be sacrificed to an overzealous and greedy industry that liquidated their own lands to make a fast cut?"

The Forest Service slowly improves in its attitude toward wildlife. It has to, for watchdog organizations now offer to drag the Service into the courts if it flouts the laws governing endangered species and critical habitat. Today the Service is carefully studying the situation vis-à-vis the northern spotted owl. The Service does not know how much old growth forest is left, but the Wilderness Society has estimated that less than 15% remains in the spotted owls' range. The remaining mature forest is so fragmented that it is of little or no value to the owl. The Forest Service's concern is shown by the fact that it is now collecting base-line data on spotted owl populations as far distant as the Gila Wilderness in New Mexico.

Another indication of the Forest Services' slow "conversion" was when Forest Service Chief Dale Robertson stopped logging of some southern national forests to protect the endangered red-cockaded woodpecker. The endangered woodpecker now exists on only four of the 26 national forests in the Southern Region. This is another sign of the importance to wildlife of aged, mature trees. This woodpecker nests only in very old live pine trees. The practice of clear cutting monoculture stands of pine endangers the bird's very existence. The Forest Service is to be commended for this courageous decision—and believe me, it did take courage to buck the logging industry which profits from mismanagement of your national forests.

To sum up, the mature forests of the Pacific Northwest have been exploited by private industry and by the U.S. Forest Service for nearly a century. An important part of our timber treasure has been shipped to the

27

Orient, where it is used to produce finished products which are now sold to Americans for far more than the value of the logs. The shortage of mature timber saw logs has nothing to do with the spotted owl. No one has suggested that owl protectors have locked up mature forests, thus causing a shortage.

It is time that we managed our mature forests for the benefit of the American people, not for the benefit of the logging industry. As is so often true, if we wisely manage our natural resources, we need not fear for the extermination of species such as the owl. Well managed forests will include enough mature timber to provide for the northern spotted owl.

Poorly managed forests will be devoid of spotted owls, but far more important, poorly managed forests will not provide a permanent supply of timber for the American public, will not protect watersheds which provide the drinking water for millions of Americans, will not provide homes for deer and elk, moose and caribou, will not prevent the soil erosion that chokes our estuaries and ruins profitable fisheries.

If we manage our forest resources for the greater good of mankind, the spotted owl will have no worries. But is that likely to happen?

When the timber industry screamed in outrage at the listing of the spotted owl, President Bush—who wants to be known as the "environmental president"—seemed to be startled by the uproar. He set up a commission to draw up a compromise plan—one which would protect the spotted owl and which would also assuage the fears of the timber industry. The Commission prepared a report which was a "watered down" version of the Habitat Preservation Act, a compromise which did not suit either side of the battle.

Strangely enough, it is not the Forest Service which the environmentalists must worry about. It is a newly discovered "weak sister" in the Cabinet of the "Environmental President"—one Manuel Lujan, Secretary of the Interior. Lujan's attitude seems to be, "Laws protecting wildlife are okay, but shouldn't be allowed to hinder timber cutting." This is the same Secretary of the Interior who remarked that "no one has shown me the difference between a red squirrel and a gray one," when discussing the endangered status of the very rare little red squirrel on Mt. Graham in Arizona. Lujan has repeatedly called for "easing" of environmental restrictions of the Endangered Species Act. When Congressman Lujan voted for the Endangered Species Act, he obviously didn't foresee the day when he might have to enforce those restrictions as part of his job as Secretary of the Interior. Secretary Lujan has made it abundantly clear that he believes that wildlife's right to exist should never threaten the opportunity to make a fast buck.

If the spotted owl continues to exist, it will be in spite of Secretary of the Interior Lujan. It will be because so many wildlifers, so many environmentalists, fought a good battle. If we cannot preserve the northern spotted owl, can we preserve ourselves?

5

Ferrets and Sparrows: A Victory and a Loss

I write this chapter with cause for joy—the apparent comeback from extinction for the blackfooted ferret.

I also write this chapter with a deep sense of loss—because of the extinction of the dusky seaside sparrow—lost despite some heroic attempts to save it. Too little and too late.

Ten years ago when I was finishing the work on the book, *THESE ARE THE ENDANGERED,* I was forced to admit that it looked like curtains for the blackfooted ferret. The last confirmed sighting of a ferret in the wild had been logged in 1979. Respected biologist Dr. Raymond L. Linder of the South Dakota Cooperative Wildlife Research Unit was in charge of the Recovery Team efforts for the ferret. I asked him if he could "tell me definitely that there is a blackfooted ferret in existence in the wild?"

Sorrowfully, Dr. Linder told me, "No one can make that statement to the best of my knowledge!" Dr. Linder added that no one could say that there was not a blackfooted ferret alive in the wild, for the simple reason that "we haven't looked hard enough." I ended up my blackfooted ferret chapter with the question, "Did the ferret become extinct while I was writing this book?"

My fears were not realized. We happily still have the ferret. Let's take a look and see why he got into trouble in the first place.

Ever since Charles Darwin penned his theories about species evolving because of natural selection, we have known that animals develop specialized abilities or traits to help ensure their survival. To balance himself on

long jumps, propelled by his strong back legs, the kangaroo developed a heavy, muscular tail. To signal other herd members across wide expanses of plains, the pronghorn antelope developed a patch of erectile white hairs on his rump. By raising those erectile hairs, the pronghorn "heliographed" alarm as if with a mirror. To allow them to fly the darkness with impunity, the bat family developed airborne sonar long before our electronic machines reached the same goal.

Specialization was the key to survival for most animal species. But too much specialization can be the cause of death for an entire species.

Before the first Spaniards saw the western plains, the blackfooted ferret had decided to specialize in eating only prairie dogs. Early French explorers named a Wisconsin area *Prairie du Chien,* the prairie of the dog. Prairie dogs aren't dogs, of course, but they do "bark" and thus their name. When the first *Espanoles* explored the American West, they found prairie dog towns that numbered in the millions of animals each. They called this land the *Llano Estacado,* the staked plain. They gave it this name because the prairie dogs, standing on their hind legs to watch the oncoming humans, reminded them of stakes driven into the plain.

Literally speaking, it would have been possible to travel from the Mexican state of Chihuahua, northward through Texas, Oklahoma, Kansas, Nebraska and Colorado, through Wyoming and the two Dakotas, into what is now Canada and on halfway up the tremendous length of Saskatchewan and Alberta—without being out of sight of a prairie dog town.

With this tremendous supply of prairie dogs, it is no surprise that the blackfooted ferret decided to specialize in eating them. The ferret is a mink-sized member of the weasel family, light tan in color with a "bandit's mask" of black across his face. Long and slim, he could travel through the prairie dog burrows at full speed. The "dog" fought back, but was no match for the killing ability of the ferret. Survival of the fittest, for ferrets, logically was survival by eating the easy meals provided by a prairie dog town.

Because ferrets are almost entirely nocturnal, no one had any idea of their numbers when the prairie dog was at its highest population. The ferrets simply moved into a prairie dog town—along with other unwelcome spongers—and lived the life of Riley with endless supplies of tasty prairie dogs, secure places to hide from bigger predators—no troubles, man!

Prairie dogs moved away when ferrets moved in, but they only moved about thirty yards. Realistically, the dogs accepted their lot in life, which was to provide food for ferrets whenever the ferrets needed a meal. Evidently, a steady diet of prairie dog did not seem monotonous to the ferret. Conrad N. Hillman of the South Dakota State Cooperative Wildlife Unit wrote:

"Ferrets were never observed to prey on animals other than prairie dogs except those made available for experimental studies."

31

While the population of ferrets and the population of prairie dogs was obviously in some kind of dynamic balance in those early years, we do not know whether or not the ferret became a part of the complicated society of a 'dog town. Burrowing owls moved into the prairie dog towns, usually choosing unoccupied burrows for their nests. Prairie rattlers and other snakes also took up residence in the towns. This was not a symbiotic relationship in the pure sense of the word. I know that rattlesnakes dined on young 'dogs because I've taken them out of the stomachs of freshly killed snakes. Snakes also dined on the eggs and young of the burrowing owl. All three species seemed to prosper in this cooperative housing project—even though the 'dogs did all of the cooperating and the snakes and owls simply "mooched" off of the 'dog town. Obviously, snakes and owls did little to reduce the population of prairie dogs, for the tremendous towns covered almost one fourth of the Great Plains in the 1750's.

Everything was going smoothly for the sybaritic ferrets who were enjoying the "endless" supply of prairie dog dinners.

Endless?

Enter man and his livestock. Prairie dogs ate grass which man wanted as feed for his cattle and sheep. Even as man's herds overgrazed the land, the destructiveness of the prairie dog was emphasized. Led by the U.S. Fish and Wildlife Service (and its predecessors) strychnine oats were used to decimate the "endless" supply of prairie dogs. Some individual dogs noticed the bitter taste of strychnine before they ingested a lethal dose. So prairie dog towns were severely cut back, but not eliminated. The few "strychnine wise" dogs swiftly repopulated the prairies. A Texas rancher once told me that "all you need to start a prairie dog town is one dog and the prairie." He might be right; prairie dog females are almost always pregnant with the next litter.

Then man came up with Compound 1080, sodium monofluoracetate. Odorless, tasteless 1080 gave no advance warning of its lethal nature. Prairie dog towns treated with 1080 oats were 99% eliminated. If the poison applicator came back in two weeks and treated the remaining active burrows, the results were 100%. In twenty years, Texas prairie dogs went from millions to the point where the Parks Department in Lubbock preserves a special park so that people can see a prairie dog or two.

The effectiveness of Compound 1080 can hardly be exaggerated. In 1957, two expert riflemen used a big dog town near Onida, South Dakota as a rifle range. The "dogs" were self-erecting targets for the high caliber rifles which were capable of almost certain hits out to 250 yards. The two riflemen each shot approximately 500 rounds per day for two weeks, getting in all the practice they could before the town was to be poisoned. Conservatively, they killed at least 10,000 dogs. But there were still as many dogs as when they started—or so it seemed! Rifles had made absolutely no effect against a big dog town. This was in 1957.

Registered Herefords needed the grass, so the 'dogs had to go. Compound 1080 was used for one week, treating the entire town. I came through one week later and could not find a single live dog—despite an exhaustive search.

Mankind called this progress, for profits from Herefords increased greatly.

But the free lunch counter for ferrets was gone. And the blackfooted ferret was almost gone.

Prairie dogs, with their great reproductive potential, had the ability to bounce back. *Their* food supply, grass, was still in good supply. The blackfooted ferret with its slower reproductive potential, found its food supply gone. For the prairie dog it was a setback, for the ferret it spelled extinction.

Catastrophe? In South Dakota, once home to millions of dogs and thousands of ferrets, researchers were only certain of one litter of ferrets each year from 1966 through 1969.

Outside of South Dakota? I saw the last blackfooted ferret I ever ob-

33

served in the wild in Southern Utah in 1970. For half an hour I watched as the ferret methodically entered prairie dog burrow after burrow, searching for its food—which no longer existed there.

Man suddenly awoke to the fact that he was seeing another case of extinction. Two pairs of blackfooted ferrets were trapped in South Dakota and sent to Patuxent, Maryland, where U.S. Fish and Wildlife scientists have worked wonders of artificial propagation. Two years later the older female produced five young—but four were born dead and the other was so weak that it lived only a few days. The younger male had cancer! The Patuxent report sums it up:

"Although two blackfooted ferret litters were produced, eight of the young were stillborn and the other two died within two days. This, in addition to other breeding difficulties and pathological processes encountered in the black foots, may be a reflection of conditions in the wild population. These conditions may be responsible for the recent decrease in the numbers of black footed ferrets in the wild. However, we are optimistic that captive propagation of this species using the techniques developed at Patuxent may still be a reality if, and when, additional young, genetically heterozygous (heterozygous means "possessing dissimilar genes") *animals can be found and taken into captivity."*

From 1974 until 1979, no ferrets were sighted in the wild!

We had lots of reasons for concern in 1981. Personally, I thought the blackfooted ferret was extinct.

Then it happened! Meteetse! A vigorous colony of blackfooted ferrets was found in this isolated Wyoming area. Since then lots of things have happened.

Blackfoots from Meteetse were captured and raised at the Wyoming Game and Fish Department's Research Center at Wheatland, Wyoming. Fearing influenza, canine distemper and other diseases which the ferret has shown an inability to resist, Wyoming scientists raised the ferrets in complete isolation. Success came quickly and the vigorous young ferrets took to captive reproduction with enthusiasm.

In just two years, the Wyoming biologists increased the captive population from 18 animals to 58! Cause for rejoicing!

Fearing an outbreak of disease or other catastrophe which could wipe out the captive flock, Wyoming canvassed the zoological world looking for the best sponsoring agencies to accept new breeding colonies of blackfoots. After an exhaustive search, they settled on two: The National Zoological Park's Conservation Center in Front Royal, Virginia; and the Henry Doorly Zoo in Omaha, Nebraska.

It was feared that transport by commercial carrier might expose the ferrets to canine diseases, because airplanes commonly carry dogs and cats. So the Air National Guard came into the act, flying the endangered ferrets from Cheyenne, Wyoming to Andrews Air Force Base in Maryland (where

Air Force One lands with the U.S. President). Then they were trucked to Front Royal.

The Front Royal colony was started on October 18, 1988—and all made the trip safely.

December 15, 1988, another seven ferrets were moved to the Omaha Zoo, where special quarters have been built for them. Now we have three growing colonies of blackfooted ferrets at three widely separated places. Recovery teams are now working on selecting prairie dog towns in the Great Plains area—dog towns which will again be the home of America's **MOST** endangered mammal.

Present plans call for the first release into the wild in 1991!

Obviously, everything looks rosy right now, unless you look at it from the viewpoint of a prairie dog. No one gives the prolific prairie dogs a vote in the matter, however, for they can outbreed the blackfoots—unless poisoned. After the blackfooted ferrets are again introduced into the wild, it will be necessary to protect their numbers for many years—until once again the ultimate mammalian specialist, the blackfoot, is again numerous on the Great Plains where he belongs. . . . a part of the original landscape.

The biggest worry for ferret scientists is that the gene pool may be too narrow, that the results of inbreeding might produce a weaker, less viable strain of blackfooted ferrets. It would surely help if another source of blackfooted genes could be located. With this in mind, the New York Zoological Society, through its subsidiary Wildlife Conservation International, posted a reward of ten thousand U.S. dollars for anyone who could locate another colony of blackfoots in the wild. The reward would have had to be claimed before December 31, 1990. Just as the colony at Meteetse was unknown and passed over for many years of searching; so it is possible that other colonies exist. Experts claim that the best places to look other than in the western United States, are near Chihuahua, Mexico and in the huge Canadian provinces of Alberta and Saskatchewan.

As we got to press with this chapter, the world's known population of blackfooted ferrets stands at a total of 120, a wonderful increase over a few years ago. There are 100 ferrets at the Wyoming State Game and Fish laboratory in Wheatland, Wyoming; 13 at the Front Royal, Virginia zoological park and 7 at the Henry Doorly Zoo in Omaha.

The prognosis for the ferret is quietly optimistic. I'll go out on a limb and say that this species will make it!

Dusky Seaside Sparrow

My reason for sadness in writing this chapter is the Dusky Seaside Sparrow. We now can add its name to the endless list of species which have become extinct. Why? Like the blackfooted ferret, the sparrow was also a specialist in that it inhabited only one special niche in the total environment. When that niche disappeared, so did the sparrow.

Bear with me while we think about the causes of this loss. When a river flows to the sea, eddies and whirlpools are formed where the water swirls against the bank. Parts of the bank are constantly being pulled into the river, forming small niches of macro-environments. These small niches are of great interest, but are they really an integral part of the main river? Or are they lost environments—doomed by being estranged from the main stream?

As the river of evolution moves along, it tries many experiments. Some succeed, others fail. Along the path of the evolutionary river, small ecosystems develop. In each of these ecosystems, species begin to evolve to fit that niche. At times, the macro-environment is destroyed by the same processes which created it—before new species have a chance to evolve. At other times, these small ecosystems prosper—and when that happens, species evolve to fit that successful ecosystem. Perhaps the small ecosystem may increase in size, even become the mainstream of the evolutionary river.

Mankind cannot decide which new ecosystem is a dead end. We do not have that intelligence, nor that ability to foresee the future. The extreme specialization of the blackfooted ferret to fit it for a singular environment —a prairie dog town—made its survival very doubtful, but we cannot be sure. That's obvious if you read the first half of this chapter. The Texas blind salamander, which evolved to fit the Stygian darkness of caves which never see the light of day, probably is an evolutionary dead end. But we cannot be sure.

The dusky seaside sparrow *Ammodromus maritima nigrescens* evolved to fit a new environmental niche. It was first discovered in 1872 near Titusville, Florida. By 1988, the sparrow was almost gone. It existed in only one strip of land one quarter of a mile wide and ten miles long, on the St. Johns River marshes and on Merritt Island, Florida.

This bird was a ground feeder, and very secretive.

In that very severely circumscribed environment, the dusky was numerous. During the scant hundred years of its known existence, it was never seen outside of Merritts Island and along the St. Johns River. There were two separate populations of these sparrows, although both were Duskies. One was on Merrit Island where the story of its extinction is abundantly clear. Flooding of the marsh areas destroyed the forb of preference for nesting Duskies. Some have blamed the demise of this population on DDT spraying to control mosquitoes, but I have been assured that at least two thousand Duskies remained after DDT use was discontinued.

On the St. Johns area, early efforts to drain the marsh showed that the soil was too salty for crops, so it was converted to pasture. It was necessary to burn the grass periodically to allow tender new growth to grow. Older aged bunch cordgrass is not palatable for cattle.

Then that specialized habitat, within which the dusky prospered, began to disappear. Man controlled water levels as an aid to reducing the mosquito population. These water control activities flooded out the forbs in which the sparrow lived, and in the St. Johns area, man drained the marsh and burned off thousands of acres.

Because Florida ranks second only to Texas in numbers of cattle, new pastures were needed. Wildfires were set to allow grass to take over. Elimination of habitat usually means elimination of some species which inhabit that habitat. This was no exception.

St. Johns Refuge personnel conducted censuses of the dusky seaside sparrow finding 143 singing males in 1970, and 110 in the same area in 1972. 1973 count was 54 singing males. Spring of 1974 saw only 37 singing males. In 1976, the count was 11 singing males, 12 in 1977 and 9 in 1978. Disaster was at hand.

Why had the sparrows coexisted with wildfire for millennia, than succumbed to wildfire losses in the 20th century? Simply because their habitat had been so severely curtailed that the loss of even one acre of suitable nesting cover was a disaster. Bunch cordgrass, mainstay of the introduced cattle herds, burns only patchily when damp. But dry seasons can allow huge areas to disappear in one fire. Drought, some of it man caused, didn't help the Dusky.

We should mention another facet—the construction of the Beeline Highway through its habitat. For endless generations, this small sparrow had existed on a pancake-flat earth. Now there were hills, formed by spoil piles left from highway construction. The duskies moved away from those hills, which were foreign to them. They moved away and disappeared. Before 1972 construction work, there were 94 singing males in the path of the road, afterwards, only 12 remained.

Drastic measures were called for. Scientists planned to locate a nest, and take the young from that nest when they were old enough. Then they hoped to raise the birds in captivity and try captive propagation as a last ditch effort to save the species. They never had the chance. No nest was located.

In desperation, biologists captured the last dusky seaside sparrows known to exist. All were males! Was it possible to raise a species with only males? Scientists replied that it was "almost" possible. They hoped to crossbreed their dusky males to similar (but different) sub-species of sparrows. Then, if the offspring was again bred back to the original dusky males we could create a new species which would be almost the same. First generation was to be one half dusky, second generation offspring would be three quarters dusky, and (if possible) third generation offspring would be seven-eights dusky. The possibility of holding the semen from male duskies, keeping it viable long after the males had died, encouraged this desperate dream.

Four crossbred dusky seaside sparrows were living at Walt Disney's

Discovery Island near Orlando, Florida, in the spring of 1989. They were housed in a special aviary, and there was a slight glimmer of hope for the plan to create a population of dusky seaside sparrows out of a males-only population.

The remnant population consisted of five crossbred individuals—a 50% Dusky female, two 75% Duskies, a male and a female, an 87.5% Dusky female and a 25% Dusky female.

What happened next remains somewhat of a mystery. According to the news release put out by Walt Disney World—

"Mother Nature took a hand, disastrously. On March 27, a windstorm threw palm tree fronds through the roof of the aviary. Morning found the important nine year old bird dead, probably from stress, although it had already outlived all expectations. Two more crossbreeds, housed together in a cage, were gone. Still another pair were lost when workers tried to move their cage to a safer place."

Several sources have told me that this is not the true story of what happened that night. Yet they refuse to tell me their version of the happenings. No one wants to criticize Mickey Mouse, it seems.

Specialists know that the two birds which escaped will not be able to live in the wild. They were born in captivity and knew only the artifical environment which Disney had carefully prepared for them. For reasons of their own, the Disney people kept very silent about the loss of the last remnants of the dusky seaside population. The Florida State Game Department didn't even hear of the demise of the sparrows for two months after their loss. Even Mickey Mouse cannot resurrect the extinct sparrow.

With great sorrow, we report that the Dusky Seaside Sparrow is now extinct. Common sense says it is so—but we were very wrong about the extinction of the blackfooted ferret, back in 1981. We can pray that we are wrong about the dusky seaside sparrow. Perhaps its buzzing trill will be heard again, in some other part of Florida—telling us that the rumors of its death were exaggerated. But it is a mighty slim hope.

6

Red Wolves and Attwater's Chickens

A subspecies of the more numerous common prairie chicken of more northerly climes, the Attwater's Prairie Chicken is one of our rarest endangered species of game bird. Although its numbers are perhaps four times the population of the whooping crane, the prognosis is not as favorable as it is for the big whooper. Why are such bad things happening to the Attwater's?

Plain and simple, it is being crowded out of its only known home. In case you hadn't noticed, there is a growing megalopolis spreading along the Gulf Coast of Texas—with gigantic Houston as its epicenter, and with earthquake-like results for a chicken which shows a stubborn refusal to change its ways to suit mankind.

Census figures for the past half a century clearly show what has happened.

1937	8,711
1950	4,200
1956	3,450
1963	1,336
1967	1,070
1970	1,440
1971	2,212
1972	1,650
1973	1,772
1974	2,004

```
1975 . . . . . 2,240
1976 . . . . . 2,088
1977 . . . . . 1,500
1978 . . . . . 1,500
1979 . . . . . 1,802
```

In 1980, we had hopes that we could arrest the disturbing slide into oblivion by setting aside areas of critical habitat. But the 1990 population of less than 500 individuals proves that critical habitat was not saved in sufficient quantity to do the trick. Are we about to lose this interesting subspecies? It certainly looks like it.

Tympanuchus cupido attwaterii yields to no species when we measure stubborness. They stubbornly cling to ancestral habitat, even when that habitat changes from a coastal marsh to an airport, a condominium or a shopping mall. An example is their refusal to change their courtship areas. Each spring, when sex rears its head, the male birds gather on ancestral "dancing grounds" to perform their dances aimed at attracting mates. Each male does a pirouetting dance with wings stiffly extended to the side so that they scrape against the ground. Their heads are stretched out in front and the yellow gular pouches on each side of the neck are inflated, while a couple of stiff feathers are erected on each side of the head to

40

further increase their strange appearance. After pirouetting, the male bird releases the air from the inflated gular sac, emitting a dull "plop". This is often referred to as "booming", but there's mighty little boom. In fact the sound is not audible very far from the performing male. While the males are strutting and pirouetting, and staging ritualistic combats with other males, the hens stroll nonchalantly through the dancing ground, seemingly uninterested.

The hens must be interested, however, for this strange ritual has succeeded in introducing male to female for millennia and the species has done quite well until man appeared on the scene in numbers.

There is one element that is absolutely needed, if the species is to continue to exist. The male must meet the female. The dancing ground is the designated meeting place. If either sex were to change the "dancing ground" the other sex would fail to meet it and the Attwater's prairie chicken would be only a memory.

So what happens when the crowds of mankind build an airplane runway where there had been a dancing ground? The stubborn chickens dance on the pavement, for some ancestral memory tells them that *this* is *the* spot. What happens when the indomitable dancing chicken meets a jet airplane? Experience has taught us that the plane sometimes crashes because of a flame-out, but the courageous chicken seldom survives the clash of wills.

The Attwater's prairie chicken likes to dance at sunrise, when visibility is not yet good. There have been times when no chicken was in sight until the jet aircraft taxied into position for the take off. The roar of the jet challenged the chickens and the dancing males came out on the runway in force.

This business of agreeing on only one place to dance and meet the girls can have disastrous results. When an air base was being planned in a Texas area, helicopters were used to "helinet" dancing Attwater's chickens and release them in another part of their known ancestral range. The birds scattered widely after release, but a few remained in the relocation area. But when spring came along, the birds had no place to dance. No dance, no pairing off. No pairing off, no reproduction and the entire stock was lost.

In 1980 we felt optimistic because of the creation of the Attwaters's Prairie Chicken National Wildlife Refuge, 5,600 acres of good habitat along the San Bernard River in Colorado County, Texas. In 1980 there were about 150 of the endangered chickens on the refuge, whose primary objective was to safeguard this relict population.

The Tatton family gave 7,500 acres of prime Texas Gulf Coast land to the Aransas National Wildlife Refuge to try to help the Attwater's. That land was appraised at one and three quarter million dollars at the time of the donation. Surely it would bring more than ten million today. The land was meant to be an addition to the wintering ground of the endangered whoop-

41

ing crane, but it was also home to perhaps sixty Attwater's at the time of the donation.

On both the Aransas and the Attwater's refuges, there has been an attempt to improve habitat by controlled burning, which converts the scrub oak thicket back to the tall grass prairie which was home to these birds long before the white man came.

In 1980 we had perhaps 200 of the endangered chickens on federal refuges and perhaps another 1800 on privately owned land. We felt that the future of the species depended entirely upon the attitude of the private landowners.

In 1990, a short decade later, we sadly count only 432 Attwater's Prairie Chickens in the whole world. Refugio County which held about one half of the total population in 1988, suffered a decline from 562 to 246 in one year, which certainly illustrates the vulnerability of the endangered population. Even Colorado County, which contains the Attwater's Prairie Chicken National Wildlife Refuge, found its population dropping from 162 in 1988 to only 90 in 1989.

To put the population numbers in perspective,

1937 we counted 8,618
1972 we counted 1,772
1987 we counted 1,108
1988 we counted 926
1989 we counted 432.

In fifty years, we lost 95% of the known world's population of Attwater's Prairie Chicken. This indicates only one thing—the species may already be genetically non-viable, and certainly is headed for extinction—and soon! There was no known remedy for the slide, but one suggestion involved acquisition of more lands for the birds, lands which would be placed in refuge status to prevent dangerous variations in the land use pattern. The Fish and Wildlife Service had an option to purchase identified valuable lands in Victoria County. This option, held by the Trust for Public Lands, was allowed to expire in November of 1988. Seemingly, no one cares.

It is worthwhile to remember that the Heath Hen was once a very populous "prairie chicken." It was found all along the eastern seaboard states. It has long since passed into the shades of oblivion. It was good to eat, and it was susceptible to mankind's introduced predators—especially household cats and to a lesser extent, dogs. By the middle of the 1800's, it was extinct everywhere except on Martha's Vineyard Island. There a refuge was provided, and the Heath Hen made a remarkable comeback to number about 2,000 individuals in 1900. One wildfire destroyed production for one year and killed many of the adult birds. By 1932 it was gone to join the passenger pigeon and the dodo. The comparison between heath hen and Attwater's Prairie Chicken cannot be avoided. By all signs, the stubborn chicken of the Texas Gulf Coast will soon be gone.

Red Wolves

Before the habitat was changed so severely, the number one predator on the Attwater's Prairie Chicken was the Red Wolf. This endangered species occupied the entire range of the endangered chicken. Management plans to help the chicken naturally had to consider elimination or lessening of predation on the chickens. Was it appropriate to poison or shoot endangered red wolves because they preyed on endangered Attwater's chickens? Obviously not.

The red wolf was about half way between a coyote and a lobo wolf in size. It had longer legs, in proportion, than did the coyote, a different shaped head—in general, a quite different conformation. In 1959, I made the rounds with trapper supervisor Johnny White of the Texas District of the old Predator and Rodent Control branch of the Fish and Wildlife Service. We found a "very typical" red wolf in a trap. Johnny White who had decades of experience with them, positively identified it as a red wolf. The skull was sent to the Smithsonian in Washington, asking for positive identification. The Smithsonian said, "Part coyote, part domestic dog."

For a long time we went by the criterion that if it weighed more than 40 pounds it was a red wolf; if less than that, it still might be a red wolf. But then we encountered a race of coyotes in Archer County, Texas, which averaged between 42 and 45 pounds. They were definitely coyotes, but whopper coyotes! We no longer had a size yardstick by which to determine whether the animal was red wolf or coyote.

There definitely was a species of red wolf in pioneer days. These animals probably inhabited the southeastern states from Texas' Gulf Coast up through Arkansas and across to the Carolinas. Bigger than the coyote, they served as a block to prevent the coyote from extending its range southward and eastward from its strongholds west of the Mississippi. Smaller than the gray wolf, or timber wolf, or lobo wolf, the red was kept out of northern and western habitats by the larger wolf. Each of the three species had their niche, and pretty much remained in that niche.

Then mankind almost eliminated the larger wolf, and at the same time severely decreased the population of red wolves. The adaptable coyote moved in to fill the vacant habitat and is now found in every corner of North America from Florida to Alaska and from the Canal Zone to Quebec.

It now seems reasonable that the red wolf simply drowned in the larger gene pool of the common coyote, *Canis latrans.* Like all members of the dog family, it's a case of "When I'm not near the one I love, I love the one I'm near." Hybridization has been a fact of record since the 1770's. It is quite possible that there is no such thing as a "purebred" red wolf i.e. one that does not have a trace of coyote in its ancestry.

Wildlife Biologist Curtis Carley, who worked with the Red Wolf Recovery Program for many years, finally decided that "If an adult male weighs more than fifty pounds, it is a red wolf. If an adult male weighs less than thirty five pounds, it is a coyote." Adult red wolves usually measure 27 inches at the shoulder, adult coyotes seldom measure more than 25 inches. All this is interesting, but it tells us only that the red wolf is a big animal, the coyote is a small animal—as a rule. Color differentiation is useless here, as both species display an amazing range of color from nearly black to nearly white.

Red Wolf Recovery teams captured what appeared to be "typical" red wolves from known red wolf territory and put them into captive propagation centers.

In 1978, research scientists determined that there were NO genuine red wolves living in Texas and only a very small population in Louisiana. Obviously, the future of the red wolf depended upon the captive breeding stock, which still numbered less than 35 in 1979. Outside of the certified breeding stock in captivity, it would have to be a very wise red wolf that knew its own ancestry.

Today, the situation with the red wolf is this. . . . there are 110 red wolves under scientific control. Of these, 24 are either released into the wild, or are in acclimation pens, awaiting release into the wild. For example, as of this writing, there are ten red wolves running loose on Alligator River National Wildlife Refuge in Florida, and another five there waiting to be released. Red wolves liberated into the wild can also be found at Bull Island NWR in South Carolina; St. Vincent NWR in Florida; and at Horn Island National Park in Mississippi. That accounts for the 24 "under management", leaving another 86 red wolves in captivity. The Red Wolf rearing stations located at Graham, Washington, holds 40 animals and is the source of most of the stock ready for release. There are 16 other projects, all in zoos, which are producing more brood stock of the "certified red wolf" strain. The Fish and Wildlife Service is hopeful of having another 30 to 40 red wolves ready for release into the wild in 1990.

Attempts to reintroduce this captive-reared red wolf into the wild have met with varying degrees of success. It is my fear that we are producing another breed of canine—as easily distinguishable from coyotes or lobo wolves as the English setter is distinguishable from the Gordon Setter—but are we "saving" an endangered species or are we developing another breed of domestic dog? After all, all dog species, from St. Bernard to Mexican hairless, came from wild canine stock.

To date, release sites have been carefully chosen—note the emphasis on island habitats—to ensure that the tiny gene pool represented by the reintroduced red wolves doesn't drown in the gigantic gene pool of the omnipresent coyote.

The prognosis for the Red Wolf is guarded at best. The only possibility of increasing its numbers lies in "farming" the animals in captive breeding programs. Like any member of the dog family, the red wolf is easily raised in captivity.

Reintroduction into the wild, however, is definitely another story. Although pen-raised red wolves seem to adapt easily to a life of hunting, and although they find their food fairly easily, there is a worrisome disease problem. It seems that captivity has reduced the species' "immune" abilities. There have been many cases of young female red wolves suffering from uterine infections. Even here there is cause for optimism, as the offspring —in the wild—of these captive-reared females seem to be free of this uterine infection. There has also been one case of pancreatic cancer in a female red wolf. This is very rare in canines and is thought to be a complete aberration, and not a cause for worry.

Researchers had their estimation of the introduced red wolves savvy raised quite a bit when Hurricane Hugo hit the Bull Island area of South Carolina in 1989. A released pair of red wolves out on Bulls Island had produced a litter of five pups. The adults had been radio-tagged for telemetry purposes. After the hurricane sent a 19 foot surge of water up and over most of the island, researchers feared that they had lost their red wolves. However, flying over the Island, they found the male and four of the pups still together. Afraid that the red wolves would find hunting difficult under the flooded conditions, they dropped "carnivore logs" (big chunks of horse meat that zoos use to feed the big cats). What had happened to the female? Researchers found her radio transmitter in some alligator droppings! Warren Parker, who heads the Red Wolf Recovery Team, reports that this was the second mate the big male had lost to alligators, but each time the male reared the pups by himself.

Many strategies have been tried to prevent captive red wolves from imprinting on humans. They've been reared behind plywood panels which completely barred the humans from sight, but we must remember that the red wolf, like the coyote and grey wolf, has a wonderfully acute sense of smell. Even when a plywood barrier prevents the young wolf from seeing a human, his nose tells him that the human is still there. Biologists working with the red wolf have no worries about the released red wolf being too friendly to humans, for experience has taught them that the released animals quickly become very wary and alert.

U.S. Fish and Wildlife Service plans call for releasing pair-bonded red wolves into the Great Smoky Mountains National Park. This will help them determine whether or not the red wolf will retain its "purebred" status when surrounded by a population of coyotes. DNA studies on red wolves and even on the big timber wolf show that the coyote genes are present in varying degrees, but are almost always there. In other words, the highly adaptable coyote has succeeded in invading the gene pool of these other two canine species. Will the coyote be the winner in the long run?

From my point of view, the *wild* red wolf is gone. His place in the wild has been taken by one of the most successful and adaptable mammals known to science, the ubiquitous coyote.

But intelligent wildlife managers are striving to preserve a wild species considered extinct in the wild. More power to them! But let's not restock the endangered red wolf into the habitat preserved for the endangered Attwater's Prairie Chicken.

7

Endangered American Birds: Large Condors and Small Warblers

The California condor is the largest of all soaring birds on the North American continent, with a nine foot wing span and a body weight of as much as twenty-two pounds.

The Kirtland's warbler is one of the smallest of all endangered bird species. You could easily close your fingers around two of them at once, and still give them room to breathe.

The little Kirtland's is definitely endangered, with its wild population estimated to contain no more than 400 individuals.

The large California condor is far more endangered. There are no longer any individuals in the wild. All known California condors are in artificial propagation facilities in San Diego and Los Angeles.

Why are these two species facing extinction? The short answer for the California condor is that he has a very low reproductive potential, not mating until his fifth or sixth year and then producing only one chick every other year. The short answer for the Kirtland's warbler is that he is too damned choosy about where he spends his summers. The warbler nests only in thick stands of jackpine, only in trees aged from five to eight years, only in Michigan's Lower Peninsula. They have never been *known* to *nest* in any other location. However, I think that the only reason we've never found them nesting outside of the Lower Peninsula of Michigan is that we haven't looked hard enough. In the summer of 1988, no fewer than eight singing male Kirtland's warblers were found by a survey team in Wisconsin. Assuming that the males had something to sing about, there may well be nesting

warblers in that state, too, which would be great news for the Kirtland's warbler and its many fans. Two of the Wisconsin males were mist-netted and color banded to help in future identification. In Minnesota a search for Kirtland's was also undertaken in 1989.

If his exact specifications as to nesting trees are not met, the warbler evidently does not nest. The warbler has a good reproductive potential— given its requirements for nest trees; the condor has a very poor reproductive potential. But there is an equalizing factor—the condor may live to be forty years old. The warbler is lucky to ever see a third summer.

California Condor

The condor has been riding the thermal updrafts ever since the Pleistocene Age, living on carrion and soaring over California mountainous areas since long before man came to watch him. Man did more than watch, of course. Man shot many of the big birds simply because they were big targets, and because—to some people—there is something repulsive about the naked head, the scavenger beak and the propensity for rotten, road-killed meat.

There is considerable evidence that the widespread use of DDT in the 1960's and early 1970's may have further lowered the already low reproductive potential for the condor. There is a belief that the speeding automobile accounted for the death of some birds, for they are notoriously slow in getting airborne when startled. They often descend for a road-kill meal, even if it is only the pitifully few bites furnished by a gopher or mouse.

In 1981, the California condor was undoubtedly the rarest bird in the world with 28 known to exist in the wild and 1 bird in captivity. The Recovery Team organized in 1973 wanted to capture the remaining wild birds and try their luck at captive propagation. There arose a great hue and cry against this. Well meaning ornithologists felt that to even try to capture the big birds would endanger their very survival. Added to this was the feeling that captive survival was not really survival at all. The Sierra Club magazine in San Francisco, the *Yodeler*, eloquently stated this idea:

If we resort to captive breeding of condors, we are not saving the bird. We are only saving the genes and feathers. . . . a condor raised in captivity is different from a wild condor in ways that we may never learn to measure, but we will know the difference in our hearts.

While we sympathized with that heartfelt emotion, we knew that the choice was between saving only the genes and feather and saving nothing at all. The risk was too great to take. Something had to be done.

In 1973, the estimated wild population was about 50 birds, give or take a quintet or so. In 1979, actual count showed a total of only 28 birds in the wild. We had lost one half of the world's population in five years. The

Recovery Team formally planned to start trapping unmated young birds in 1980. The threat of legal action stopped that in its tracks. The obstructionist tactics were led by *Friends of the Earth*, a group led by radical environmentalist-writer Cleveland Amory.

Intransigence of these pseudo-conservationists delayed the program, but all obstacles were overcome and artificial propagation capture was begun. Aviculturists had already begun propagation of the very similar Andean condor, practicing against the day when they would have the future of the California condor in their hands. In December of 1988, biologists released Andean condors into the wild in California, each bird fitted with a radio transmitter to allow radio telemetry to check their travels. There is no worry about establishing a foreign population of Andean condors in the Condor sanctuary area, because only female birds have been released. Because the Andean condor is also an endangered species, biologists will recapture all of the Andean condors when the experiment ends in 1990 and the female Andean condors will be released into habitats in Colombia from which they have been exterminated. Their prospective mates, six males which are being held in the Los Angeles Zoo and the San Diego Wild Animal park, will be released into those same Colombia skies, hopefully to reestablish the species there.

One of the released Andean condors hit a power line in flight and died. Another had to be recaptured as it showed very little ability to survive in the wild. The others are doing very well.

As for the captive birds—well, one California condor laid an infertile egg on February 20, 1988 at the Los Angeles Zoo. In San Diego, captive condors laid two eggs, one of which was fertile. Hopes began to rise.

Buoyed by successes in artificial propagation methods such as cross-fostering, double-clutching, recycling—techniques which had worked with the peregrine falcon, even with the whooping crane, captive propagation of California condors was started. The only alternative would have been to stand by and record the demise of a species.

Now, in 1990, what is the situation? No California condors soar through the dry mountain air of the Sespe region of California. BUT. . . .

On April 29, 1988, the first ever condor chick hatched out in captivity! In an effort to avoid having the chick imprint on its keepers—and think it was a human itself, zoo personnel used a puppet hand, carved and painted to resemble a real live condor to feed the chick on regurgitated mice. The chick seemed to prosper.

As of May 1988, there were 28 condors in captivity, up one from a couple of months before. It was too early to determine the sex of the newcomer. It was encouraging to note that the other 27 captive birds consisted of 13 males and 14 females. To avoid putting all of our condors in one breeding basket, 14 are housed at the San Diego Wild Animal Park and the other 13 at the Los Angeles Zoo.

Now we move the story up to April 19, 1989, when the second ever California condor chick conceived in captivity emerged from the egg, with the assistance of staff at the San Diego Wild Animal Park. Three other fertile eggs were being incubated as of that date—one of them produced by the Los Angeles Zoo, a first for that facility. There was hope for an increase of four—building the world's captive population to 31 birds in the fall of 1989.

As of this writing, the California condor is extinct in the wild state, but is alive and well in captivity. This does not satisfy our desire to have this graceful creature soaring over the California desert areas again, but so far it is the best we can do—in fact, the only thing that could have been done. To leave the decreasing flock in the wild state would only have ensured its extinction.

On the plus side, aviculturists are doing a great job of producing condor chicks in captivity, and are improving their knowledge of "how to" release birds into the wild when their numbers increase to the point where we dare to chance release into the wild. There definitely is hope for the perpetuation of the California condor. There was no hope just a few years ago; so this must be deemed to be progress.

A late update on the California condor . . .

Tom Hanscom of the San Diego Wildlife Park says that thirteen condor eggs have been laid so far this year and that even more are expected. San Diego has already hatched two eggs and the Los Angeles Zoo has hatched another—more are expected to hatch. The world population of California condors now stands at 35, all in captivity. There is now a faint glimmer of hope.

Kirtland's Warbler

In 1981, I wrote that the Kirtland's Warbler now numbered less than 500 individuals in the entire world. This warbler is the only tail-wagging warbler with a gray back. If you want to see one, you'll have to go to the Lower Peninsula of Michigan, for that is the only place where it is known to nest. After spending its four month summer in the pleasant jack pines of Michigan, this tiny bird migrates all the way to the Bahamas to spend the other eight months of the year.

It would seem that this bird is too choosy for its own good. Not only does it nest (as far as we know) only in one part of Michigan—the counties of Crawford, Oscoda, Iosco, Roscommon, Kalkaska and Ogemaw—but it nests only in dense stands of jackpines of a certain age group. To suit the warbler, these trees should be in dense stands and be only six feet tall. When they get much bigger, the Kirtland's warbler doesn't seem to have anything to do with nesting there.

When forest fires caused by lightning were a normal part of life in the Michigan forest (and presumably in the Wisconsin, Minnesota and Ontario forests) the Kirtland's warbler found all the nesting sites he wanted, as the young jackpines grew back after fires. Enter Smoky the Bear sentiment against forest fires. Modern fire protection practices changed our opinion of wildfire. No longer a creator of habitat, it was thought of as a great calamity for wildlife—and of far more importance, it was thought of as a destroyer of profits from forests. Tremendous areas of forest were protected from fires and grew to full maturity, even-age stands of pines which were completely unacceptable to the warblers. Again, over-specialization rears its ugly head as one of the reasons for the decline of a species. More accurately, man's imposition of his ideas of what life should be caused the decline of the warblers. In 1979, a singing male census found only 210 singing males.

Since it first attracted attention in 1903, bird watchers have reported the tiny bird from fifteen counties in Michigan and widely scattered locations in Minnesota, Wisconsin and Ontario. But let me repeat: The Kirtland's warbler has never been found to have nested outside of the Lower Peninsula of Michigan.

In 1953, Harold Mayfield organized a census of the entire world's population of Kirtland's warblers. They found 432 singing males, and estimated the population to be double that. In 1961 a similar census found 502 singing males. In 1971, they found only 201 males. Obviously, elimination of its particular nesting habitat was causing the decline. It does us little good to become exasperated and say, "Why can't this silly little bird learn to nest in other habitats?" It does us little good, because the fact remains that the warbler will not *choose* to nest in other habitats.

Action was taken to help the remaining population. First, Michigan Recovery teams identified the remaining good nesting habitat and posted it against trespassing during the critical nesting period—in an effort to ensure maximum results from minimum habitat.

Because the parasitic cowbird was known to lay eggs in warbler's nests to the detriment of the warbler's own brood, Michigan workers trapped and destroyed the cowbirds thus minimizing the possibility that the warbler would rear only the unwanted cowbird and allow her own smaller young to starve while the bigger cowbird baby got all the food.

Of greatest importance, the Recovery Team secured the dedication of 135,000 acres of jackpines, suitable for nesting, and in the right place. They planned to manage this habitat to produce at least 35,000 acres of perfect habitat per year. This would lower timber profits on the area, but would surely help the Kirtland's warbler.

In 1981, little was known about the wintering whereabouts of the warblers, although it was known that they had been sighted in the Bahamas. How much more is known ten years later? There was a drastic decline in

53

numbers of singing males counted from 210 in 1986 to 167 in 1987. But there was a dramatic rebound in 1988 when 215 single males were counted. However, these figures are suspect for the reason that the populations of Kirtland's warblers move as certain tree groups become too old for their liking, and they move into new age-groups of trees which are just right. As a result, they may be missed in the first census after they move and then discovered in time for the second census after they move. A dramatic example of this was found in the 1988 census when 78 singing males were counted in the New Mack Lake Burn area, an increase of 50 singing males over 1987. We now feel that the problem of providing undisturbed nesting habitat—in trees of the right age and size—has been solved. In addition, trapping and removal of the parasitic cowbirds seems to have that problem under control, although it obviously requires periodic repeat to be effective. There is finally reason to be optimistic about the future of the Kirtland's warbler.

Optimistic, yes, but not complacent. The small population base we are working with points up the delicacy of the situation. The total number of singing males censused by year is as follows:

Year	Count	Note
1951	432	
1961	502	The all time modern high population
1971	201	
1972	200	
1973	216	
1974	167	The all time modern low population
1975	179	
1976	200	
1977	219	
1978	200	
1979	211	
1980	243	
1981	232	
1982	207	
1983	215	
1984	215	
1985	217	
1986	210	
1987	167	
1988	215	

As we finished writing this chapter, another threat to the Kirtland's warbler was noted. Scientists at the University of California, studying the global warming situation, predicted that the jackpine forests of Michigan will get hotter in the next century. They also pointed out that the jackpine forests will react to this warming by slowly extending their range to the north and contracting their range to the south. Yes, a forest species can move to suit changing environments, albeit the movement will be very slow. It seems that the preferred habitat of 1990 in Michigan will move northward to provide the same conditions in Ontario in the next century or two. As if the Kirtland's warbler didn't have enough problems, now it must plan on a move in a hundred years or so.

The future for these two birds—one the biggest of endangered birds, the other one of the smallest of endangered birds—holds an omen for mankind. Surely we must know that if we cannot save tiny warblers and majestic condors from extinction, we probably cannot save ourselves.

8

America's Bald Eagle

Way back when America was a young nation, Benjamin Franklin argued that the wild turkey should be selected as our national emblem, rather than the bald eagle. Ben wasn't kidding. He told the truth about the bald eagle, that the regal-looking bird was a scavenger that loved to feed on carrion killed by some bird or animal stronger than the eagle. He pointed out that the eagle was not above robbing the weaker birds, that it customarily forced the more expert fisher, the osprey, to drop its fish after it caught it. The eagle then swooped down and caught the fish in the air and fed on the kill of another.

Ben Franklin pointed out that the wild turkey, on the other hand, was a resident species which withstood the cold of winter instead of migrating away from that cold. Native to all of the original thirteen states, the turkey provided the only meat that many of the earliest settlers could kill for their own use. Ben admired the intelligence and wariness of the turkey—and as a turkey hunter, I agree with him more than two hundred years later.

But the fact remains that the regal-looking, white helmeted bald eagle is the symbol of the United States of America. It was so chosen by our elected representatives.

A painting by famed wildlife artist Bob Hines helped to familiarize thousands of Americans with the bald eagle. Hines' painting, created for the Department of the Interior, was distributed by the Superintendent of Documents, of the U.S. Office of Printing and Engraving, in poster size. In 1989, another famed wildlife artist, Robert Bateman, produced an even

more beautiful and lifelike painting of the regal bald eagle. His beautiful art, unlike the easily available Hines poster, is a "limited edition" print and quite costly.

Is the bald eagle in danger of disappearing as a species? Absolutely not. It does not really belong on our list of endangered species. It **IS** endangered peripherally, in the 48 contiguous states. Peripherally? Yes. That means that it is in danger in part of its range. It certainly is **NOT** endangered in Canada nor in Alaska. In fact, in Alaska, it is exceedingly common and certainly in no danger of disappearing. I've seen as many as sixty bald eagles in one tree along Alaska's salmon streams. Haines and Skagway are winter homes to large concentrations of bald eagles brought to those spots by the abundance of food provided by the dead and dying spawning salmon which clog streams running into the ocean. In Alaska, the bald eagle is an opportunist which frequents salmon streams at spawning time—to take advantage of natural mortality. This opportunism of the bald eagle is further demonstrated in the southern extremes of its range. Here bald eagles regularly patrol around the edges of flocks of wintering waterfowl. The bald eagle is not a fast enough flyer to catch a flying duck, but the eagle has learned that it pays to flush the resting birds every once in a while. When the waterfowl flock takes to the air, the eagle notices that individual waterfowl remain on the water. Then the eagle swoops in for the kill. By thus cleaning up the dead and dying birds, the eagle performs a useful purpose as a scavenger and demonstrates its ability to take advantage of any concentration of wildlife. The biggest concentration of eagles I've ever seen in the lower 48 was at the Lake Andes, South Dakota National Wildlife Refuge. There we counted more than 200 per day—patrolling the edges of a flock of a quarter of a million mallards.

But the eagle definitely was in trouble in the lower 48 states. The biggest part of the blame was laid at the feet of agricultural pesticides. More specifically, DDT. Remember that the bald eagle is a fish eater by choice and that it is at the top of the food chain. Pesticides enter the food chain in the bodies of dead insects. Fish eat those insects and accumulate the DDT in their body tissues. Small fish are eaten by larger fish, which again serve as "bioaccumulators"—increasing the concentration of the deadly DDT in their tissues. The lordly eagle swoops down and his talons pierce the body of a trout or salmon. The eagle eats the fish, and again serves to concentrate the DDT in its tissues.

Sad experience has shown that an abundance of DDT in the tissues causes the bird to lay eggs with shells so soft that the egg cannot withstand the rigors of incubation—if indeed it is even hard-shelled enough to survive being laid in the nest. DDT was not the only pesticide or insecticide, of course; it is just the one we know most about.

Any large bird used to be a target for people with guns, and the bald eagle suffered losses to the uninformed who thought that every hawk or eagle was a threat to flocks of chickens and turkeys. Passage of the federal law entitled the Bald Eagle Protection Act slowed illegal shooting to the point where it became statistically negligible. Under terms of this Act, the killer of a bald eagle could be hit with a fine of up to $5,000 or a year in jail, or both.

Harvesting of very large trees also had a deleterious effect upon eagle populations. Those big trees provided nesting spots for the eagles. These big birds build very big nests, and add to them from year to year, often nesting in the same spot all through their lives. When *THEIR* nesting spot was gone, the eagles sometimes did not nest at all that year.

Eagles declined drastically in numbers, especially in their eastern and southeastern habitats of the lower 48 states. They have been staging a comeback in the last decade, however, and there is now increased hope that they can be removed from the "endangered peripherally" list. Alaska continues to boast great numbers of salmon-eating eagles.

Reasons for the comeback are 1) banning of DDT and reduced usage of other chemicals, 2) an educational campaign to teach Americans that the bald eagle is not to be shot on sight, but rather is to be treasured, and 3) protection of nesting sites.

As part of the campaign to save the bald eagle in the Lower 48, state and private conservationists cooperate in a nation-wide count of wintering bald eagles. In 1990, they counted more eagles than in the wintering ground counts fifteen years ago! Credit for this increase, in part, should go to the National Wildlife Federation's program of offering a reward for information leading to the conviction of any person shooting a bald eagle in the United States. They began in 1971 with an offer of $500, and granted the reward money 14 times since. That means that only 14 convictions resulted

—but the "educational value" of the reward was very great. People learned that there actually was a reward for information leading to a conviction, which meant that their own neighbor might well turn them in if they shot an eagle. Now, in 1990, the National Wildlife Federation has doubled its reward amount to $1,000 to make up for inflation and to further focus attention on the majestic bald eagle and our attempts to safeguard it. Credit also should be given to the enforcement branch of the Fish and Wildlife Service for greatly stepped up programs to curtail the sale of eagle feathers used in ceremonials.

With improved law enforcement, and with improved public attitudes toward large raptors, the bald eagle is in fairly good shape in the lower 48 and doing fine in Alaska and Canada. The biggest worry is the destruction of habitat, which continues apace, and possible shortages of prey species. But the prognosis for the American bald eagle, as a species, is just this: Doing all right! We have another species, the golden eagle, which is common throughout most of the western United States. Although often accused (wrongly) of killing sheep, the golden eagle seems to be holding its own against shooting from airplanes, against sheepmen and their rifles. Never numerous, it seems to be doing all right.

But there are four other species of eagle that truly are endangered. They are the Greenland white-tailed eagle (*Haliaeetus albicilla groenlandicus*), which inhabits Greenland and nearby Arctic islands; the Harpy eagle (*Harpia harpyja*) of southern Mexico to the Argentine; the Philippine monkey-eating eagle (*Pithecophaga jefferyi*) obviously of the Philippines; the Spanish Imperial eagle (*Aquila heliaca adalberti*) of Spain, Morocco and Algeria. These four eagle species are endangered and in peril of extinction.

9

The Peregrine Falcon

A peregrine falcon is a bird with slaty blue and black markings, having a wingspread of about three and one half feet. It has lighter colored undersides with distinct barring marks on the belly. Does that describe a peregrine falcon?

No way.

A peregrine is a falcon of regal bearing, fierce of eye and manner, capable of unbelievably fast level flight which shifts into "the speed of light" when it stoops from the heights to hit its flying target. Its flight movements are like those of a pigeon, but much faster. Does that describe the peregrine? No, but we're getting closer.

I'd rank the peregrine second only to the gyrfalcon of Arctic climes as the most interesting of all raptors. And we almost lost it. In fact, it was extinct as a breeder in the eastern half of the United States. However, peregrines that breed on Greenland migrate along the eastern seaboard to wintering areas in North, Central and South America. We almost lost it entirely because we were so busy fighting insects with the effective insecticide known as DDT that we didn't notice that DDT and its metabolite DDE were eliminating birds by making them incapable of producing egg shells.

When we awakend to the catastrophe, the peregrine was gone from the eastern half of the 48 states. In the fall of 1979, I traveled near Pea Island NWR in North Carolina. I was pleased to see a peregrine chasing a mourning dove. In overdrive, both birds flashed across the sand dunes, with the dove jinking for dear life, the peregrine close behind. Failing to overtake the speeding dove in level flight, the peregrine broke off the race and swung atop a telephone pole to rest. I put the binoculars on it and was certain that it was, indeed, a peregrine. Did that mean that the peregrine was again a resident along our Atlantic seaboard. No, it simply meant that the peregrine migration from the far north was in full swing.

Later that day, I twice saw hovering peregrines suddenly stoop from a height of three or four hundred feet to hit mourning doves in full flight. With the added speed generated by its "free fall" the peregrine was much too fast for the panicky dove and hit the dove in mid air, killing it by the impact; then the peregrine dropping lower to catch the dead bird before it hit the ground. I do not believe any small bird has a chance against a "stooping" peregrine. With the added advantage of complete surprise the blue thunderbolt is bullet fast and remarkably sure in its attack.

At that time, the eastern peregrine was extinct, but northern and western races were in fair supply. Cornell University became the repository of all knowledge of the peregrine, and quickly became known for its ability to rear young peregrines.

Let's take a look at the history of these populations. In 1942, Dr. Joseph Hickey found that there were 275 known nesting sites of peregrines in the eastern United States. He felt that 210 of these sites were active in 1942 and estimated that there were 350 active nesting aeries in the east—estimating that he had failed to locate a large percentage of active aeries. At the same time, there were 133 known nesting aeries in Greenland and Canada.

In 1964, growing concern over the plight of the peregrine led to a more intensive and extensive search for aeries, and 209 were located in the eastern US. But not one of these aeries was in use! For all practical purposes, the peregrine was extinct in the eastern part of our nation.

Nothing happened for eleven years, sadly. In 1975 a further study confirmed our worst fears, the peregrine was gone. It was obvious that DDT was to blame. Researchers documented a 25% loss in egg shell thickness in the peregrine at the same time that the bird was losing population so rapidly. Fortunately, DDT was not in use in the Arctic.

Cornell University, using Arctic and western peregrine falcon breeding stock, refined the ability to produce young to the point where Dr. Heinz Meng raised seven young from one captive pair. (In the wild, the peregrine lays two to four eggs per year). Soon, Cornell University was able to raise 200 young per year.

A Recovery Plan was formulated and put into action immediately. The plan called for a complete inventory of all suitable nesting spots in the eastern half of the country. These sites were ranked in order of suitability for reintroduction of the species. Emphasis was placed on stepped-up captive reproduction, for stepped-up enforcement to protect migrating birds through the eastern states, and a good public information program to gain popular support for the peregrine.

Selecting brood stock for the program was a problem for geneticists. After much soul-searching, birds were taken from the Arctic race, from the Aleutians and Queen Charlotte Island in the north Pacific and from Scotland and the Mediterranean areas of Europe. It was felt that this would provide the genetic diversity to ensure a healthy race of falcons.

"Hacking" is the process of liberating young birds into the wild—slowly and easily—while still providing food for them at the liberation site. This gives the birds a chance to learn how to feed themselves, to gradually become less dependent upon man and able to survive in the wild. Hacking has the added advantage of starting the "imprinting" process. It was felt that the bird would become accustomed to the area in which it was released, and would return to that area to nest. It worked! Of the first 152 young birds released in this manner, 112 lived to the stage of independent existence.

In the spring of 1979, wild falcons paired, nested and produced young in the eastern half of the United States for the first time in twenty years.

One of the most fascinating stories to come out of this resurgence is the story of Scarlett, a female which took up permanent residence on the 33rd floor of the U.S. Fidelity and Guaranty building in downtown Baltimore. Skyscraper ledges and window openings provided a habitat similar to the cliffs that peregrines preferred in the original landscape. Although Scarlett seemed to have all her needs supplied, including a never-ending supply of domestic pigeons—an easy meal for the blue thunderbolt dropping out of the 33rd floor to strike far below at supersonic speeds.

Without a mate, Scarlett built a nest up on the skyscraper and went through all the necessary moves—but had no mate. Enlisting the aid of the Chesapeake and Potomac Telephone company, Cornell researchers placed a pen atop a nearby building and released an adult male—called Blue Meanie—into that pen. Scarlett became very excited and repeatedly flew to the cage. She accepted quail and pigeons offered to her at Blue Meanie's pen.

Then the dramatic moment came! Blue Meanie was released. He immediately flew up to the 33rd floor and Scarlett joined him with ecstatic cries. They flew off wing tip to wing tip, and researchers began to dream of an ending which went "and they lived happily ever after." But it was not to be. Blue Meanie flew off into the sunset and Scarlett returned alone to her nest, where she laid infertile eggs.

After what would have been a normal incubation period of time, researchers removed the infertile eggs and substituted downy young falcons from the propagation program at Cornell. Scarlett was a good mother and fed the chicks. She successfully fledged two males and two females.

About that same time, Secretary of the Interior Cecil Andrus authorized the project to hack young falcons atop the Interior building in downtown Washington, D.C. One thing I will agree to—there was an abundant population of domestic pigeons. There was great interest in the project and the Department of the Interior set up a closed circuit television system to allow the public to see the young falcons without disturbing them.

Why encourage peregrines to nest on skyscrapers? Three good reasons. First of all, these buildings have ledges which furnish nesting spots similar to those used by the wild birds on the sides of cliffs. Second, the food supply—domestic pigeons—is plentiful and expendable. Third, updrafts occurring against the sides of tall buildings help the peregrine to climb to its nest while carrying a fat pigeon to its young.

While the eastern race of peregrines was benefitting from a well thought out and beautifully implemented recovery program, peregrines in Alaska and our western states were in a different situation entirely. Never extirpated, they suffered a drastic population loss. Reasons for the decline were the same as on the east coast.

The earliest educated guess as to numbers of the remnant population in the western coastal states (plus Nevada) was made by Bond in 1946. He compiled a list of 136 known nesting sites and made a "gloriously wild guess" that there would be twice that number. Breeding populations remained stable until 1950, then declined rapidly. By 1969, only ten known nesting sites remained in California. As DDT spread its doubtful blessing over the agricultural West, conquering malaria and other insect-vectored diseases, the peregrine falcon was being decimated.

Egg shell thinning was a problem in the west as it had been in the east. In an effort to keep aeries active, researchers introduced healthy chicks into failed nests. Interior populations had better luck than did coastal birds. California took an active role in the attempt to rescue the peregrine.

Californian attempts to increase peregrine numbers included double clutching, cross-fostering and hacking back young birds that are captive and incubated from wild eggs.

Double clutching refers to the proven technique of removing the first clutch of eggs laid to induce the female to produce another clutch. It works.

Cross-fostering is the practice of putting peregrine falcon eggs in the nests of other species of hawks to be incubated, hatched and reared as wild birds. Many hawk species are very tolerant of this procedure, even to the point where one hawk nest hatched out chicken eggs. We still chuckle at the thought of those hawks bringing dead mice to the young chicks—and wonder what went through their heads when the chicks refused good red meat?

Hacking back refers to the practice of slowly releasing into the wild young peregrines that have been hatched in an incubator from eggs taken from the wild.

Recovery Team efforts proved successful in the east have been used in the west. Results, while not as spectacular, are very encouraging. As we

64

prepared this chapter, a National Wildlife Federation report came to our desk. Let's quote it in its entirety—

"Five peregrine falcons released in downtown Denver earlier this year have left their urban perches for the winter, but Colorado's 'Peregrine Partnership' is hopeful that the birds will return in 1991 and help spur recovery of the endangered raptor.

"The birds were the second group to be released as part of the Partnership, a three year cooperative project between the Colorado Wildlife Federation, the Colorado Division of Wildlife and several businesses. The program got underway last year when five peregrine chicks were placed in hack boxes atop the 23 story Civic Center in downtown Denver.

"Hacking is hand feeding a bird while slowly acclimating it to life on its own. The same building houses the offices of the Colorado Wildlife Federation.

"The five eyas released this year were fed and cared for by volunteers until the nestlings could hunt on their own. One clue the project is working came recently when a wild peregrine falcon was seen interacting with the project birds. Diana Blomeke, CWF staff member, said this was a good sign proving the birds can make a home in the confines of a metropolis.

"CWF anticipates the return of the first year's falcons next March when the birds will have reached breeding age. Blomeke says, 'We have high hopes for last year's peregrines returning.' The Partnership's goal is to have at least one mating pair return to the high rise and breed.

"Also next summer the final group of peregrine chicks will be hacked from the same building.

"Releases of peregrine falcons in urban areas have proved successful in the past. Los Angeles, Salt Lake City and other cities have been hosts to the falcons."

Re-introducing peregrine falcons into city habitats seems to be successful and this makes me happy for many reasons. I rejoice at the resurgence of a regal bird, a proud raptor, one that kills pigeons for its dinner. Most cities have no love for the "barn" pigeons which infest their public buildings and befoul the walkways. Of course, there are many who like to see the pigeons. Hundreds of people feed them daily, simply because the pigeon comes close to providing "wild birds" to the unnatural habitat of the city.

If the peregrine can ever become numerous enough in city habitats to have any effect at all on the hordes of filthy barn pigeons, we will have a perfect solution to two problems.

As of today, the prognosis for the peregrine falcon is one of guarded optimism. Recovery is on the way; it is not yet here.

Gray Whale

10

The Great Whales

In the book of Genesis in the Christian bible, we read, "And God made Great Whales."

Man has very nearly undone the work of the Creator. Mankind has nearly exterminated several species of great whales and sadly reduced numbers of all great whales.

The Blue Whale is the largest animal that ever lived, bigger than any dinosaur that ever lived, and it still lives—but it is in danger in both the short term and the long term. Everything about the great blue whale is big. Calves measure as much as 25 feet long when born, and gain weight at the rate of 200 pounds per day, while feeding only on mother's milk. When man began thinking about numbers of wildlife species, it was estimated that only 210,000 of these monsters existed. That was in the mid 1850's. In 1985, that number had been reduced to approximately 11,000! Ninety-five percent of the blue whales were gone!

The bowhead whale fared even more badly, dropping from 100,000 to about 4,000. Gray whales, never numerous, almost disappeared from the eastern Pacific and did disappear from the western Pacific. They are now staging a small but encouraging comeback on America's side of the Pacific. Sperm whales once numbered a million and one half; in 1985 a quarter million drop in their population had been noted.

Sei whales numbers dropped from about 200,000 to only 80,000, and the Minke whale decreased from 360,000 to about 250,000.

These population figures might or might not approximate the facts—it is very hard to census whales which ply all of the world's oceans and do not reply to questionnaires. But it is very obvious that we have severely diminished all whale species and several of them rate the term "endangered."

Why has this happened? Let's look at the history of whaling.

Eskimos have killed, and used whales since time immemorial. But Eskimo numbers were always small and whale numbers always great. Furthermore, the whaling season was very short. During only one and one half to two months of the year was it possible for Eskimos to hunt whales. Their impact was unimportant.

About 1300, Basque sailors in the northwest corner of what is now Spain found out that they could harpoon and kill whales in the Bay of Biscay. They killed the whale and towed it in to shore to be butchered and rendered into whale oil. For almost three centuries, these hardy pioneers enjoyed a world monopoly of whaling. They killed only the "right" whale. It was called "right" because it was the right one to kill, for it floated when dead and could be towed to shore. When the Basques found the whales scarce in the Bay of Biscay, they adventured across the Atlantic and worked rich whaling grounds off New England's shores and up along the Canadian Maritime Provinces. Probably they knew of the North Atlantic whale populations from the stories of cod fishermen. Portuguese fishermen, pursuing *bacalao*, were familiar with many ports in Newfoundland and Labrador long before the "discoverers" came to stake their claims as the first to see these new lands.

This brought whaling to the attention of seafaring nations whose sailors no longer feared falling off the edge of the world. England, Spain, Portugal, Norway, Scotland, Russia and the United States (once born of Revolution) got into the act, and the death knell for many whales was sounded. Norway got into the act with a vengeance, finding rich stocks of whales in their Arctic reaches. Near Spitzbergen, they founded Smeerenburg, which translates into "Blubbertown." Japan got into the oceanic whale-killing race very late in the game, but seems determined to make up for that lapse by continuing to kill whales that are near extinction. New Bedford and New London became whaling ports from which American ships set out on voyages which sometimes lasted more than three years—hunting down the leviathans of the deep. Herman Melville's *Moby Dick* told of that era, an era of great courage, great privations and great fortunes being made from the decimation of whale populations.

Whaling efficiency continued to grow. Steam-powered killer boats now could chase and catch the fastest whale. Whaling pioneers sought only the bowhead, right and sperm whales, the ones which floated when dead. The swifter and more elusive *rorquals* sank when killed, and were too heavy for primitive whalers. But when Sven Foyn invented the harpoon bomb in 1864, the biggest of the rorquals was fair game for the modern whaler. Foyn's invention consisted of a harpoon fired by a cannon, and containing in its "warhead" an explosive. The cannon delivered the harpoon deep into the whale's vitals. When the whale (or the ship) tightened up on the attached line, backward slanted "barbs" on the harpoon broke vials of sulphuric acid which ignited the charge of gunpowder inside the harpoon. That detonation in its innards killed almost every whale on the first shot—but if needed, a second bomb could be fired into the dying whale. When the dead whale was "reeled in," a pipe was shoved into its innards and compressed air pumped in to make sure the whale floated. Then it was hauled to a factory ship, or to a shore station.

A real innovator, Foyn built an "accumulator" into his line-handling system which provided the stretch and give necessary to keep from breaking a line when hauling a twenty ton carcass in a heavy sea. No species was immune and even primitive observers noticed that whale numbers were dropping in the North Atlantic.

Whalers began to work the Arctic and Antarctic waters and all of the western Pacific. Many nations paid a "licensing" fee to Great Britain for the privilege of setting up shore stations on South Georgia, so that they would work the whale populations of Antarctic waters. The resourceful Norwegians set up a floating whaling station—one that could be towed to the edge of the pack ice and moored there to boil out the oil, cut out the whalebone or baleen and—not incidentally, build huge fortunes for whaling companies.

By 1712, American colonists were taking sperm whales. We became very good at it. After the War of Independence from England, whaling became an American game, with American whalers dominating the scene in the 1800's.

In 1859, petroleum oil was discovered in Pennsylvania. This was not noted by whalers at the time, but it spelled the end of big profits from sperm oil, needed for lamps and candles. Kerosene was better and you didn't have to go to sea for three years to get it. About the same time, spring steel was becoming cheap enough to undercut and displace the springy whalebone which was used—among other purposes—to shape the figures of 19th century women.

Note well the date of 1859, because after that date there was no valid economic reason to ever kill another whale—except for food. Eskimos used the whales for food, so did primitive tribes along the northern edge of the Euro-Asian land mass. The protein-hungry islands of Japan had now developed a taste for whale meat—to match their taste for all other seafoods. The Japanese are still loath to leave the whaling arena in 1990! Called "whale beef" the meat of whales is prized in Japan, and the Japanese pay high prices for it. Interestingly enough, good red *cattle beef* can be sold in Japan cheaper than whale meat—but Japan continues to invent excuses to keep American beef out. Tokyo alone has 8.5 million seafood lovers and most of them still like whale meat.

As a junior officer in the U.S. Navy during World War II, I was serving aboard a ship which used a surfacing grey whale for target practice, firing our three inch cannon at the surface-basking animal. When I argued volubly against this waste of life, the skipper told me, "Don't be a damned fool! There are lots of whales and we don't get a chance to shoot at something resembling a submarine very often!"

I'm happy to relate that our marksmanship was lousy and we didn't even scare the whale. Everybody but me got a good laugh out of the incident and we went on toward the Solomon Islands. The whale went on sunning himself.

The International Whaling Commission was founded in 1946. Ostensibly formed to help whales, it was completely lacking in enforcement authority. Member nations used the IWC as a lobbying place to guarantee the continuation of their whaling activities. The IWC was a total failure at first. As late as 1964, 23 factory ships were still operating and the total catch that year was estimated at 63,000 whales.

But world opinion was turning in favor of the whale. In 1972 the United Nations called for a ten year moratorium on the taking of all whales. A splendid gesture, but no one had the authority to catch and punish those whaling nations which violated the moratorium.

In 1981, Bantam Books published Farley Mowat's A Whale for the Killing. This book had nothing to do with commercial whaling, but it attracted a lot of attention to the subject of whales.

Then the IWC discovered a way to put teeth into its directives which sought to reduce whale killing by setting quotas. The United States Congress legislated against the products of nations which violated the whale killing ban. Ousting Japanese fishing vessels from U.S. Coastal waters did much to bring the Japanese around—at least closer—to the IWC directives. The fact that the United States is the world's greatest open market was not lost on nations that wanted to sell their seafood to us.

Slowly, but inevitably, the IWC has gained respectability. As we write this, only Japan and South Korea continue to flout its directives, but they are slowly coming around.

In 1986, the International Whaling Commission voted to ban all commercial whaling after 1986. Japan, Norway and the USSR filed objections to this closure and—again—the IWC lacked enforcement authority.

Moreover, the proposed ten year moratorium proposal had a weak link. An effort to count worldwide stocks of whales was to be undertaken during the ten years. In 1987, the Japanese hypocritically proposed to kill 1,650 Minke whales in the Antarctic as a "research tool, aimed at determining the size of the Minke population." Surely there must be a better way to count Minke whales than to kill them!

To further expose the hypocrisy of their action, the Japanese continued to sell the meat and oil taken from this "research" killing of Minke Whales.

Perhaps we could swallow their "research" story if the profits of the slaughter of Minkes were turned over to the IWC for enforcement purposes.

Using this same excuse of "research," Iceland killed fin whales in 1986 and 1987. Like Japan and South Korea, Iceland has asked for "research killing quotas" in 1986. In June of 1987, the IWC refused. Yet 80 fin whales were taken by Icelanders before U.S.-Iceland talks produced a stop to the whale killing. Iceland, which prospers by the export of its considerable seafood industry, fears a possible U.S. embargo on their products.

Elephants and whales are the only living beings whose brains are larger than ours. Unfortunately, we do not make use of our brains when we should.

In an successful attempt to curry favorable public opinion, Russian icebreakers and ships cooperated with U.S. and Alaskan agencies to free a pair of whales trapped by ice in Alaskan waters. Whether or not these two whales lived through their delayed migration down to the west coast of Mexico, Gorbachev and company found out that American and world public opinion was definitely on the side of the whales.

As the International Whaling Commission grows to adulthood and takes its rightful place as the controller of whale killing, we can look forward to restoration of whale numbers—IN THE SHORT TERM—to the point where we will have absolved humanity of its sins in killing whales with the harpoon.

But—IN THE LONG RUN—Whales and all other denizens of the oceans are in growing danger. That danger comes from the increasingly appalling pollution of the oceans. Take one small example out of many. New York City hauled its sewage and waste out to sea for many decades. It was so convenient to dump it over into deep water and have it gone for good—out of sight, out of mind. Now we find that it is not gone for good, but rather is rolling back in upon our beaches, fouling our seaways and posing serious health hazards. Unable to stomach our sewage, the oceans are beginning to vomit this filth back on our beaches. Once we thought that the ocean was too large to ever notice the effects of our littering its bottom with our wastes. We now know better. The sludge is coming home to roost.

Fouled beaches are bad enough, but what of the animals which must live in those polluted waters? It is time to start thinking about how we can save wildlife if we destroy their habitat—the greatest habitat niche in the world, the oceans. In 1972, I wrote in the book, *WAYS OF GAME FISH*, the following:

"Man's filth is now flowing into the oceans at such a rate that conditions for the reproduction of game fishes are no longer right for their survival."

Obviously, ocean pollution was bad in 1972. Eighteen years later, ocean pollution has increased to catastrophic proportions, far beyond my worst fears of 1972.

Whales seem to have survived the harpoon and the flensing lance; they have a fair chance of surviving the Japanese seafood market. No longer are

71

the world's largest animals being processed into pet food. The short term danger only lasted for a thousand years. The long term danger is very real and whales are not safe from mankinds' filth. The long term prognosis for survival in a filthy ocean is not good.

If present pollution trends continue, the world's largest brains will disappear from the earth, because we didn't use ours.

11

The Hawaiian Picture

In the geologic sense, everything about Hawaii is new. Every form of life that exists there had to come there, for Hawaii was created by volcanic eruptions which built up lava from the sea bed until it broke through the surface of the sea and became dry land. This process continues to this day. Over millennia, erosion by wind and water carved the lovely shapes of the main islands while wind and sea brought new forms of life to the newly-created islands.

Seaborne coconuts probably got a foothold on the edge of the igneous rock and prospered, for Captain Cook found them in great profusion when he became the first European to discover the lovely "Sandwich Islands," so named for the Earl of Sandwich. The droppings of birds carried seeds of life from other islands, even life from the mainlands of Asia or North and South America. These seeds grew and prospered in the constant warm temperatures and plentiful rainfall of the Hawaiian Islands.

Some scientists believe that if Charles Darwin had reached the Hawaiian Islands instead of the Galapagos, he would have written his Evolution of Species ten years sooner—for the evidence was so much stronger and easier to decipher.

Bird species reached these fire-born islands and liked what they found. They were in a closed environment, with no enemies and with lots of food available. Evolutionary processes were speeded up, because they operated without many extraneous pressures—such as losses to predation of a mutant species. Evolution of separate species, to fit separate niches, proceeded with unusual speed. If a specially downcurved beak would allow access to a special food, some species of bird promptly (in the geologic sense) developed that necessary downcurved beak.

73

The first humans to reach the Hawaiian archipelago were Polynesians who sailed dugout canoes across great expanses of the Pacific with consummate skill, relying on intuition, knowledge of the stars, even sensitive senses of smell, to allow them to find these tiny dots in the vastness of the Pacific Ocean. These first human intruders caused the extinction of many species—species which could not sustain the pressure of human hunting, for they had evolved without dangers and were defenseless against it. At least 44 taxa were exterminated by the Polynesians and the mammals they brought with them, *prior* to the arrival of Europeans in 1778.

Should we weep for the species of bird life which became extinct? Or did they, in their turn, exterminate other life forms which preceded them? As each wave of arrivals came to the Hawaiian Islands, they had a drastic damaging effect upon the earlier waves of arriving immigrants. In many cases, new arrivals completely displaced earlier arrivals.

But the Polynesians were all conservationists compared to the white men who came after them. Ranching, logging and other agricultural practices changed the habitat, crowding out many species. For example, on far away Laysan Island there was a different arrival—the rabbit. The rabbit ate the vegetation of Laysan Island, almost eliminating it. The Laysan millerbird, the Laysan honeycreeper and the Laysan rail all became extinct. The Laysan rail and Laysan finch had already been translocated to Midway Island in an effort to broaden their chances for survival. But the common rat was accidentally introduced to Midway Island in 1946 during the Second World War and the rats eliminated the translocated species from Midway, along with the Bulwers petrel which lived on Midway.

White settlers brought dogs and cats as pets. The incredibly varied bird populations had no fear of these efficient predators and suffered great losses. Lush tropical vegetation was cleared to make way for grass pastures, fertile lowlands were drained and plowed to make way for sugar cane and pineapples. Man simply crowded out many species of Hawaiian avifauna. The state bird, the Nene goose, was almost exterminated at this time, for its nesting habitat and feeding areas were expropriated from their rightful owners (the birds) and given to pineapple and sugar cane growers. In addition to his land use sins, the white man brought two more species of rats, barn owls and the Indian mongoose to this birders' paradise. Defenseless bird species were eliminated *en masse*.

In summation, the damage has been terrific and is still continuing. What is amazing is not that so many bird species suffered so greatly, but that Hawaiian avifauna remains among the richest and most varied in the world today! In 1986, bird researchers in the high forests of the big islands found bird densities as great as three thousand birds per square kilometer! Last year, approximately one million seabirds of 17 different species located their colony nests on Laysan Island, for a density of nearly a quarter of a million birds per square kilometer. These seabird nesting colonies find their food in the sea. All they ask is that they be left alone. The establishment of the Hawaiian Islands National Wildlife Refuge has been a giant step toward providing the privacy they need. Maybe privacy is the wrong word, for the birds nest in crowded colonies where their own din is unbelievable and no one bird is ever alone. But they've known that situation for millennia, and prosper under those conditions. The refuge serves the main purpose of keeping man away.

The Townsends Shearwater is an interesting case history. Young birds on their fledgling flight became confused by man's electric lighting and fell from the skies in great numbers. Cooperative people brought the fallen birds to recuperation centers where they were nursed back to health and reintroduced onto the beach areas. Cooperative power and light companies developed different systems of lighting, systems which sent the light down where it was needed, but kept it from disorienting the birds which flew above the lights. Results have been encouraging, but the Shearwater still falls from the skies and the problem is still with us.

Other species are menaced by introduced mammalian predators. Trapping programs to remove mongooses and rats, fencing projects to exclude goats and cattle, all have been shown to be helpful in allowing the native birds to nest successfully. U. S. Fish and Wildlife experts have used an anticoagulant drop bait to kill the introduced mongoose and the introduced rat. They can use the mammal-specific poison safely because there is only one native mammal and that is the Hoary bat, which does not pick up and eat the poisoned baits.

Perhaps the most important change on the far-flung islands of the Hawaiian chain is the change in public awareness. Now it is well known that introduction of exotics like the mongoose and the domestic cat was a terrible mistake. Educational programs have made Hawaiians aware of and proud of their unique avifauna. This lends support to improvement projects. Attempts to reintroduce captive propagated birds into their former habitats have met with varied results. If the causative factors of their disappearance have been removed—the reintroductions prosper. If the same conditions which caused their demise are still operative, the reintroductions fail. This has proved especially true in the case of the five species of waterfowl which are indigenous to the islands. The Laysan duck, which nests only on Laysan Island, has increased from a low of about 20 individuals in the wild in 1915 to the point where several hundred now nest on *their* island. NWR operations on Laysan bode well for the future of this duck. In addition, there are a great number of Laysan ducks in captivity around the world, all reproducing readily. This does nothing to help the wild population at present, but it does ensure genetic diversity for possible reintroductions in the future.

A second species, the large Hawaiian duck (koloa) is holding its own on mongoose-free Kauai. These ducks have also been introduced onto Oahu and Hawaii itself. There is a grave danger, however, that the introduced mallard duck crossbreeds with the Hawaiian duck. It is quite possible that the Hawaiian will hybridize with the mallard to the extent that another species is lost. This hybridization with mallards has effectively removed the Mexican duck from the list of continental U.S. species, and the same thing may happen here.

Even as America's national emblem, the bald eagle, is threatened (not endangered) on the 48 contiguous states, so the Hawaiian state bird, the Nene goose, is endangered. This goose breeds easily in captivity and large stocks are present at zoos and aviaries around the world. But reintroduction into the wild on the Hawaiian Islands has not proved to be the panacea it was once thought to be. Released birds bred and prospered until their colonies attracted predators—especially the introduced mongoose. Poisoned drop baits are now being used on nesting colonies of nenes to control predation. Perhaps it will work, but the dangers from exotic predators—such as your pet cat and my pet dog—are very real for the endangered nene.

The appendices at the end of this volume list the endangered bird life of Hawaii in more detail, and the list is surprisingly long. What makes the situation so desperate is that most of these species, if not all of these species, are found in the wild nowhere else in the world.

The name "Io" is well known to crossword puzzle fanatics. It is the word you write down when the definition reads, "Hawaiian hawk", for there is only one hawk native to Hawaii. It seems to be quite adaptive and seems to be secure in its very small range, the same small range it occupied in pre-Polynesian times. Perhaps man is not to blame for its small population.

Where there once were five species of honeyeaters in Hawaii, now only one *individual* is known to be alive deep in the Alakai Swamp. If this really is the only individual of the Oo species, we can add another to the long list of extinctions in Hawaii.

The richness of the speciation of Hawaiian birds is perhaps best demonstrated by the honeycreepers. There are still 20 species remaining out of 48 known pre-historically. Although evolving from one species that arrived on Hawaii in the prehistoric past, the honeycreepers adapted to various ecological niches with great originality. The study of their differences would require a lifetime for a scientist. Honeycreeper bills range from the seed crusher bill of the *palila*, through the crossed bills of the *akepa* to the downcurved beak of the *iiwi*.

Exotic introductions have been the greatest enemy of Hawaiian wildlife. The introduction of humanity was the worst mistake, as far as the avifauna is concerned. Introduced cattle have wrecked habitat, introduced goats have trampled the eggs of nesting seabirds, introduced dogs and cats killed many species entirely and have greatly reduced other species, the introduced mongoose has been a disaster for ground nesting birds, introduced feral pigs have rooted up the habitat of many birds with bad results. Even in the field of snails, we have a disastrous introduction. The poo-uli evolved as a

76

snail eater, and found its food in the moist floor of the high tropical forests. The introduced garlic snail eats other snails and competes with the poo-uli for food. Introduced avian diseases, especially avian malaria, have had a bad effect upon bird numbers.

Man has severely damaged paradise in Hawaii.

We are now trying to make amends where it is not too late. Active programs for the control (better yet, elimination) of the introduced mongoose, rat, feral pig and feral goat are showing good results. Experimental fencing to keep unwanted ungulates out of habitat niches shows much promise and more of it is being done each year. Removal of grazing animals from lower slopes of some of the islands has allowed the reforestation of these lower elevations and allowed the endangered bird species to extend their ranges down from the higher habitat into which they have been forced.

Research is leading the way in forest restoration, too, and this may have the most important long lasting effect. Here, as everywhere else, habitat seems to be the key. Given good habitat, most species can withstand predation, although they are often powerless to defend themselves against *introduced* predators.

In Hawaii there has been heated debate over the possibility that remnant populations should be taken into captivity and reared artificially—as a last ditch effort to prevent extinction. Proponents point to the mainland efforts to breed the California condor artificially in captivity and to the case of the whooping crane which has been successfully reared in captivity. Opponents of these programs point out that captive reared whoopers have not added materially to the wild population, being unable to compete in the wild and are unable to find mates in the wild. They also note the failure of the dusky seaside sparrow captive rearing project, begun too little and too late, in Florida. (See Chapter 5 of this book). Sadly, opponents of captive propagation point to the fact that large scale reintroductions of the state symbol, the nene, have not succeeded in increasing the wild flock numbers. Captive propagation of the nene has succeeded in greatly increasing the number of nenes in captivity, but not in the wild.

The wonderful birdlife of Hawaii was, and still is, a textbook of evolution's ability to create different species to fit different ecological niches.

The catastrophic loss of Hawaiian bird species is a textbook example of how man crowds wildlife into extinction.

The prognosis for most of the endangered species in Hawaii is not good—because man continues to crowd these species out of their living space. Valiant efforts by conservationists have worked minor miracles in this tropical paradise, but as long as the human population of Hawaii continues to increase, the number of endangered species will decrease— decrease because so many more will become extinct, thus effectively removing themselves from the list of endangered.

12

Florida Panthers
and Sea Cows

Mankind has altered the habitat for wildlife in Florida perhaps more than in any other state. The unique meeting place of water and land which was Florida has now given way to a thousand miles of seaside developments, of big cities crammed with immigrants from Cuba and with untold thousands who came to Florida seeking the dream of inexpensive, sun-warmed retirement.

Man has partially drained the tremendous ocean of water and grass called the Everglades. Of many species which are in danger of extinction in Florida, let's talk about two as widely different species as can be found anywhere—the manatee and the Florida panther.

Manatees were first reported by Columbus' sailors who thought they looked like mermaids, which proved that these sailors had been away from home much too long. Shaped like a fat sausage, the near ton of blubber has a whiskered face which bears aboutely no resemblance to a beautiful woman. Slow moving and inoffensive, the manatee consumes as much as 200 pounds of green vegetation per day. Like a big cow grazing underwater, the manatee produced some tasty "manatee beef" and was hunted eagerly by the first European inhabitants of Florida and the Caribbean Islands.

But a far greater danger emerged when boats of all sizes invaded the manatee's habitat. A big propeller can actually slice a manatee in half. All sizes of propellers can cause gashes in the hide of the manatee, often killing them through loss of blood—sometimes by infection which enters the propeller wounds. Unfortunately, Florida has more registered boats than any other state, and the number continues to grow.

Aware that they were losing their manatees, Florida officials gave them complete protection from hunting, then set aside large areas needed by the manatee. In these areas, boating traffic was either slowed or prohibited entirely, reducing the chances of slashing a manatee. Many manatees are lost when they get their flippers entangled in crab pot lines, or other fishing gear. Research has shown that the manatees are fairly quick to learn and have good memories; yet they seem incredibly stupid in failing to get loose from such entanglements.

Manatees cannot stand marked drops in water temperatures. Some of them get through the fairly warm Florida winter by using the "warmed" water coming out of power plants' cooling systems. This dependence upon artificially warmed waters has its dangers. It leads to crowding, which increases chances of disease and puts the manatee in the vulnerable position of having all of its eggs in one basket. If the water cools suddenly, the manatee may die—for it does not tolerate temperature changes very well. We had physical proof of the manatee's inability to withstand temperature drops in the first week of 1990. A statewide quick freeze did tremendous damage to garden crops and some damage to the state's important citrus crop. Within 24 hours of the onset of the freeze, word came in that manatees were dying. If the newspapers were correct, no less than 26 of the big sea cows were found dead in the next ten days! It was a sad sight to see the big bodies towed behind a motor boat—victim of a sudden cold snap.

The original range of the Florida subspecies extended up the Atlantic coast as far as Virginia, but none winter north of Florida now. Our manatee, properly called the West Indian Manatee (*Trichecus manatus*) once was found all around the beaches of the Caribbean and along the Atlantic coast of Brazil, nearly down to the Tropic of Capricorn. It is very rare throughout that range today. Hopefully, there are more than 1,000 of our sea cows in Florida today.

Other manatee subspecies have not fared as well as ours. The Steller's Sea cow was found all the way up the northwestern coast of North America, well into icy waters. Unfortunately, whalers exterminated it for food and for oil produced by melting down the manatee's blubber.

The Dugong (*Dugong dugong*) once was found all along the northern beaches of Australia, throughout Indonesia and Malaysia and through the Philippines. Its numbers have shrunk alarmingly, and it is not common anywhere.

Another species, the Amazonian manatee (*Trichecus inunguis*) was once found throughout the Amazon basin, even up to the headwaters near the Andes. Little is known of its numbers today.

A hopeful note about our Florida manatee. Dr. Jesse R. White, Veterinarian at the Miami Seaquarium and adjunct professor at the University of

Florida, has been having good success with his program of breeding mana-tees in captivity. Where others had failed to reproduce manatees in captiv-ity, Dr. White had good luck when he changed the diet of the grazing "sirens" by adding a daily supplement of calcium and phosphorus. Then he improved their iceberg lettuce diet by adding commercial trout food, ap-ples and carrots. Invigorated by better food, the manatees promptly repro-duced. Now the captive breeding system grows a mixture of wheat and oats—hydroponically—to provide three times as much protein as native plants.

There is definitely hope for our subspecies, the West Indian Manatee. Captive-reared manatees are now being released into the wild, and their whereabouts traced by means of radio telemetry. Results appear promising. The public awareness program administered by the Florida State agencies has produced good dividends and lethal collisions between propellers and manatees are decreasing. Perhaps extinction is not inevitable in the case of the Florida manatee—a blob-like, shapeless, slow-moving vegetarian easily located in the water. The prognosis is guardedly optimistic in USA waters, very poor in other habitats with the other subspecies.

THE FLORIDA PANTHER is something else again . . . a very secretive, nocturnal animal which is very difficult to locate because it is very wary, quick moving and fond of the thickest thickets found in Florida. While the manatee is very visible, easily approached and not at all wary, the Florida panther is very mobile, secretive, almost entirely nocturnal and very diffi-cult to observe.

The Florida subspecies of the panther is but a slightly different animal from the common mountain lion *Felis concolor* which ranges from Alaska to Patagonia and most parts in between. Today, there is definitely no endan-gered mountain lion—his numbers are fairly constant across a huge area of the Rocky Mountain states from Montana and Idaho down through Wyo-ming, Colorado, Utah, New Mexico and Arizona and he still exists in the rugged Sierra Madres of Mexico.

This Florida subspecies is quite a different matter entirely. Once fairly common through the southeastern USA, from Florida to Arkansas and north to the Carolinas along the Atlantic coastal tier of states, its numbers have shrunk to the "nearly gone" point where we estimate less than 50 ani-mals still alive. This remnant population is confined entirely to Florida; at least it appears that way.

Let's review the bidding—when Columbus came to these shores, or near to them, there were far fewer deer than there are now. There definitely were more panthers than there are today. To make sure no one misunder-stands, that panther name is applied to the same animal that most of us call mountain lion or cougar or puma.

Mountain lions subsisted almost entirely on deer. They had eaten deer since time immemorial. They hadn't hurt the deer population in the centuries that they fed on deer. But the white man brought his agricultural practices to this continent and weighted the scales heavily in favor of the deer. We removed the mature forests and substituted row crops such as corn. Deer loved this change, for it gave them lots of "edge" cover, and provided escape cover right next to a good food supply. Man also removed the adult forest wherein the cougar felt safe, and the deer did not feel safe.

Monoculture became the "in thing" in forest planning, and these stands of even-rowed pines were definitely not to the panther's liking.

Man wanted deer; pioneers did not want cougars. Man trapped the lion, hunted it with dogs and removed its home ranges. Lion numbers fell drastically while deer numbers mushroomed. Again, we have a case where man interfered with a functioning predator-prey relationship. The range of the mountain lion shrank and there appeared a big gap in the range—a gap where lions were very scarce across the prairies and plains from eastern Colorado and New Mexico all the way to the remaining forests in deep east Texas and Louisiana and Arkansas. This effectively separated the two populations of mountain lion. Under effective management as a game animal, the western mountain lions are in stable condition from the Rocky Mountain states all the way up into British Columbia and on to the edges of Alaska.

The southeastern variety has almost died out. Biologists named it a separate subspecies *Felis concolor coryi* but its own mother can't tell a *coryi* subspecies lion from a regular *Felis concolor concolor*. The taxonomist recognizes a few differences. The Florida panther is characterized by slightly longer legs, with shorter and stiffer hairs in its pelt, darker in color than *concolor,* a skull which boasts a relatively broad, flat frontal region with remarkably high and arched nasals. Almost all Florida panthers have white flecks on head, neck and shoulders.

For decades the Florida panther was protected from legal hunting, but man's crowding into Florida was worse than legal hunting. More than ten years ago, the head of the Florida Panther Recovery Team, biologist Robert C. Belden, and his associates recommended acquisition of a sizable chunk of Florida as a refuge for the endangered cat. Even then, they had a hard time finding out whether or not a certain area held any panthers or not.

To get an idea of the panther's whereabouts and to track its movements, Florida biologists called on Roy McBride, lion hunter and all around good outdoorsman from West Texas. I had worked with Roy way back in 1961 and knew him to be a thorough-going professional. Roy and his dogs went to Florida and proved that they could trail and tree the Florida panther. Radio telemetry collars were attached to the panthers which were then released.

In 1981, the chances of being able to preserve the remnant population looked mighty dim. Speeding automobiles killed a few, but the biggest problem was reduction of habitat for the cougar requires a wide territory in which to range. Essentially solitary, except when the female comes in season, the cougar found its numbers steadily shrinking. Studies continued, and an educational program sponsored by the Florida Game and Fresh Water Fish Commission changed the attitude of the public toward the elusive cat. But the fact was obvious that the panther needed a home of its own, a place where it would be safe.

83

In 1989 came the big news. The U.S. Fish and Wildlife Service was able to buy 24,300 acres of critical panther habitat, to form the nucleus of the Florida Panther National Wildlife Refuge. Eventually the refuge will measure 30,000 acres of land. The more than twelve million dollar purchase price came from the Land and Water Conservation Fund. The remaining acreage is expected to come through land swaps.

With the establishment of the Florida Panther NWR 35 miles east of Naples, Florida, all three known population centers of this feline are now safe. The other two areas are the Big Cypress National Preserve and the Everglades National Park.

Establishment of the Florida Panther NWR is the most encouraging sign in the long struggle to save this subspecies of Florida panther. Will it be enough to turn the tide in favor of the panther? There is hope. But there is also the worry that the genetic base of this sub-species population is too small to allow its preservation. Prognosis: Not too good, but hopeful.

13

The Masked Bobwhite Quail

This quail, which wears a black mask like the *bandidos* of B movies, is slightly smaller than its far more numerous northern cousin. In 1990 it is known as *Colinus virginianus ridgwayii*, which makes it but a sub-species of the familiar northern bobwhite, which is simply *Colinus virginianus*. It's recent history can be divided into two chronicles, the time before Jim and Seymour Levy, and the time after Roy Tomlinson was assigned to work with the beleaguered species. Let's recount the history.

Masked bobwhites were found in goodly numbers over the wide grasslands of Arizona and Sonora in Old Mexico when the white man moved in. The settlers' cattle and sheep overgrazed those pastures which were home to the quail, doing irreparable damage to the habitat. During the three decades starting in 1870, cattle numbers in southern Arizona rose from 5,000 to 1,500,000! The masked bobs problems were compounded by the severe drought of the 1890's.

By January 1, 1900, you could not find a single masked bobwhite in the United States of America!

Pioneer ornithologist Ligon said that the bird was also extinct in Mexico by 1950. He was almost correct—almost but not quite. In 1964, Jim and Seymour Levy, sportsmen and amateur ornithologists from Tucson, found unfamiliar feathers in the nests of the cactus wren. This was in Sonora, near the tiny hamlet of Benjamin Hill. After positively identifying the feathers, the brothers Levy started searching for live masked bobs in Sonora. They found a few individuals, captured some, and tried to raise them in captivity back home in Tucson. There were two separate efforts, one at the Levy home and the other at the Arizona-Sonora Desert Museum. Vandalism and the destruction of the pens caused the museum to give up the propagation effort, but the Levy brothers didn't give up easily. They put pressure on the U.S. Fish and Wildlife Service to do something about the dire straits they found the masked bobwhite to be in. When an artificial propagation effort was started at Patuxent, birds from the Levy effort formed the nucleus. Inbreeding caused poor production in this first effort.

Yielding to the pressure from Arizona, the Fish and Wildlife Service assigned Spanish speaking biologist Roy Tomlinson to look into the plight of the masked bobwhite. He traveled widely through Sonora carrying a pair of mounted masked bobwhites, and a set of quail pictures. He went from rancho to rancho, always asking the same question, "Have you seen a bird that looks like this?"

He suceeded in locating two separate small populations of masked bobwhites and began a systematic, scientific study of the birds' habitat and of its needs. I had the privilege of making the rounds with Roy, over some of the worst roads in all of Old Mexico, while he documented the deteriorating habitat conditions in bobwhite range.

At the same time, Roy was studying historic habitats in southern Arizona, looking for an area that would provide the tall grass habitat that the birds seemed to require. Tomlinson got the Fish and Wildlife Service, the Bureau of Land Management and the Arizona Department of Game and Fish, and the University of Arizona cooperating in programs to restore habitat in Arizona.

After successfully negotiating the diplomatic protocol hurdles, Roy got permission to live-trap some of the Mexican birds and to take them out of the country. Tomlinson livetrapped Mexican birds in 1964 and again in 1970. They were flown first to Mexico City, then to Patuxent, Maryland where their progeny were easily raised in captivity. The original breeding stock furnished to Patuxent consisted of 57 birds live-trapped in the wild near Benjamin Hill, Sonora, and four pairs of captive-reared birds donated by the Levy Brothers in Arizona. One of the first uses of the new crop of masked bobs was to repay Mexico for the original live-trapped birds. But both Mexicans and Americans found that the captive-reared birds had very little chance for survival in the wild. They lacked the wariness needed to avoid predation. They didn't even bother to hide when a hawk flew overhead. They became high-priced hawk food very quickly. Within two months of their release, all had perished.

Various release methods were tried to give the captive-reared birds a better chance of survival. I remember nights when volunteer students from the University of Arizona slept on cots beside the gentle release pens in southern Arizona, trying to protect the birds while they learned the ropes of survival.

By now the artificial propagation program in Patuxent was in high gear, and there was a good supply of birds with which to experiment. Habitat was being improved and there was some hope for survival in the wild. Then Dr. David Ellis thought of a new idea.

"Why not use wild-trapped adult male bobwhites from Texas to teach the broods?"

"Because those live-trapped birds will hybridize with the masked bobwhites," he was told.

"Not if we use caponized males!" was the retort.

That experiment worked. The adult Texas males were introduced to their brood of young birds during the normal brooding season. They were given a couple of days to get accustomed to each other, then they were released—very gently—into the wild. The adult male taught his brood to freeze at his signal, to remain motionless when danger flew overhead. It worked, and the young masked bobwhites grew up wild and wary.

Populations introduced in 1976 with the caponized male system may have persisted to this day in some coverts in southern Arizona, on the Buenos Aires Ranch in the Altar Valley. By 1980, we had small—but thriving—populations living in southern Arizona. In 1990, the situation has grown markedly better. Now there is a Buenos Aires National Wildlife Refuge in Arizona and Manager Wayne Shifflett reports that masked bob populations are larger than ever before. Biologist Steve DeBrott located 17 coveys numbering at least 175 birds in the summer of 1989. The total pre-nesting population is at least twice the 175 number. Habitat on the refuge, protected from overgrazing, is greatly improved and the refuge people plan to introduce as many as 2,000 more captive-hatched birds this summer. The limited success achieved at the Buenos Aires NWR must be viewed against the undeniable fact that thousands of masked bobwhites have been liberated there, yet we only have at most 350 birds there. Success or failure of the re-introduction at the refuge cannot be judged until a few years after the restocking efforts are stopped.

The situation seems but slightly improved in Old Mexico.

Overgrazing of the semi-arid pasture lands of Sonora still continues. Pasture improvement measures in Old Mexico seem to center around the introduction of the very hardy buffelgrass. This offers some hope at first, as it does provide the tall grass cover needed by the birds. However, if buffelgrass becomes the only crop grown—a real monoculture, which is very possible—the masked bobwhites will not survive in the purely buffelgrass pastures. Buffelgrass in mature stands is too rank, with no space between the plants—and this rules out the masked bobwhite. Already, in 1990, biologists are beginning to rule out the buffelgrass, feeling that it has become a blight, rather than the panacea needed by the masked bobwhite habitat.

We must remember that these birds have evolved a different reproductive schedule. They hatch their eggs in late August and early September! It makes good sense. In July and August, the rains come to the ancestral range of the masked bobwhite quail. With the rains comes a plentiful supply of insects, supplying the necessary high protein food that the newly hatched quail need. Back in 1980, we held out little hope for the Mexican population because land management practices in the dry lands of Sonora and Sinaloa remained poor, with very little grass left for the birds. It seemed that the few remaining birds prospered when autumnal rains came on time, but almost disappeared during a dry fall. It is true that the situation in Mexico seems almost hopeless as of this writing, but we must remember that the Mexican population still existed after it had been considered extinct for twenty years. The masked bobwhite is a tough customer and he does not go gladly into that dark night of extinction.

With financial help furnished by the U.S. Fish and Wildlife Service and the Nature Conservancy, Mexican biologists are now working to improve the situation for the masked bobwhite in Old Mexico, operating under the aegis of the *Centro Ecologico de Sonora.*

The pioneer work begun by the Levy Brothers and Roy Tomlinson has been carried on and improved through a fine cooperative effort between the Arizona Game and Fish Department and the U.S. Fish and Wildlife Service. Steve Dobrott and David Brown, John Goodwin, Wayne Shifflet, Dr. David H. Ellis and Dr. Jim Lewis have all been part of this fine effort.

It is well to remember that the masked bobwhite has survived only through the international cooperation between the United States and the friendly folks south of the Mexican border. Birds were taken from Mexico several times. Birds went to Mexico from the United States several times. There is a continuing effort on both sides of the border, with dollars now going from our side to their side to pay for continuing work.

The prognosis for the masked bobwhite is that he will continue to prosper in improved habitats in southern Arizona and hopefully will continue to make the scene in Old Mexico—where we got our birds to start their long climb back from the brink of extinction.

14

Endangered SUBspecies

Sometimes we get all excited about the endangered status of a SUBspecies, when the full species is doing okay. I'd like to discuss a few instances of this phenomenon, just to put things in perspective. Let's start out by talking about squirrels . . .

The fox squirrel is a very successful species, with a range which extends over much of the nation and far into Canada as well. But one particular subspecies, called the Delmarva fox squirrel, is not doing anywhere near as well. In fact, with its habitat decreasing steadily as a result of mankind crowding into its world, it now is maintaining its numbers only because there is complete protection and good habitat on state and federal refuges. The squirrel gets its name from DELaware, MARyland and VirginiA—the three states which form its principal range. Once it ranged well up into Pennsylvania and even into southern New York State, but lost out in much of its range because of habitat changes. The big, sometimes two pounds of squirrel, Delmarva fox likes big trees, with lots of open parkland in between. White oak, which grows to great size and provides a steady source of mast, was plentiful on the Atlantic Seaboard in colonial times, but these valuable woods were severely reduced as civilization moved in.

It is easy to distinguish the Delmarva Fox Squirrel from its (often) symbiotic relative the common gray squirrel. Twice as big, the Delmarva subspecies of fox squirrel, prefers more open forests than the gray chooses, and the more fearless Delmarva spends a lot of its time on the ground, while the gray is much more timid and spends most of its time in the semi-safety of the trees.

As the mature forests were eliminated, second growth trees took over, providing a dense understory, which the Delmarva does not find to its liking. As always, reduction of suitable habitat results in reduction in population of numbers using that habitat. The Recovery teams have concentrated on stopping the loss of habitat and on the re-introduction of Delmarvas into habitats which are safe, and which can be expected to remain safe. They have successfully started a colony on Chincoteague National Wildlife Refuge using squirrels live-trapped on National Wildlife Refuges in Maryland.

Public pride has been enlisted to help the endangered Delmarva fox squirrel—and this seems to be getting results—as people protect "their" squirrels, found nowhere else. But the question remains—just how much should we get worried about the status of a very small population of squirrels which exhibit only minor differences from the prospering big species, the common fox squirrel? The people in this peninsular region—the Delmarva—intend to save *their* particular squirrels and that is good, for wildlife benefits by the increased concern of any population of humans. But we must ask another question. If the Delmarva fox squirrel disappeared from the earth, and its place were taken by the common fox squirrel, would we really have suffered a loss?

In a small town in Missouri, there exists a wonderfully interesting colony of squirrels. They are common gray squirrels, but they are all white! Some albino specimens showed up several decades ago, and local people liked the white ones. An insurance man named Smart took a special interest. He helped Mother Nature out by trapping and relocating the "normal" gray squirrels, leaving the white ones to rule the roost by themselves. In so doing, he actually affected the evolutionary outcome of this tiny population of fox squirrels. His culling out of normal fox squirrels made it certain that albino would mate with albino. Over the generations, the chromosomes carrying the albinism gene became the dominant fact of life for these squirrels. Now there is a population of about 200 pure white gray squirrels, but no one suggests that we call this a SUBspecies. Albinos seldom succeed in the wild, because their coloration makes them the target for every predator, and they cannot hide. The protection afforded by the humans in this Missouri town tips the balance in favor of the white ones, and there is no chance of a crop failure wiping out this colony of white squirrels because the human caretakers will guarantee that no white squirrel starves. Obviously this is an artificial situation.

No one would argue that a *human created* variation would justify concern for the possible extinction of that variant species. Should we become exercised about the danger to a *naturally occuring* variation? What is the real difference in the two situations?

Far beyond the obviously artificial situation of the Missouri albinos and the almost natural situation of the Delmarva squirrels lies the situation with the endangered Mount Graham red squirrel found only in the mountains of Arizona. Listed as endangered since 1968 *Tamiasciurus hudsonicus grahamensis* is very much in the news of late. It seems that mankind is really crowding in on the *lebensraum* of this Arizona subspecies. The University of Arizona is big in astrophysical research and they want to upgrade their abilities in this line. Specifically, they want to build an astrophysical observatory atop Mount Graham. The U.S. Forest Service manages the land for its owners, the American public. The Forest Service said, "Go ahead and build the observatory."

All hell broke loose now that the permit to build was issued. The Sierra Legal Defense Fund filed suit on behalf of the Sierra Club, the National Wildlife Federation and the Arizona Wildlife Federation, alleging that the Endangered Species Act was violated by the permit-granting. The court is asked to declare unlawful any further "site-disturbing" activities on Mount Graham.

"We are unwilling to stand by and watch a species be driven into extinction by federal agencies that ignore the law," says Lee Kohlhase, President of the Arizona Wildlife Federation. The National Audubon Society and Defenders of Wildlife also joined in the suit.

What are we talking about here? There are perhaps only 140 individuals left of this subspecies of red squirrel, and they all live on Mt. Graham, at 10,720 feet above sea level in the Pinaleno mountains. They have not really held their own in recent years, and the environmentalists are obviously afraid that even more human crowding-in will exterminate this pitiful remnant of the Mt. Graham red squirrel. The low numbers suggest that the subspecies is already "non-viable" simply because the gene pool is too limited.

The University of Arizona filed a request for permission to build their observatory way back in 1984. They planned to clear off 60 acres of forest to allow construction of 13 telescopes, including the world's largest. The Forest Service has okayed permits calling for construction of three telescope buildings, a support building, a workshop building and residence for engineers, a *helicopter pad*, a parking lot, a *picnic area* and a paved access road.

Environmentalists argue that Arizona is a big state, people can picnic in other areas—while the squirrel cannot move successfully. While granting that the clean air over Mt. Graham is attractive to the observatory people, they also point out that they do not object to observatories as such—they just object to this observatory being placed on the only habitat of the endangered species. The Forest Service definitely is cooperating with the observatory proponents and dragging their feet in observing regulations which protect endangered species and their habitat. The matter is obviously going to be decided by the courts.

Can the needs of less than 150 small squirrels be considered against the $261 million dollar observatory? Remember that the snail darter postponed construction of the huge dam in the Tellico controversy. Personally, I hope the Mt. Graham squirrel backers win out. Surely they will if the matter is decided strictly on its legal merits. Perhaps the University of Arizona ought to shift its plans to Kitts Peak?

Sometimes we've listed as endangered a subspecies which has little claim to recognition as a separate subspecies. A good example of this is the Sonoran pronghorn, which we've agonized about for several decades. This "sub" species of the common pronghorn (*Antilocapra americana*), differs in the least details from the main species. Some taxonomists claim that the only discernible difference is that the Sonoran is slightly lighter in overall coloration. If that is true then the Sonoran pronghorn is not worthy of special protection. I prefer to think that the Sonoran is a disappearing segment of the very successful main body of pronghorns. I hope the Sonoran will continue to have special protection, for it survives in the cruelest, most inhospitable section of North America.

A Recovery Team was named for the Sonoran pronghorn in 1975, but five years later that team had not come up with a Recovery plan. How could they? The Sonoran ranges very widely across the cruel desert along the US-Mexico border. I've photographed them in the bone-dry, searing heat of the Cabeza Prieta Game Range in Arizona, and I've watched a pitiful remnant of this subspecies moving like mirages in the shimmering heat waves of the Scammons Lagoon area of the southwestern desert of Mexico. In the six or seven hundred miles between these two deserts, there are no known Sonoran pronghorn antelope, and now most biologists think that the antelope of Scammons Lagoon's shores is still different from the Sonoran pronghorn.

Although the Arizona Game and Fish Department has made a valiant effort to learn more about this animal, no one can give an account of their numbers, nor even an intelligent estimate for the Mexican segment. In 1980, they estimated that about 80 Sonorans existed in the Grand Canyon State. In 1989, the estimate is approximately 100 Sonoran pronghorns in Arizona, according to James C. de Vos, Jr. Research Branch Supervisor for the Arizona Game and Fish Department. Noting that recent published estimates put the Mexican population as low as 15–20 antelope, Mr. de Vos says that is low. Based on observations on both sides of the border, de Vos feels that there are in excess of 100 Sonoran pronghorn in Old Mexico. He admits that this is strictly a guess.

The Sonoran has adapted to life in the desert. We know very little about his or her needs, or food preferences. Most of us are not accustomed to thinking about plants like lecheguilla, tasajillo, ocotillo, cholla, palo verde, boojum trees and saguaro. Water is a very scarce commodity all over the range of the Sonoran. On the Cabeza Prieta I watched them come to water at Charlie Bell Well and at Papago Well. The names of these widely separated watering holes are easy to remember for they hold the balance of life or death in a great stretch of Sonoran pronghorn antelope range.

The situation in the U.S. is slightly better than it was ten years ago. The situation in Mexico is slightly worse than it was ten years ago. All we can say for sure is that a very small number of pronghorns, differing only slightly from the main species, ranges across huge acreages of desert, but they are not holding their own. If they really rate the distinction of being a separate subspecies, we are not succeeding in saving this "endangered" subspecies.

If I were a pragmatic "manager" of desert livestock, I would see to it that the gene pool of the Sonoran pronghorn was enriched by an injection of healthier pronghorns from Wyoming or Montana or South Dakota—but environmentalists would scream at the sacrilege of interfering with the process of natural selection. Come to think of it, the pronghorns which withstand the winter blizzards of the Red Desert in Wyoming probably would not last a week in the furnace heat of the Cabeza Prieta. But if they lasted long enough to breed some of the Sonoran does, it would surely help the chances of survival of this endangered group of antelope. What do you think?

In any event, the Sonoran pronghorn antelope has not gained much attention from the public because it is such a small matter, in an environment so far from centers of population, in conditions so hostile to mankind that few of us ever go to see how the Sonoran pronghorn is doing.

Taxonomists are to be classed as either "splitters" or "lumpers" depending upon whether or not they feel that slight differences are cause for sub-speciation in the taxonomic lists.

For one example of this situation, we offer the Canada goose. It is *Branta canadensis canadensis* or is it one of the many subspecies? Is a difference in size reason enough to call it a separate species? There's a good argument for the size differential, for we have the Giant Canada which weighs as much as 25 pounds, and we have the lesser subspecies which weighs no more than 3 pounds. Surely they are different?

Or is coloration a reason for differentiating between subspecies of Canada goose? You can get an argument on both the question of size and the question of coloration. Let's look at the situation with one endangered subspecies of goose, the Aleutian Canada Goose.

Looking remarkably like other subspecies of Canada goose, the Aleutian variety evolved to fit conditions on the cold, wet and barren Aleutian Islands west of mainland Alaska. There were no mammalian predators on these islands, so the Aleutian goose evolved as a ground nester with no fear of predators. Then humans crowded in with the idea of "farming" valuable fox pelts. The situation worked like this: Investors bought a few pairs of foxes and turned them loose on these uninhabited islands. The islands were uninhabited by humans, but were the habitat of the Aleutian goose. With a few breeding seasons, the fox population had quadrupled and the investors moved in, harvested the fox pelts and reaped a nice harvest. But the Aleutian goose reaped a harvest of near extinction on those islands. En-

93

tirely unwary, the native goose was devoured by the non-native foxes. Man made a buck or two, but the goose lost out.

Take the case history of Agattu Island. In 1923 four Arctic foxes were introduced, five more in 1925 and another 23 in 1930. By 1936, at least a thousand foxes had been harvested on this one island. The explosion of Arctic foxes was due to an abundance of good nourishing food—for which read, "Aleutian geese."

The U.S. Fish and Wildlife Service was charged with protecting Alaska's wildlife in the period before statehood. The Service live-trapped Aleutian goslings on Buldir Island and removed them—first to Monte Vista NWR in Colorado and later to Patuxent, Maryland. There a captive flock grew in numbers, making sure that the gene pool would not die out entirely.

Before the Aleutian subspecies could be reintroduced to the wild, it was necessary to make some of the Aleutian Islands again suitable habitat. Which is a fancy way of saying that we had to eliminate the Arctic foxes, which should never have been there in the first place. Using strychnine baits and the incomparably more efficient and species selective Compound 1080, the Fish and Wildlife Service began the elimination of foxes on the big island of Amchitka in 1949. By 1967 they were able to say that no foxes remained on Amchitka.

Similar fox control programs were undertaken on several other islands in the Aleutian chain—islands named Alaid and Nizki and Agattu. While the foxes were being eliminated, the Aleutian goose flock prospered in Patuxent.

The first reintroduction to the wild went to Amchitka in 1971, and failed for unknown reasons.

In 1974, the Fish and Wildlife Service tried again, with 41 wing-clipped adult geese from Patuxent. Four pairs nested and produced a total of five goslings. 139 more were released on Agattu in 1978 and another 244 went to Agattu in 1979. Nine wild-reared birds were captured on Buldir Island and brought to Agattu for release with the Patuxent products.

Late in the winter of 1980–1981 biologists of the California department and of the Fish and Wildlife Service confirmed that Buldir Island raised geese were present on the wintering grounds again. It seemed that progress was definitely being made in restoring the endangered subspecies of Canada goose, the tiny, newly rescued Aleutian goose. The moral of the Aleutian goose story should be evident: Introducing exotic species into habitats where they never existed before is not something to be taken lightly. In almost every case, it causes great harm to the native species. Buldir Island joins the Hawaiian Islands, the Galapagos, Australia, New Zealand and many other cases where exotic predators eliminated, or almost eliminated, native species which had no defense mechanism.

Should we work hard to preserve subspecies when the species itself is in no danger? I feel that we definitely should, simply because that subspecies is evolving to fit a particular niche. In so doing, the subspecies is preparing the way for further evolution to even more selective habitat niche requirements. If natural evolution created the subspecies, we should fight to save it. If man created the subspecies (as in the Marionville, Missouri white squirrels) we have no duty to protect that subspecies. I fully recognize that taxonomists do not consider albinism as a subspeciation, but rather as an anomaly. Just the same, I sure do hope that the white gray squirrels of Marionville are protected and fostered by concerned humans and that they go on to even bigger and better populations.

15

The Kit Fox

As a boy growing up on the North Dakota prairie, I don't believe that I ever heard of a kit fox. When I was a State Game Warden in North Dakota I saw my first kit fox (also called swift fox) in Morton County, when a local trapper brought one to me for identification. He thought it was a freak, a red fox with different coloration, stunted in size and sporting huge ears. I was able to show him a picture of one in my reference books. The pelt was never worth much in comparison with red fox or even with coyote. It is my impression that the tiny fox was never common in the Dakotas before 1950.

It should be mentioned here that the big lobo wolf kept the population of coyotes down on the western plains. The coyote, in turn, kept the population of red, gray and kit foxes low in areas where the wily coyote was numerous. I know that the big wolf killed and ate the coyote; I am not convinced that the coyote caught and killed the red, gray and kit foxes. However, the red fox was scarce in the middle of North Dakota in the period of 1950–1954 and the expansion of the red fox into the entire state coincided exactly with the decrease in coyote populations.

The coyote decreased as a direct result of poisoning programs which used the very effective Compound 1080 (sodium monofluoracetate). With coyote numbers greatly lowered, the red fox began to show up everywhere west of the Missouri River. It is strange that the foxes might benefit from the results of 1080 poisoning programs, for Compound 1080 is highly species-selective (aimed at the canines) and kills foxes as surely as it will kill the target species—the coyote. One explanation might be that the 1080 poisoning program removed the coyotes (at least removed 75% of them) and **THEN** the fox species moved into the niche vacated by the coyote.

Anyone who has ever been privileged to see a kit fox run down its rabbit prey, capturing the big hare through blinding speed, always describes the running ability of these lithe animals in glowing terms. A single coyote, or a single red or grey fox, has no chance of running down and killing a northern white-tailed jackrabbit, but the kit fox does it regularly. I've never seen it in the wild, but I remember seeing a 16 millimeter camera film of that unequal race. It reminded me of a film showing an African cheetah running down one of the African plains antelope. Once locked on to its individual prey, the cheetah follows every desperate twisting and turning and finally grabs its prey through blinding speed. Exactly the same is true of a kit fox chasing a jackrabbit or cottontail.

In the years I worked in South Dakota, I saw several kit foxes in the western stretches of that prairie state. These diminutive speedsters evidently form a strong pair bond. In Harding County, South Dakota, I found the poison-killed body of a female kit fox lying stretched out on the snow. Something or somebody had tucked 45 mice, by actual count, under the edges of the dead body, neatly outlining the dead fox with dead mice. The only possible explanation is that the male of the pair had brought food to his dead mate, not accepting the fact that she was dead.

So far we've been talking about the northern kit fox (*Vulpes velox hebes*) which seems to be holding its numbers over a very large part of the central United States—from Colorado to the Dakotas, western Minnesota to Montana's mountains. This animal is listed as endangered in the Canadian part of its range.

But one of its subspecies (*Vulpes macrotis mutica*) is in more danger. Commonly called the San Joaquin kit fox, this is the largest of the subspecies, longer-legged, and slightly more heavy boned than the Northern kit fox. Like all of the desert kit fox subspecies, it suffered as a result of the 1080 poisoning programs in livestock country through the late 1950's and all of the 1960's, but it suffered far more at the hands of crowding humanity.

When rangeland is "developed" to prepare it for agriculture, kit fox denning areas are simply erased from existence. When all of the available land is converted to intensive agriculture, the kit fox is only a memory.

Prior to 1930, the San Joaquin kit fox was thought to range over most of that part of California described as running from Tracy, San Joaquin County and La Grange, Stanislaus County in the north, down through the valley to Kern County. In those days the range was thought to be populated by one kit fox per square mile—this was an educated guess, only.

By 1975, the San Joaquin kit fox was found only in *parts* of the valley from Contra Costa and San Joaquin countries in the north down to Santa Barbara and Kern countries in the south. Remember that the fox was found only in parts of this range, not all of it.

In 1975 the best estimate of the total population of the San Joaquin kit fox was 6,961 animals, total!

The reason for this decrease in numbers was plain. Man was crowding the kit fox out of its ancestral home by bringing in irrigated farming on a very large scale. In 1979, 93% of the total land acreage of the San Joaquin valley south of Stanislaus County was tilled and developed for irrigated farming, thus effectively erasing the kit fox due to loss of denning habitat and to loss of most of the rodent population. Unlike the adaptable coyote, and the even more adaptable red fox, the kit fox does not seem to be able to live in close proximity with man.

Another cause of kit fox depletion is *overgrazing*. Where grazing is moderate the little fox prospers and is evidently not hurt at all by the intrusion of cattle. On the other hand, overgrazing is generally detrimental to the kit fox. But mankind has so many different ways of crowding out the swift fox. Oil field development removes denning and hunting areas. 24 hour drilling causes the kit fox to desert its dens. Too much noise, too many vehicles moving around its range and the kit fox is gone. Long after predator control use of Compound 1080 was a thing of the past, this lethal stuff was still used in rodent control with oats or other grains as bait. California researcher Schitoskey found that the kit fox died after consuming just one kangaroo rat whose cheek pouches held just one gram of poisoned grain. This result was under laboratory conditions and from this result was extrapolated the belief that secondary poisoning was a dire threat to the kit fox after rodent control poisoning. In many years of field experience with the question of secondary poisoning by Compound 1080, I seriously doubt that conclusion. Secondary poisoning, although theoretically possible, just didn't seem to occur in any of the trials I followed when I was an employee of the old Predator and Rodent Control Branch of the U.S. Fish and Wildlife Service.

Kit fox pelts have never commanded high prices and trapping has usually not been a factor. Loss of habitat is the culprit in this as in so many other cases of endangerment. The Recovery Plan prepared by the Recovery Team calls for the acquisition of some high priced California land to protect habitat for the fox. This will be very difficult, if not impossible to accomplish.

As of mid-1990, I was unable to get a population estimate out of any of those people working with the San Joaquin Kit Fox. I think it is pretty obvious that no accurate population estimate can be made at this time. Nevertheless, the San Joaquin Kit Fox is definitely endangered.

These foxes, of all subspecies, are beneficial to man for their rodent-eating activities, and hardly ever cause any damage to man's interests. It will surely be shameful if we cannot find room for this beautiful, interesting animal to live with us on this crowded planet.

I was able to learn much more about the northern kit fox than I could about the California subspecies. Nell McPhillips of the South Dakota offices of the U.S. Fish and Wildlife Service, did a good job of clarifying the taxonomy of the kit fox, and I quote:

"Although some have lumped the swift fox *Vulpes velox* and the kit fox of the southwest *Vulpes macrotis*, I believe the majority of evidence supports their consideration as separate species.

"Some have thought that the swift fox actually consists of two subspecies, *Vulpes velox hebes*, the northern swift fox, and *Vulpes velox velox*, the swift fox. This theory for separate subspecies was still prevalent when the northern swift fox was listed as endangered under the Endangered Species Act and in Appendix 1 of CITES for Canada. . . . The swift fox was not formally listed as threatened or endangered at that time because the taxonomic status of the subspecies and its distribution were not sufficiently known. . . . In 1986, Stromberg and Boyce published a paper of the *Systematics and conservation of the swift fox Vulpes velox in North America*. They found that subspecific status for northern populations of the swift fox is probably not justified after measuring dental and cranial characteristics of 250 swift fox specimens. . . . In conclusion, the U.S. Fish and Wildlife Service recognizes *Vulpes velox hebes* as endangered in Canada and *Vulpes velox* as a species that will possibly warrant listing. Additionally, the Service presently recognizes *Vulpes velox* and *Vulpes macrotis* of the Southwest as two separate species. The San Joaquin kit fox *Vulpes macrotis mutica* has been listed as endangered since 1967." End of quotation from Nell McPhillips.

In this personal communication to me, biologist Nell McPhillips stresses that the future of the northern swift fox may be tied in with the future of the prairie dog ecosystem in the northern great plains. She feels that the recent publicity about the blackfooted ferret (see Chapter 5) has awakened the public to the importance of the prairie dog ecosystem, and that this may help the northern swift fox, which shares that ecosystem. She points out that re-introduction procedures for both ferrets and northern swift fox are being worked out.

Canadian authorities have decided that the northern swift fox became extinct in Canada prior to 1980. Yet, with the cooperation of Mr. and Mrs. Miles Smeeton, kit foxes have been reared in captivity near Cochrane, Alberta, and the resulting progeny was released into the wild in 1983. Coyotes killed some of the released pairs, confirming earlier theories as to what caused their demise earlier. First results of these re-introductions were good, and there has been reproduction in 1984 and 1985. The program will be continued as planned. Public response in Canada has been very enthusiastic, as the small fox poses almost no threat to man and his livestock.

For the student of wildlife extinction, the situation of the San Joaquin kit fox is very precarious. It is unlikely that the trend toward "Californication" of its habitat will be reversed. With onrushing "development" in that valley, the San Joaquin kit fox is probably doomed.

In the wide open spaces of Colorado, Wyoming, Nebraska, the Dakotas and on into Saskatchewan and Alberta, the northern swift fox is probably going to make a comeback—because it has room to run, and friends to help it exist.

16

The Everglades Kite

In 1981, in the book *THESE ARE THE ENDANGERED*, I told the following story:

There used to be a small gourmet restaurant in the old city of Quebec, Canada, which served the most delicious *escargot* I've ever eaten. Snails removed from the shells were placed in round holes in a stone cooking dish. Under each snail was a teaspoonful of excellent cognac. Above each snail, covering the entire cooking plate, was a creamy white sauce, mostly cheese, but flavored *à la Française*. Those snails simmered in the boiling cognac, while that tangy flavor permeated every cubic centimeter of their tender molluscan bodies. If I could eat that wonderful dish at every meal, I would probably never order anything else. But that might be dangerous. I might get so specialized that I would starve, if something happened to eliminate that meal.

Which is exactly what happened to the Everglades kite.

The kite is a small hawk-like bird of about eighteen inches in length, with a wing span of two feet. This bird loves snails. In fact, the only thing it will eat is snails. Worse yet, the only thing it wants to eat is the apple snail.

Over thousands of years of evolution, the Everglades kite stuck to its choice—apple snails or nothing. It became beautifully adapted to the pursuit of apple snails. It's flying ability allowed it to hover, almost motionless, while its sharp eyes searched out the apple snails in its favored swamp habitat in Florida and Georgia. Its talons were perfect for grasping the almost perfectly round shell of the apple snail. Its curved and pointed beak was perfect for extracting the snail from its shell.

Our endangered Everglades kite is one of many snail kites which flourished in the wet areas stretching from northern Florida down across all the Caribbean and Central American countries all the way to the Amazon drainage in the unbelievable bird wealth of South America.

Many perils assailed the kites. By 1980, there were only 165 known Everglades kites known to be alive in Florida. They were restricted to ranges on the headwaters of the St. Johns River, to the West side of Lake Okeechobee, parts of the Loxahatchee Slough and the Loxahatchee NWR, and to the northern part of the Everglades.

Drainage had almost eliminated the apple snail, hence the highly specialized apple snail eater, the Everglades kite, was in dire peril. Without apple snails to eat, the Everglades kite disappeared from most of its former range. But there were more troubles.

Man introduced the water hyacinth, and its lush green growth prevented the kite from finding the apple snail. Man's plants were crowding out the apple snail and the Everglades kite which fed upon that snail. The Everglades kite seemed completely unable to shift its menu to anything else. It was too specialized and this caused its downfall.

Florida has given legal protection to the Everglades kite since 1943, and the Endangered Species Act added federal protection. A severe drought in 1971 struck still another blow at the Everglades kite.

The kite has many friends. The National Park Service gives excellent protection in the Everglades National Park. The National Audubon Society sent Alexander Sprunt to protect the birds in the Okeechobee region, and he performed admirably for many years. The Loxahatchee National Wildlife Refuge tried hard to increase populations of apple snails and to stabilize water levels in kite habitat. But the fact remains that we had all of our kites in one basket, for they existed only in small parts of Florida. It looked like the species was going to become extinct as a result of two factors: Our alteration of its habitat and it's own extreme specialization insofar as diet is concerned.

In 1990, there no longer is a Recovery Team working with the Everglades Kite. The latest information on this very endangered bird is this:

We now know that the Florida kite *will* eat other things, and may not starve to death in the absence of the favored apple snail. Observers have noticed that they ate other species of snails, some small turtles and even rice rats. Adaptable? Not really, but not so severely specialized that it can eat nothing else.

The highest population in recent years occurred in 1984 with an estimated 668 birds. After a drought in 1985, the population dropped 39% down to only 407 birds. The kite has usually been censused in December. Population counts (not estimates of population) have been as follows:

1969–98 birds; 1970–120; 1971 after severe drought-72 birds; 1972–65; 1973–95; 1974–81 birds; 1975–110; 1976–142; 1977–152; 1978–

267; 1979–431 kites; 1980 up to 651 birds actually seen. In 1981 they counted only 109 birds after another severe drought, but kite biologist Beissinger wasn't satisfied with that count. He went back two months later and counted 230 kites.

1982 counted 312 kites; 1983 counted 437, up to 668 in 1984 and back down to 407 in 1985 as Florida experienced another severe drought.

Workers decided that an interim population of 650 birds, on average, over a ten year period would be a sign of success in the fight to save the Everglades Kite. As you can see from the up and down counts of kites in the first half of the 1980's, it would appear that we are achieving our goal. But the kite is very definitely still in dire straits. The struggle against extinction in this species is apt to be long and protracted.

First requisite for survival seems to be correct management of water levels and water flows, although water quality may be of over-riding importance in the long run. Man has crowded into Florida in great numbers over the past 25 years. As a result, competition for every drop of water is ongoing. Water supplies for agriculture, for livestock and for municipal water supplies can never be great enough for the increasing human population. Water cannot be managed only to suit the needs of the kite. The needs for recreation and for agriculture are often opposed to each other and certainly opposed to the needs of the Everglades kite.

The future survival of the Everglades kite can only be achieved by total cooperation of a distressingly large number of agencies—agencies whose aims are diametrically opposed in many cases. Fortunately, the Everglades kite does not seem willing to go "gladly into that good night." The prognosis is guardedly optimistic. A lot depends upon human perceptions of the importance of the many endangered species in Florida—manatees and panthers and sea turtles and kites. There IS hope.

17

Saving the Reptiles

Most people instinctively dislike reptiles! The fact that this is not logical has nothing to do with it; many people shudder at the sight of a snake. Hardly anyone gets sentimental about a crocodile or an alligator. Yet most reptiles are beneficial, and many species are endangered. Let's take a look.

Crocodiles and alligators are widely distributed around the world wherever warm waters are available. Only the icy waters are totally without reptiles, which cannot regulate their own body temperatures. Because they take on the same temperature as the water they inhabit, reptiles will never spread into the Arctic. We feel that the dinosaurs perished because they couldn't cope with a global cooling, but our theory is challenged by the fact that the crocodiles and alligators survived the same cooling off which exterminated the dinosaurs.

The *crocodilia* have been around for more than 300 million years, but now it appears that extinction looms for at least 20 species of crocodiles.

Several subspecies of crocodile regularly dine on large mammals, including man. This is particularly true of the Nile crocodile, a monster reputed to reach thirty feet in length. It is hard to drum up support for an animal which might use us as food. Still, crocodiles are very valuable in many parts of the world.

Ten years ago, we listed the American alligator as endangered. This was true of the 'gators which occupied Florida and a part of the south Atlantic coast of the United States. Louisianans claimed that they were up to their hip pockets in 'gators and objected strenuously to listing the 'gator as an endangered species. Total legal protection for the alligator caused an up-surge in numbers and Louisiana finally got permission to hunt and use alligators. Wallets, purses, cowboy boots and shoes again made their appearance. No one presently worries about the future of the alligator in America—it is farmed for meat and hides—and farmed profitably. Limited hunting seasons are allowed, which serves to keep the wild population in check.

The American alligator becomes accustomed to humans very readily—far too readily to suit residents of some of our waterside communities. In 1971, on the Aransas National Wildlife Refuge in south Texas, a ten or twelve footer became so used to people that he would crawl out on the bank when tourists banged on the side of their car to call him. These tourists fed bread to the big 'gator, much to the chagrin of the refuge manager. Anticipating the lawsuit he would face if that big fellow decided to put a human between two slices of bread, he ordered cyclone fencing to separate man and 'gator.

Hunting ducks in the southeast corner of Texas, I watched a big gator approach a duck which I had shot. The duck floated in the middle of a shallow pond. Although he waited for at least half an hour before engulfing the dead duck, I didn't take advantage of the opportunity to fight him for "my" duck.

The American crocodile is another story entirely. It has almost disappeared from Florida waters. Its close relatives—the Orinoco crocodile, Cuban crocodile and Morelets crocodiles—are all endangered. In Africa, the Nile, Congo pygmy, African slender-snouted and West African crocodiles are all endangered. Only in Zimbabwe is the giant Nile species off the endangered list.

In India, the Muggers crocodile and the very rare gavial are endangered, along with the Chinese alligator and the false gharial of Indonesia. Australia has the very large saltwater crocodile and the Johnson's crocodile, which seem to be safe from extinction, despite unregulated hunting for hides in years past. The inaccessibility of the Australian species is their best protection. Biologists studying the big crocs in Australia report that there once were millions of them, but in 1978 they estimated less than five thousand.

Man must take the blame for the extermination of some crocodiles and for the precarious position others find themselves in. Man wanted to use their hides to make high-priced cowboy boots, ladies shoes, purses and wallets. It seems incongruous that a species which survived the age of the dinosaurs, a species whose family tree predates ours by at least one hundred million years, would be exterminated to satisfy the whims of fashion.

Mankind can also take the credit for preserving the remnant species of crocodilia. Happily, these reptiles take readily to captivity and do well in crocodile farms. In captivity they breed readily and increase in numbers beyond belief. Alligator farms in Florida and Louisiana are able to satisfy the growing appetite for alligator meat, and the long time market for skins.

In South America, Brazil, Ecuador and Venezuela protect the caiman by law, but enforcement is absent and export permits are easily obtained. The future of all South American caimans is bleak.

In Asia, India protects the very rare gavials in its Nandankanan Biological Park and propagates the gavial (sometimes called gharial) in the Kukril Crocodile Rehabilitation Center with an eye to restocking the big reptile in the wild. In Thailand, the Siamese crocodile is profitably farmed, although it is now considered extinct in the wild.

In Australia, crocodile aficionados realize that the job of rallying public support for the croc is difficult. One crocodile expert wrote me that "Every time we seem to be winning a few people over to our side, some crocodile takes a child on one of our beaches and this sets us back fifty years."

That, it would seem, is understandable.

Crocodiles and alligators and snakes are sinister looking and seem to arouse an atavistic revulsion in most humans. Watch people coming into a reptile house in the zoo. They are in no danger whatsoever from the reptiles. But a shudder of revulsion is the commonest reaction of people seeing their first snake, or first crocodilian. Perhaps this is inborn as a result of experiences of millennia before man gained the upper hand over the reptiles. Perhaps it is silly; but it exists.

Can mankind overcome the feeling of revulsion long enough to prevent extinction of reptilian species? Good progress is being made in this aspect of human behavior. Schools now teach children—by allowing them to touch harmless snakes—that snakes are dry-skinned and cool, not slimy and nasty. But it will take generations to change our basic attitude toward snakes, and this is a big problem for those who work to preserve species of snakes. Especially poisonous species of snakes.

Several of our many North American species of rattlesnakes are listed as threatened—which is the next step above endangered. One example is the New Mexican ridge-nosed rattlesnake, found in my home state of New Mexico. Are people really working to protect these poisonous snakes?

New Mexico and Texas herpetologists are working in the Sierra San Luis mountains of Mexico, studying the ridge-nosed rattler there. In September of 1988, this team surgically implanted radio transmitters into five of the rare snakes. In April of 1989 they were able to learn the location of four of the radio transmitters. This subspecies is found only in the Sierra San Luis of Old Mexico and in the rocky country of Hidalgo County in New Mexico. There are so few of them that a team of five experienced herpetologists found only one in six days of searching. One adult female ridge-nosed rattlesnake was located in the Peloncillo Mountains of New Mexico, but she probably doesn't have a chance of finding a mate, for no young have been found. There is a lot of work going on to find out why the ridge-nosed is threatened. Who is doing the work? Texas and New Mexico biologists are helping. Bonnie Raphael, a veterinarian researcher with the Dallas Zoo, volunteered her time to surgically implant the radio transmitters. This is the first time that surgically implanted transmitters have been used in any study of the ridge-nosed rattler. The Fish and Wildlife Service is funding part of the expenses. Two graduate students from the *Universidad de Nuevo Leon* in Mexico are helping with the field work as part of the contract with the University of Texas.

I think it is a plus on the human side of the equation that humans are working to perpetuate a species (in fact many species) which can kill mankind. Is it a sign that man is becoming more civilized?

18

Worthless Species?

It is easy to get our dander up about the possible extinction of the mighty African elephant, but are you worried about the possible extinction of the Texas blind salamander?

Two Texas-based species are similarly endangered. One, the whooping crane, is the object of continent-long protection, lots of fund-raising, has a refuge or two devoted to its fight for survival—it's even the symbol of mankinds' efforts to save endangered wildlife. The second species, the Houston toad, doesn't arouse such fervor for its protection. It is small, sedentary in nature, doesn't migrate, is hard to find. But is that the real reason why we do not struggle as hard to save it as we struggle to save the whooping crane? Or have we subconsciously set ourselves up as judge and jury in deciding which species shall live and which shall be allowed to die out?

A friend of mine says that a true test of religious faith is to find yourself facing the collection basket in your church and all you have is a twenty dollar bill. Do you have the faith to contribute when it really costs you? The same may be true of our ecological faith. Do we feel a stirring of outrage at the extinction of a salamander, or a toad, or a periwinkle? Should we?

Just north of San Antonio, Texas, there's a limestone escarpment (the Balcones escarpment) which divides the "hill country" from the flat expanse of south Texas. In this limestone escarpment there is a series of caves which have been sculpted by water down through the countless centuries. In one of those caves, where sunlight has never penetrated, at least not in the last ten thousand years, there exists a blind salamander.

Did this salamander decide to choose this eternal blackness for its home, or did some freak of geological events entrap it in that Stygian darkness? No one will ever know.

Evolution has a way of eliminating unused parts of the body. After thousands of years of never using eyes, the salamander lost its eyes. When there is no light to fall upon a retina, evolution eliminates the retina. Sometimes it takes thousands of generations to remove an appendage which is no longer needed. Take the case of our tail bone, a relic from the days when we had tails. It is no longer needed, but we still have it. But we are a species with a long life span and with a very slow (relatively) reproductive rate. The salamander, on the other hand, has a much shorter reproductive cycle, regenerating itself every year.

Because there is no light, the salamander lives without eyes. Because there is no possibility of seeing color when light is absent, the Texas blind salamander lives without color. Is this an endangered species which must be preserved at all costs, or is this one of thousands of evolutionary dead ends which we cannot save from extinction, even if we wanted to?

How about toads? We may still believe that handling a toad can cause warts on humans, but not many of us do that. But if a toad is in danger of extinction, do we worry about that? Should we?

The Houston toad is a case in point. Biologists have described this relict population, found only in Burleson and Bastrop Counties, Texas, as a subspecies of *Bufo americanus* and sometimes as a subspecies called *Bufo terrestris* in deference to its known proclivity for burrowing underground and staying there for long periods. More correctly, we should call it *Bufo houstonensis* in deference to its type locality.

But the taxonomist himself has trouble with this species—or subspecies. The classical description includes a dorsal pattern consisting of dark spots on a tan background, coupled with obviously thickened postorbital and interorbital cranial crests. Then the scientist goes on to say, "...the absence of the obviously thickened postorbital and interorbital crests in some specimens leads to confusion." I will agree with that statement.

The best identification mark for the Houston toad is its song. Once heard and identified, the call is easily separated from the songs of other toads and frogs. This secretive toad spends most of the year buried in the loose soils of the loblolly pine country in Texas. Active only at night, and almost unknown except in breeding season, the Houston toad is one of the hardest species to locate, much less to count.

Reproduction of the Houston toad is associated with the existence of breeding ponds. When these water areas are present at the right time, the males go to those water areas and start singing their high pitched call. The females swoon at the sound of that masculine serenade and become receptive. If the spring is too dry and water areas are not present, the males don't sing and the females don't swoon and there is no reproduction that year in that locality.

Males in which the mating urge is strongest will go hunting for other water areas. Often they find permanent water areas which are frequented by other species of toad. They sing their songs and they find mates—but often they find mates which are of other subspecies. The resulting hybridization is just another case of a tiny gene pool being drowned in a much larger gene pool of a common species.

Scientists are interested in preserving the authenticity of the Houston toad gene pool. They have discovered that it is relatively easy to propagate the subspecies in captivity, simply by providing the conditions which the romantic males seem to need. For several years now they have propagated the toad and liberated its offspring into the wild in state parks in Bastrop County. As long as this continues, the Houston toad can be saved. But is there sufficient interest to preserve this subspecies indefinitely? Or should we allow evolution to take its course and eliminate the Houston toad by hybridization with other, more successful, toad species? Or did we upset the evolutionary apple cart by altering the land use of the East Texas loblolly pine areas?

Obviously, it is easier to raise money to save the giant panda than it is to save the blind salamander—easier to preserve the whooping crane than to preserve the Houston toad. But who gave us the right to choose life or death for a species that shares this planet with us?

19

Parrots of Many Lands

Thirteen parrots and nine parakeets are on the endangered species list, along with three macaws. Nine of these species are endangered in South America, with Brazil heading the list because of the inroads being made into that wonderful rainforest which provides much of the world's oxygen, and which is being ruined by misdirected agriculture programs and by greed for the money represented in tropical woods.

The list of endangered includes:

Forbes Parakeet from New Zealand, the golden parakeet and the golden-shouldered from Brazil, the Mauritius parakeet from the Indian Ocean, the ochre-marked parakeet from Brazil, while Australia lists four endangered parakeets—the orange-bellied, the paradise, the scarlet chested and the turquoise.

Parrots on the endangered list number an unlucky thirteen: Australian parrot, Cuban or Bahaman parrot, ground parrot from Australia, the imperial parrot, the Puerto Rican parrot, the red-browed parrot and red-capped from Brazil, the red-necked, the red-spectacled, the St. Lucia parrot and the St. Vincent parrot from the West Indies, our own thick-billed parrot, and the vinaceous-breasted, also from Brazil.

Most of these species have suffered from being captured for the pet trade, and from the destruction of their rainforest habitat. The causes of decline in parrots and macaws and parakeets are as varied as the appearance of these colorful birds. Some live on tropical islands, some high in the mountains. Some live in steaming rainforests, some live on the rocky slopes of arid mountains. Because several of them can learn to mimic human speech sounds very well, they have commanded great sums of money on the pet market. Unfortunately, they also carry many parrot diseases, which has complicated their importation and which handicaps efforts to reintroduce them into the wild.

Let's take a look at the situation with several species of parrots.

Puerto Rican Parrots

The Puerto Rican parrot was almost lost in 1971, with only thirteen birds remaining in the wild. Their only home was on the Luquillo Mountains in the Caribbean national Forest. By 1989, the wild bird count had inched up slowly to 47 birds. Due to fine inter-agency cooperation there were 54 Puerto Rican parrots in an aviary, a protected breeding stock. Then Hurricane Hugo roared over the Puerto Rican Commonwealth and *aficionados* of the Puerto Rican parrot feared the worst. However, counts found 24 parrots in the wild, a reduction of one half in the wild population. Once again, the wisdom of keeping a captive stock had been demonstrated. Aviculturists have done wonders working with the Puerto Rican parrot. One fledgling that developed weakened feathers unable to support the bird's weight in flight, had a complete set of wing and tail feathers from molted birds transplanted in him to replace the weak ones. Amazingly, the bird promptly flew! A Puerto Rican parrot egg was cracked. Aviculturists actually patched it and it was incubated and hatched!

In 1978 fertile eggs were produced by captive parrots in the Puerto Rican aviary for the first time. Since then there has been considerable success with the captive propagation program, which now boasts of 54 birds.

Thick-Billed Parrots in Arizona

Customs officials confiscate parrots at border crossings when such parrots are of species whose entry is illegal, or when the species is one of the many on the endangered species listings. The thick-billed parrot is endangered across its range, which once included all of Mexico and extended into southern Arizona. Despite its endangered status, the thick-billed parrot still is taken through Customs. When it appears, it is confiscated.

Using these captured specimens, Arizona's Game and Fish Department has begun a captive breeding flock, and progeny of that flock have been reintroduced into the Chiricahua Mountains of the Grand Canyon State. Several of the released birds had been fitted with tiny radio transmitters to allow for monitoring of their movements. In 1989, the released flock left their wintering quarters in the Chiricahua Mountains and headed north for cooler climes. Airplanes searched for the radio signals and found them—and the thick-billed parrots—way up on the Mogollon Rim (for those not familiar with Arizona's geography, Mogollon is pronounced "muggy-owen").

Some of the thickbills remained behind in the Chiricahuas and three more birds (from the Aviculture Institute) were released and promptly joined the stay at homes. Another bird from the San Diego Zoo was released, bearing a radio transmitter, and this helped the Arizona Game and Fish Department in their attempts to keep tabs on the birds. Considerable pairing has been observed and several pairs have been observed copulating. Many nests have been explored, but no reproduction in the wild flock has been noted as of this time.

Please don't get the idea that these are "pet shop" birds unable to take care of themselves in the wild. They are strong fliers, and radio tracking by airplane has verified the fact that they make long, sustained flights from roosting areas to feeding areas and back again. They were once native to southern Arizona and the prospects seem bright that they will once again nest there.

To support the reintroduction effort for the thickbills, Captive breeding projects are underway at several American locations and even at the Jersey Wildlife Preservation Trust in England—a long way from the Chiricahuas. Cooperators in the U.S. include the San Diego Zoo, Los Angeles Zoo, Sacramento Zoo, Arizona-Sonora Desert Museum, Phoenix Zoo, Gladys Porter Zoo, Tracey Aviary and the Tyson Research Center.

The Tyson facility is of greatest importance in the project, because they are equipped to handle large numbers of the birds and because they are willing to tolerate birds for long-term quarantine. During this quarantine period, the birds are used in the captive breeding program—which may increase to as many as 60 breeding pairs at one time.

Thick-billed parrots seized in illegal trade have been found to harbor psittacosis, salmonella, Pacheco's disease and parrot-wasting fever—even after they have cleared U.S. Customs quarantine. There is a lot of interest in these parrot diseases, and many nations are closely following the reintroduction project in Arizona.

Arizonans are very interested in the project and "parrot-watching" has become the "in thing" for many in that state. It is even tax-deductible to make a contribution for this cause. Private individuals and organizations have helped make the Thick-Billed Parrot Reintroduction Project possible by matching funds contributed by federal agencies and by Arizona's Nongame Wildlife Income Tax Checkoff. The Checkoff provides a funding base for the nongame and endangered wildlife efforts of the Arizona Game and Fish Department. If you want to help this project—which is already surveying likely places for reintroduction of thickbills into Old Mexican habitats, send your contribution to:

Thick-Billed Parrot Project
c/o Terry B. Johnson
Arizona Game and Fish Department
2222 West Greenway Road
Phoenix, Arizona 85023-4399

20

Tracking the Rails

Have you ever noticed that we Americans get more excited about an ecological disaster far from our shores than we do about an ecological disaster happening in our back yard?

Lately the newspapers have carried several good stories about the massive effort being launched to rescue the Guam rail and the Micronesian kingfisher. Since 1984 a gigantic effort has been underway to stop extinction of these two species from their ancestral homes on Guam, familiar to many who served in the Pacific theater during World War II. Under the guidance of the U.S. Fish and Wildlife Service, the Smithsonian, the Guam Division of Wildlife and Aquatic Resources, and the American Association of Zoological Parks and Aquariums—34 Micronesian kingfishers and 21 Guam rails were airlifted to the United States and captive propagation was begun. The kingfishers are doing nicely, having increased from 34 to 57. But the Guam rail has exhibited a population explosion, the original 21 increasing to 150! We are even now liberating Guam rails on the island of Rota—a close neighbor to Guam. It is hoped that the birds will prosper on Rota and allow for their future reintroduction into Guam.

Two questions come immediately to mind. 1) why don't we commit money and resources to the plight of our own California-endangered lightfooted clapper rail? and 2) why did the Micronesian kingfisher and the Guam rail get in such a precarious state?

I'll leave the answer to number one up to you.

Question number two is easier to answer. For millennia, these bird species and others now extinct, prospered on Guam. But shortly after the end of World War II, which changed the universe for Guam and Rota, biologists began to notice a severe decline in native bird populations. Scientific investigations began immediately and the finger was pointed at pesticides and habitat loss and avian diseases. None of these theories proved out. Then the native islanders suggested that the problem was that the brown tree snake was eating the birds. Simple as that. This theory proved to be correct.

The brown tree snake was evidently introduced into the Guam habitat by either the Japanese army or the American army. Each army was a temporary overlord of Guam during the last months of World War II. It's not important whether the blame goes to Japan or to the island-hopping U.S. forces. The fact remains that the ill-tempered reptile has eliminated nine species of forest birds—most of them not found anywhere else except on Guam!

John Groves, curator of reptiles in the Philadelphia zoo, went to Guam to survey the snake population. After eight days in the rain forests of Guam he reported that there were at least one million brown tree snakes on Guam! He also stated that there was no way to save the remaining bird populations on Guam, for he had no idea how to eliminate the snakes.

So we are now raising these birds in zoos in the United States, with great success. As captive populations increase—fending off extinction—some will be re-introduced onto Rota as a way station pending elimination of the brown tree snake from their real home, the bigger island of Guam. So far, no one has come up with a sensible suggestion as to removal of the snakes.

Even on Rota, the Guam rail is definitely not out of danger. The native Chamorro people love to shoot anything that flies, and they like to eat the flightless Guam rails that are being reintroduced onto Rota. They also like to shoot and eat the big Marianas fruit bat, which is also an endangered species. But even here on these (formerly) idyllic islands in the blue Pacific, species are being crowded out by man. Golf courses and resort hotels planned for the ten mile long island of Rota will eliminate about one half of the existing habitat for these rare birds. We are again crowding out wildlife species—either by introducing an exotic such as the brown tree snake on Guam, or the mongoose on Hawaii, or by sheer weight of mankind's own numbers. How important is the desire to play golf? Do the wishes of the American and Japanese tourists override the critical habitat needs of these very endangered birds?

Now let's consider the situation with one of the rails much closer to home. The lightfooted clapper rail is a native of Californian seacoast habitats. This is one of 26 separate subspecies of the clapper rail.

Original range of this clapper rail is thought to extend from Santa Barbara County in California all the way down the Pacific coast to San Quintin Bay on the Baja California Peninsula. There have been no sightings in Santa Barbara County since 1875. Has this rail been endangered that long?

There is evidence that a marsh which formerly held zero lightfooted clapper rails has repopulated, so the birds do move from one marsh to another. Yet they are essentially non-migratory and remain in one marsh for most of their lives. Big enough to furnish meat on the table, they have long been hunted for sport and food. Nevertheless, it doesn't seem that the hunter has been the *main* cause of their demise. This rail nests—and lives its life—where sea and land meet. This puts them at the mercy of wind and weather. An exceptionally high tide will cause great mortality among them, drowning out their nests in the cordgrass and destroying young and old alike if the weather is bad enough. They have always had to contend with the weather, and it didn't keep the clapper from surviving for millennia before the hunter came on the scene.

No problem with finding food; the lightfoot eats almost everything and finds a goodly supply of its favorite crustaceans in the muck of its marshes. But when DDT came on the scene shortly after the end of World War II, the clapper rail found itself at the top of a food chain which concentrated DDT and DDE metabolites at dangerous levels. Was this the major factor in their decrease? No one knows, and it is too late to find out this long after the termination of indiscriminate spraying with DDT. Certainly egg shell thinning blamed on DDT had some effect. Overshooting by hunters also had some effect; we cannot assess it with any degree of reliability.

But the greatest cause of the near extinction of the light-footed clapper rail is undoubtedly the draining and reclaiming—for which read destruction—of coastal salt marshes. An early Recovery Team report stated that coastal salt marshes between Santa Barbara County and the Mexican border had shrunk from 26,000 acres to less than 8,000 acres. Again mankind is crowding out a species of wildlife.

In 1981, Recovery teams hoped to stabilize the U.S. population of lightfoots at 400 nesting pairs! This was the goal, not the low number of rails! The California Department of Fish and Game was trying to restore the Bolsa Chica marshes. The problem is not merely that of saving coastal salt marshes, for the tidal flow must not be interrupted. It is the ebb and flow of salt water into the marshes which provides the food and the habitat needed by this small remnant population. But land values in Southern California have skyrocketed and are now among the highest in the nation. It is one thing to want to restore tidal flows in what once were marshes; it is quite another to be able to do it. Even a decade ago, many scientists questioned whether the existence of the lightfoot was worth the astronomical costs of preserving it? In my mind, there is no greater tragedy than the extinction of a species which can be blamed on man's actions. In my mind, each and every species is worth the astronomical cost. We blithely spend billions on silly schemes like the "Star Wars" concept, which no one sincerely feels is possible, and for which no one can realistically can find a need. In comparison, I'd blithely spend a billion or so on the lightfooted clapper rail. How about you?

In any event, the 1990 situation is this: the lightfooted clapper rail clings precariously to life in a very few salt marshes on the California coast—coastal marshes that are desired by "developers" with fat wallets.

Are we rushing into captive propagation for the lightfooted clapper rail? Perhaps we ought to stock them onto Rota, where they'd be far enough away to attract our attention.

21

Some Endangered Fishes

Many species of fishes face extinction. The situation with fish is very different from that of endangered mammals or birds. Most of the fishes which are endangered are "one habitat specific." In other words, they evolved to fit a specific limited habitat. As that limited habitat changed, the situation often became life-threatening for that particular species. We do not have to look very far for examples.

Glacial action formed millions of small lakes across the southwestern part of the United States. Fishes evolved and prospered in those waters, as long as it was possible to move from one habitat niche to another. But the southwest continued to dry up—and is still drying further. Water became in short supply. Lakes disappeared or became very small and shallow—which meant that their waters got hotter than they had been before.

Streams which held prosperous populations of trout suffered from reduced stream flows. Then their lower reaches warmed up as they flowed down onto desert levels. Trout which lived in the higher elevations were cut off by the warming of waters. They still did well in the small streams flowing off of mountain snow and ice. But they died if they ventured into the warmer—sometimes hot—lower reaches of their streams. Unable to transfer from one habitat niche to another, they held on only in the isolated upper reaches.

Without any chance of widening their gene pool, these relict populations began to develop individual characteristics—to sub-speciate—to a remarkable degree. For example, the Gila trout (*Salmo gilae*) and the Apache

119

Devil's Hole Pupfish

trout (*Salmo apache*) undoubtedly developed from the same parent species. Locked permanently into their small stream habitats, they developed in different ways, although fairly close together geographically. They developed slightly different colorations, and they became smaller (or at least did not evolve into larger) fishes to suit their small stream habitat.

The Apache trout was not even known or technically "described" until 1972. About the same time that famed fish taxonomist Bob Miller of the University of Michigan described the Apache trout—and muddied the waters by calling it the "Arizona trout", the White Mountain Apache tribe of Indians became interested in protecting this species. Perhaps they felt that they, too, were left over from a bygone age and thus felt a kinship with the small fish which shared their name. They cooperated with state and federal fishery experts to fight off another danger—hybridization with the introduced rainbow trout. The hardy, and desirable, rainbow trout had been introduced into most waters of Arizona and New Mexico. They worked their way upstream into what had been prime Gila or Apache trout waters and promptly hybridized with the colorful little natives—thus drowning the specific gene pools in the much larger gene pool of the rainbow.

When fishery biologists Jack Hemphill and Andy Anderson (and others) explained the situation to the Apache tribe, they received full cooperation in preserving the very few habitats left to the native fish—habitats unsullied by introduced genes of the rainbow. Apache trout populations, placed off limits to anglers by tribal action, prospered in some of the headwaters of the Black and White Rivers in Arizona. The conservation efforts of the White Mountain Apache Tribe earned them the Conservation Award of the Department of the Interior. Tenuous at best, the Apache has a fin-hold in about fifty miles of trout streams on the reservation, where every effort is being exerted to keep them pure and unsullied by the rainbow trout. If the fight for survival is won, there will be no gain for the sport fisherman who finances this rescue mission—directly and indirectly—because the restricted range and small size of the fish makes sure that they'll never be numerous enough, nor big enough to give the angler pleasure.

But what about the Gila trout? Work still goes on in New Mexico. In mid-1989 biologists took about 100 Gila trout, which they now designate as *Oncorhynchus gilae* from remote South Diamond Creek in the Gila Wilderness area. They used mules to pack them out of the mountains to where they could be trucked to the Mescalero National Fish Hatchery in New Mexico. Females were hand-spawned at the hatchery and about 5,000 eggs were removed, thus providing another supply of this endangered species which will be transplanted into wilderness streams that have been cleared of (non-native) rainbow trout to make way for the original inhabitants.

Forest fires in the high country which harbors both the Gila and Apache trout pose a danger to the fish. Removal of shade trees by fire allows stream temperatures to rise, endangering the fish. In addition, ash blown from the fire contaminates the streams, clogging the gills of fish and killing them.

It is possible that the small Apache trout might grow larger if stocked in reservoirs. But if that happened, the larger Apache trout—protected at such great expense and effort—would only make that lake off limits for the equally big, and equally attractive to the angler, rainbow trout. If the tiny gene pool of the Apache—or Gila—trout were to be lost, would mankind be the loser? We do not know . . . therefore we cannot take the risk. If it is possible to save these relict populations of trout, we should do so. But it *is* something like keeping a human patient alive by heroic means in a hospital, using respirators and intravenous feeding.

Pupfish

There were once large lakes in what is now the desert southwest of the USA. Over millennia, these lakes shrank and some dried up entirely. Just like the case of the high altitude trout we now call Apache and Gila, other species were locked into restricted environments by the shrinking of the lake system—forming isolated pockets which experienced extreme sub-speciation as they evolved.

To cite a huge example of this, we look at glacial Lake Lahontan, which formerly occupied as much as 8,000 square miles of Nevada and California. Glaciers receded and inflow to the lake was reduced, and the lake began to get smaller. As inflow from feeder streams stopped, there was less and less chance for transfer of populations from one drainage to another, further limiting the evolution of the species. As water volume decreased, water temperatures rose and percentages of dissolved solids were greatly increased. Some lakes became alkaline to the point where they lost their entire fish population. Others were able to maintain a fish population despite the change in alkalinity.

One part of Lake Lahontan dwindled down to become the Pyramid Lake—Lake Winnemucca—Truckee River habitat.

A geologic moment in this drying up cycle might last for thousands of years. During one of these moments, the white man came to Pyramid Lake and found the cutthroat trout there growing to greater size than known elsewhere. He also found the *cui-ui,* a sucker-like fish, present in tremendous numbers. The dessication of former Lake Lahontan had obviously reached a plateau which contained optimum conditions for these two species.

It took just an "eye-blink" of geologic time, but in a few decades mankind crowded in. He used the entire Truckee River to irrigate crops grown in the desert. He dried up the Truckee, and he caused the extinction of the Pyramid strain of cutthroat. Extinction is forever, and the Pyramid cutthroat can never be brought back. Mankind is definitely the poorer for this.

The *cui-ui* has decreased in numbers to the point where it is reared only in hatcheries now.

The damage has been done. Decreased stream flows into once magnificent Pyramid Lake can be blamed on the geologic evolution of the Great Basin, for which man cannot blamed. The Pyramid cutthroat was given a boot down the road to extinction by man's unwise use of the Truckee River. Who's to blame? Split the difference between mankind's greed and "desertification" of the southwest climate.

But there are other species facing the same problems. The Devils Hole pupfish is the best known of this group, but it also includes pupfish subspecies named Comanche Springs, Desert, Leon Springs, Owens and Warm Springs. Their very names tell the story, showing that they are extremely specialized small fishes which exist only in widely separated small waters, usually only a spring or a seep. Leon Springs in Texas is very far from Warm Springs in Nevada, but the problem is the same. Their future is dark, except where they are kept alive by superhuman means—in order to say that we can do it.

The Tecopa Springs Pupfish was once listed as endangered, but before the official listing was completed, the existence of the Tecopa pupfish was completed. They became extinct. They were the first species removed from the endangered list by reason of extinction. They will not be the last.

A related subspecies, the Shoshone pupfish, was also declared extinct by the U.S. Fish and Wildlife Service. This one had never been listed; so it did not need to be de-listed. Who mourned the passing of these two subspecies of two inch long fish? Who *should* have mourned?

The Nevada family of pupfish also includes the smallest of them all, the Warm Springs pupfish. Their tenuous lease on life is threatened by man's irrigation systems, which lower the water level in their very limited habitats.

These tiny relict populations of pupfish can obviously be sustained by putting them into aquaria where mankind has control of all phases of their environment. But would the aquarium-reared fish be the same as the wild fish? Obviously its future evolution in an aquarium would be different than the evolutionary path it would have had to follow in the wild. By collecting these subspecies into captivity and managing them, man would not be preventing extinction of a subspecies. Instead, man would be developing a completely different subspecies—a creature of man, not a development of the great river of evolution. If pupfish disappear, who will be to blame? It will certainly be us, the only species that changed the habitat by draining underground reservoirs with his irrigation pumps.

Endangered Darters

Perhaps the mightiest fish of all is the snail darter. Although only 88 millimeters in length, this tiny fish stopped construction of the Tennessee Valley Authority's Tellico Dam. Let's recount the history.

Congress authorized the Tellico Project in 1942, but World War II stopped development, and Congress again authorized the project and appropriated funds in 1966. Construction started on May 7, 1967. On the 28th day of December, 1973, the Endangered Species Act became law.

In August of 1973, Dr. David Etnier of the University of Tennessee found a new species of little fish while he was snorkeling in the lower reaches of the Tennessee River. He hand-caught an individual fish and listed it taxonomically as being *Percina tanasi* of the subgenus *Imostoma*. We called it the snail darter.

That was a sad day for the dam builders.

Scientists petitioned for endangered species listing for the snail darter and pointed out that its critical habitat would be eliminated by completion of the Tellico Dam. The Secretary of the Interior in 1975 concurred, to the consternation of the dambuilders. Lawsuits and counter lawsuits went all the way to the Supreme Court where the nine wise men decided that the Endangered Species Act *did* apply to projects authorized even before the Endangered Species Act was enacted into law. The snail darter had stopped construction of a dam. But not for long . . .

A pragmatic Congress passed legislation which specifically exempted the Tellico Dam project from the strictures of the Endangered Species Act. Was all the hullabaloo about the Tennessee River snail darter worth it?

Well, scientists took a population from the Tennessee and introduced them into the Hiawassee River, where they did well. In addition, it focussed attention on this tiny fish, and other populations were found that had not been known before.

There were, and are, other species of darter in danger. For example, the Watercress darter, found only in Glenn Springs, at Bessemer, County of

Jefferson, in Alabama. Despite efforts to locate other populations, it was unknown away from its watercress-choked habitat in this one spring. The entire population was estimated at 400. The danger here was man's filth, for the runoff from man's septic tanks was increasing the coliform bacteria count in this limited habitat. Then the Recovery Team also found this fish at Thomas' Spring and at Roebuck Springs. Attempts to transplant the species into a very similar habitat at Prince Spring failed entirely.

In some of the habitats used by this fish, abnormally high counts of nitrogen in the water, caused by mankind's septic tanks and fertilizers, allowed vegetation to completely choke the habitat. Yet it provided increased supplies of insect life, upon which the darter fed. Some success was had with introducing grass carp to control vegetation—with bad results for the watercress darter. It seems particularly tragic that the future of these species is threatened by man's filth and by man's mistake—the introduction of an exotic species into a limited habitat.

Then there's the Okaloosa darter, a far more adaptable subspecies. Nine-tenths of its range is on Eglin Air Force Base in Florida—the same place where refugees from Cuba and Haiti are currently imprisoned until their cases can be adjudicated. This little darter prefers fairly fast flowing streams which hold dense stands of vegetation for protection against predators.

Let me end my discussion of the tiny endangered fishes of the United States with a bit of personal philosophy.

Should a small fish of absolutely no economic value to man be allowed to stop or to delay a big water impoundment project? Is the prevention—or delaying—of extinction that important? My answer is an unqualified yes. There is no crime greater than causing the extermination of a species: conversely, there is nothing more foolish than trying to prevent the extinction of a species which has failed to make the grade—due to its own inherent weaknesses, not to any action of mankind. The dilemma facing managers of this planet's wildlife is that we do not know whether we are valiantly trying to save a worthwhile species or foolishly trying to delay the disappearance of an unsuccessful mutation in the evolution of a species. Because we are not gifted with supreme intelligence, it is far better to err on the side of preserving every species—if we have that ability.

22

Who Wants to Save a Bat?

Sidelight to bat history is the Bat Tower, listed on the National Register of Historic Places. In 1929, Righter Clyde Perkey wanted to get rid of the mosquitoes who were plaguing his fishing clientele on Sugarloaf Key in Florida. Knowing that bats ate mosquitoes by the millions, Perkey built a Bat Tower, modeled after one in Texas. His tower was designed to furnish good daytime roosting for the bats. To lure the bats to his tower, Perkey even imported a load of smelly bat manure—guano—to make the flying bug traps feel right at home. The bats did not take up residence in the Bat Tower. Still "bat-less" it can be seen on Sugarloaf Key, restored and protected by the Historic Key West Preservation Board.

That bat tower was built in 1926, but long before that time mankind had learned that bats are our friends. The majority of humans have never seen a bat, but they have benefited from the insect-eating habits of the flying mammals. At dusk, millions of bats of many species leave their daytime roosts—usually in a dark corner of a cave, in a church belfry—any place where they can sleep the sunlit day away in peace. These untold millions of insect eaters fly almost nonstop through the dark hours, and all the time they are flying they are eating airborne insects.

Many Americans have made the acquaintance of bats by watching the spectacular departure of the Mexican freetailed bat from Carlsbad Caverns in southeastern New Mexico. After the sun sets, but while it is still twilight, a steady stream of bats pours forth from the opening to this most beautiful of all caves. Their numbers fluctuate widely, from well up in the millions down to five hundred thousand. The National Park Service, which manages Carlsbad Caverns, tries to minimize human interference with the bat flight—but also provides a Ranger to lecture visitors about the bats.

Okay, bats eat insects all night long, which makes them our friends. But horror tales about vampire bats and the Count Dracula type stories have given the bat a very bad press. Education is perhaps the best way to help the bat. Let's start by noting a few facts:

Bats are warm-blooded mammals which suckle their young. They spend the sunlit hours hanging upside down from the roof of a cave. Their droppings pile up on the floor below, forming a very rich source of fertilizer called guano. Man has "mined" this guano for countless centuries. In some cases this guano-mining activity has caused the bats to leave their cave. Study of some of these guano deposits reveals that bats have used that particular cave for more than five hundred years.

What else is interesting about bats? Well, they developed sonar—or radar—long before man did. They emit high-pitched squeaks in flight and are guided by the echoes of those squeaks. They are able to fly in complete darkness, and are even able to avoid thin wires hung in their path. On a very dark night, they bounce their sonar off of tiny mosquitoes to locate their prey. Certainly their tiny eyes are not specialized to see in dim light, like owls, for example.

All the bats ask is to be let alone. Is that too much to ask?

Many species of bats are in good supply and are not endangered. Some other species are in trouble—their existence threatened by man's activities.

In 1976, Dr. John S. Hall of Albright College and Dr. Michael J. Harvey of Memphis State University asked that two species of bat—the Virginia big-eared and the Ozark big-eared—be placed on the list of endangered species. Three years later, these two species of big-eared bats were placed on the endangered list. Public comments were solicited and the Service proposed to purchase a cave to provide critical habitat for the Virginia subspecies. However, the Kentucky Fish and Wildlife Resources Commission knew that all this bat needed was to be left alone. They resisted the proposal to name Stillhouse Cave as Critical Habitat, arguing that to name it would be to invite attention to the rare bats—and remove their necessary insulation from man.

The gray bat weighs less than 16 grams and is one of the largest of its species. It is the only representative of its particular group—having its wing membrane connected to the ankle bone instead of to the first toe as is the case with most bats.

At one time there were individual hibernating populations of gray bats numbering more than one million individuals. By hibernating in great crowds, the bats saved vital body heat and kept temperatures high enough to ensure survival. If someone or something disturbed the colony, they did not "just find another cave." Often that particular colony is simply lost.

Young-rearing time is the most critical for the bat colony. By crowding together, mother bats are able to keep their young warm with the expenditure of less energy to produce "body heat." But it takes a lot of bats to maintain the high temperature. If the colony is reduced in size, the young bats die from lowered temperature. The gray bat simply cannot live in small colonies; it requires "group warmth" to reproduce successfully.

Exceptionally rigid requirements characterize gray bat survival. They prefer to winter in deep caves where temperatures range between six and eleven degrees celsius. Summer caves should have high-domed ceilings which trap and hold the warmer air. Because they prefer to feed over water areas, the summer (maternity) caves are located within one kilometer of the water, preferably with forest growth between cave and water feeding area.

The greatest threat to the gray bats is disturbance of maternity colonies by visiting people. If you enter the cage and the bats flurry around for five minutes, then settle back to their roosting positions—no apparent damage has been done. But the body temperatures of the young have been lowered. Several such arousals of the roosting flock and the young die.

Disturbing a wintering colony is even more deadly. The bat which is disturbed must use up a lot of energy—coming from stored body fat—before it settles back into hibernation. A single disturbance can cause the gray bat to come out of hibernation in the spring in a weakened condition. Several disturbances in hibernation and the bat will not live to see spring. One important study of hibernating bats shows that the dormant animal uses only .01 gram of body weight per day. Yet when disturbed from hibernation, that same bat will lose as much as .48 gram in the first hour of disturbance.

Spelunking, the sport of exploring caves, has been one of the biggest dangers to bat populations. Spelunking clubs have shown restraint in this matter and now schedule explorations around the bats reproductive schedule when possible. It is hoped that spelunkers will continue to improve their practices in this light, for disturbance is the biggest enemy of the bats.

Another peril for bats is the use of insecticides. Evidently the bat is something of a bio-accumulator for residues in bat caves have contained PCB's, heptachlor epoxide, lead and other elements at dangerous levels. DDT was particularly dangerous to bats before it was banned for most usages in this country. After banning DDT in America, Americans hypocritically continued selling it overseas, which may have caused loss of bat species in undeveloped countries. We may never know that story.

In the 1981 book, *THESE ARE THE ENDANGERED*, I discussed the endangered status of the Indiana bat. What has happened in the intervening decade? I am sorry to tell you, but the truth is that the Indiana bat has suffered a decline of approximately 55% in numbers. More than half of them have been lost in ten years!

We know more about cave dwelling bats than we do about those which roost in other places, simply because it is easier to census bats in large concentrations. But there are other species which are important to us in other ways, about which we know very little. For example, there are several species of long-nosed bats which live in the semi-arid Southwest. They feed on the nectar of the desert flowers during their annual migrations. Plants such as the agave and the huge saguaro cactus are pollinated by these bats as they gather the nectar. We have seen a great decline in the picturesque saguaro cacti all over the southwest—a decline so marked that "cactus-napping" is now a common crime in states like Arizona. Should these bats be on the endangered listing? The question was answered in the winter of 1988, when both Sanborn's long-nosed bat (*Leptonycteris sanborni*) and the Mexican long-nosed bat (*Leptonycteris nivalis*) were added to the U.S.Fish and Wildlife Services list of endangered species. Some students of the southwestern biota are worried that entire ecosystems may be eliminated if those ecosystems lose the pollinating services of these long-nosed bats.

Worldwide, it appears that the best friend the bat family can claim is one Dr. Merlin D. Tuttle, founder and President of Bat Conservation International, with headquarters in Austin, Texas. Post Office Box 162603, zip code 78716, if you wish to write for more information.

Merlin found that he had to have good photographs of the many bat species if he wished to help save them. Starting from near scratch, he became one of the world's foremost authorities in high speed photography. Most bats were photographed in complete darkness with the aid of high speed electronic flash. Tuttle showed great ingenuity in devising methods for tripping the shutter at the exact millisecond to get spectacular photographs. His articles describing different bats and their habits around the world have been featured often in the National Geographic Society's magazine. Due to his efforts, millions of people now know that some bats catch and eat fish, that others are called flying foxes and are the size of a small dog, that some bats are relished by primitive peoples who eat them, that other bats live almost entirely on frogs captured by homing in on the frogs' "croaking" sounds, that some bats live entirely on fruits, and most important of all, they have learned that bats are harmless creatures, helpful to humans and that only one species, the vampire bat, feeds on the blood of cattle. In the continental United States, all bats are helpful—no bat poses any threat to any human being. Rabies danger to people is so infinitesimal that we can safely ignore it.

It's sad that humans *do* pose a threat to bats.

There are approximately 950 different species of bats in the world. Yet the IUCN's listing of endangered species lists only 33 species of bats as being endangered. This does not point to the other 917 species being out of danger. Far from it. It simply means that we do not know enough about the other species of bats to list them as endangered! Of the 33 species so listed, North American species account for five positions.

There are only 39 known North American bat species, and five of them are endangered. If this same percentage holds true for all species of bats worldwide, it means that no fewer than 123 species are endangered worldwide. Why the high percentage of US species being listed as endangered? Simply put, we have studied these bat species while most of the world has not.

If bats are not left undisturbed in their caves, we may need other means of controlling insects. What do you think is more economic—control of insects by dangerous chemicals or by the millions of unpaid workers known as bats?

Surely man has a big stake in the survival of bats.

23

Sea Turtles at Risk

Five different species of sea turtles are presently endangered, at risk of disappearing from the face of the earth because of our carelessness! There is no more damning evidence of our inability to manage wildlife than this!

Sea turtles spend 99.99% of their lives at sea, returning to land only for the egg laying ritual. I first saw this spectacle near Stuart, Florida. We walked quietly along a darkened beach, and waited for the big females, some of them weighing more than sixty pounds, to laboriously drag their bodies up on the sand. Their eyes glowed lambent fire in the reflection of our dim flashlight. They knew we were there, but they came ashore anyway—as they must come ashore if their race is to continue. Using their front flippers to slide their heavy bodies across the wet sand, they sought the high water mark. Then they used their flippers to excavate a deep hole, down into the sand. Front flippers scraped the sand away and the back flippers tossed the sand down the sloping beach.

It took more than half an hour to excavate the nest hole. The female rested for a few minutes and then went about the work of extruding dozens and dozens of eggs, dropping them into the hole in the sand. Water streaming from her eyes as she worked gave the impression that she was crying real tears. These tears made rivulets in the sand.

When the last egg was laid, she pivoted ponderously and used her flippers to cover up the eggs. When the beach was returned to its former appearance and her job completed, she crawled awkwardly back into the sea. On land she was an ungainly beast, definitely out of her element. But once in the sea, a graceful wave of her flippers propelled her into the ocean—her real home. Once in the ocean, the female sea turtle seemed to disappear from our view unseen and unknown until the same moon of the next year when it all happened again.

Along sheltered beaches across the world, that drama is reenacted regularly as the sea turtles come ashore to lay their eggs. Once, most tropical or sub-tropical beaches boasted egg laying sea turtles. The action is now limited to a surprisingly few beaches—and fewer and fewer turtles are climbing out of their element, into an alien world, to assure the continuation of their race.

After the nesting period is completed, the eggs are immediately in danger. Native peoples dig them up and eat them, but this happens less and less often than it used to. Raccoons and other predators dig up the eggs and eat them. Mortality is heavy.

Yet after the tiny turtles hatch out and dig their way to the surface does the mortality become horrendous. Wading birds, herons and ibises and others, consider the tiny turtles a delicacy as do alligators, hawks, crows, owls, raccoons, coyotes, foxes, coatimundi and fishes. When the hatch is in full swing, predators gather by the hundreds and the tiny turtles run a fearful gauntlet to gain the still-dangerous, dubious safety of the ocean. There big fish wait to eat them.

Perhaps less than one turtle reaches maturity out of 500 eggs laid. Nature could sustain that terrible mortality because of the sheer profligacy of the sea turtle egg-laying process. Upon reaching adult size, the sea turtles lead a relatively safe existence—if we discount man—and each female may return to the egg-laying beaches, year after year, for more than two decades, thus increasing the odds for survival of the species. Wasteful as it may seem, this reproductive process seemed to work well enough, for sea turtles inhabited almost all of the warm waters of the world's oceans. We know of very little mortality among the adult population. Surely big sharks may take a few, and there are a number of places where intrepid natives sail the calm seas at night, spearing the adult turtle whose eyes glow in the light of a small fire carried in the boat. I sailed with such a *camaguerero* in the Sea of Cortez. He harpooned the turtle with a special "stopper" on his lance to prevent penetration into the vitals of the turtle. The harpoon's barbs hung in and under the carapace and he was able to pull the turtle into his boat. Ashore, he remedied his lack of refrigeration by the simple expedient of keeping his turtles alive. With their flippers tied behind their backs, the turtles wait in mute patience until a buyer shows up—which often may be weeks. Call me a sentimentalist if you want to—I bought his captive turtles and took them five miles down the beach and turned them loose again.

Modern man has invaded the world of the sea turtle. Many of the prime egg-laying beaches in North America have been developed into condominiums and marinas, and we can only imagine what happens when the female turtle returns to the beach where she has laid her eggs for many years, and finds only concrete sea walls and boat slips.

When we woke up to what was happening, we found that five species of sea turtle nesting in American waters were in danger of extinction: the Kemp's ridley, loggerhead, leatherback, hawksbill and green turtle species. Why had sea turtles come to this desperate situation? Was it man's crowding them out of their nesting areas? Surely that had an effect, but there was a far greater danger out in the ocean, where they had formerly felt themselves to be safe.

Commercial fishermen tow long trawl nets to catch shrimp. The mouth of the trawl is spread wide to funnel the tasty shrimp into the net, and the net narrows down to a bag at the end, where the shrimp are packed together by the force of the towing motion. This is the method which produces the bulk of the world's shrimp catch.

It is also the method which seems to be exterminating the sea turtle. Although sea turtles can stay submerged for a long time, they must breathe air! Forced into the purse of the net, they are covered with hundreds of pounds of shrimp and other fish species. Unable to get out, the turtles drown.

The National Marine Fisheries Service—an organization known more for its sympathies with the commercial interests than with the environmentalists—estimates that at least 11,000 sea turtles, including the most endangered Kemp's ridley turtle, die each year in the shrimp trawls in the Gulf of Mexico and the southeastern coast of the U.S. I suspect that the actual loss of endangered sea turtles is much higher. I base this guess on having spent a few nights with shrimp trawlers working the Sea of Cortez. The trawler I shipped on killed at least a dozen big sea turtles with each lifting of the trawl. Multiply this loss through the entire fleet and multiply that by the number of nights the trawlers worked the shrimp waters of the Cortez and we come up with losses in the hundreds of thousands in this one great body of water alone!

To realize the size of the danger posed by shrimp trawls, we must point out that about 7,000 commercial vessels operating offshore tow their trawls for four to five million hours per year. Add about 11,000 smaller vessels which work inshore where Turtle Excluder Devices (more about TED's later) are not required, and you begin to realize the magnitude of the problem for the sea turtle. Shrimp trawlers dispute the claims that their trawls drown many sea turtles, claiming that pollution or disease kills the turtles which wash ashore. However, wherever TED's are used, the numbers of dead turtles washing ashore always goes down. Sincere shrimp captains state that they have worked their trawls for years without drowning a single turtle. This is possible in some areas, but in the prime sea turtle areas, the trawl is a deadly danger to the endangered turtles. The shrimping industry is a big one. Americans eat about two and a half pounds of shrimp each per year. In 1988, 331 million pounds of shrimp worth 506 million dollars were landed in the United States. Another half a Billion (yes, that's right BILLION) pounds are imported from other nation's shrimp fleets. More than 30,000 fishermen and their families rely on shrimp. But shrimp trawling is eliminating sea turtles rapidly. That's the problem.

There is a solution!

TED stands for turtle excluder device. The device is an ingenious contraption which is fitted about half way back on the long net of the trawl. It intercepts the turtle with steel bars, and slides it up and out the top of the trawl. Ten thousand hours of tests conducted by impartial observers prove that it does work.

The problem lies not in designing a turtle excluder—the problem is in getting shrimpers to use them.

So the Congress reenacted the Endangered Species Act. Under the authority of this act, regulations were promulgated to force use of the proven TED on May 1 of 1989. Although the TEDs cost only $400 each, the shrimp industry rose up in red-eyed wrath. It wasn't the cost of using the TEDs they objected to. It was their contention that the TEDs lowered the shrimp catch by as much as 40%. According to tests, this contention was arrant nonsense.

Salt water commercial fishermen are a tough breed. They fight the elements to earn their living. They don't take lightly to any organization telling them what to do. They are as independent as a hog on ice; always have been a breed apart. They are not famed for listening to reason, not if it interferes with their independent way of life. I usually find this trait very praiseworthy, but not this time when the existence of five species of sea turtle is in danger.

Shrimpers in Florida, Georgia and South Carolina began obeying the law and didn't seem to be having any trouble. The numbers of dead sea turtles washed up on the beaches of those three states went down markedly. Gulf Coast shrimpers fought the regulation, and flatly refused to use TEDs. Then they started lobbying the Bush Administration to get rid of the TED regulation entirely.

Secretary of Commerce Robert Mossbacher caved in to the pressure. First he postponed the enforcement of the regulation for sixty days. This sign of weakness served to increase the pressure against the regulation. Mossbacher caved in again and on July 13, 1989, he suspended enforcement of the regulation entirely! This showed a flagrant disregard for the law of the land. Mossbacher's legal counsel informed the Commerce Secretary that he was himself in violation of the law.

Frightened into action by this warning, Mossbacher swung the other way and reinstated the regulation. Many observers felt that he "reinstated" the regulation and quietly urged "non-enforcement" of that same regulation. All hell broke loose on the shrimp ports of the Gulf Coast. Determined to

133

show their total defiance of the law of the land, shrimp boats blockaded ports, threatened the Coast Guard, and even threatened the law-abiding shrimpers who were going along with the law. Caving in again, the wishy-washy Secretary Mossbacher issued a blanket suspension of the regulations which mandated TEDs.

Conversation organizations promptly took the Secretary to court. There the judge told the Secretary that he was breaking the law, but told him that he did NOT need to stop breaking the law. This inexplicable ruling cannot possibly hold up under appeal, but it is effective in that it removes the turtles' protection for the rest of this shrimping season.

What we have here is an example of how the future of the turtle is endangered by the federal government's callous flaunting of the laws governing endangered species—a cowardly caving in to vocal pressures from commercial interests—a shameful refusal to obey the law of the land. When the rights of turtles are measured against the (alleged) loss of a dollar, we learn which side the federal administration is on. And it isn't on the side of the endangered species.

The Bush Administration will obviously lose the fight on this one—but will the decision come too late to save the sea turtles in American waters? The Audubon Society has called for a blanket boycott of shrimp and shrimp products as long as the shrimp fleet refuses to obey the law by trawling without the legally-required TEDs.

There are only about 600 nesting female Kemp's ridley turtles left in the world. TEDs may help save them, but shrimpers refuse to use TEDs.

Does your shrimp cocktail still taste as good?

But the turtle faces other dangers. Many are found dead after eating plastic materials, materials which they mistake for their favorite food—jellyfish. Shrimp fishermen are irate at the TED rules. Some of them go so far as to kill every sea turtle they run into. Their reasoning is that if the endangered turtles become extinct, they won't be endangered any more. In what we can only hope was an isolated instance, a shrimper off Fort Myers, Florida was arrested when he cut the throats of three nearly drowned loggerhead turtles.

PROGNOSIS: Given public cooperation and given real enforcement of the regulations, it MAY be possible to save these endangered sea turtles from extinction. But the battle has just been joined and there's a long, tough road ahead. We are not optimistic!

How about the other three quarters of the world? In Pietermaritzburg, South Africa, I interviewed Dr. George Hughes, head of the famed Natal Parks Board and an important member of the working group (on sea turtles) of the International Union for the Conservation of Nature. Dr. Hughes earned his doctorate with a comprehensive study of sea turtles in the Indian Ocean.

According to Dr. Hughes, Maputaland, on the South African coast, just south of the big island of Madagascar, is a favored breeding spot for five species of sea turtles. These are the hawksbill, green, olive ridley, loggerhead and leatherback. The same listing as ours, except that he studies the Olive Ridley while we worry about the future of the Green Ridley.

Happily, Dr. Hughes was able to report that none of these species is endangered in any way in his corner of the world. When we asked him about shrimp trawlers, he told us that they troll very deep in Indian Ocean waters, far below the levels used by the sea turtles; thus the trawls are not a significant danger. Leatherbacks weighing upward of 700 kilograms lay their eggs on Zululand beaches, according to Dr. Hughes. He adds that South Africans are proud of their heritage of sea turtles and that vandalism of the nests is almost unknown. The Natal Parks Board has been researching these big wanderers of the seas for 22 years now, and has tagged 4,700 loggerhead females on the egg laying beaches, making a giant contribution to sea turtle lore the world over.

Sea turtles are definitely better off in the Southern hemisphere than in our hemisphere, and that is nice to know. But the plight of our big sea turtles is serious!

24

Important Federal Laws for Endangered Species

After long wrangling in Congress, and due to the unrelenting push for its passage by wildlife interests, the Endangered Species Law became effective December 28, 1973. This is undoubtedly the most important action in the entire century-long fight to protect endangered species from extinction.

There have been many assaults upon the Endangered Species Law and its companion law—the Critical Habitat Act—since that day in 1973, but the essential purpose and scope of the Law remains the same.

The Endangered Species Act (ESA) applies to all forms of life that merit federal protection by reason of their endangered status. This protection is extended without regard to whether or not the species has any commercial or sport value.

Theoretically, it protects the Tooth Cave Spider of Texas just as much as it protects the Whooping Crane; it is aimed at preservation of the Judge Tait's Mussel in Alabama just as much as it preserves the peregrine falcon or the blackfooted ferret. ESA governs the taking of any individual of that protected species, regulates interstate commerce in specimens or parts of that animal, and provides the legal authority for the acquisition of land to protect that species. Of greatest importance, perhaps, is the fact that the ESA provides federal money to several states and even to foreign countries to prevent extinction of endangered species.

The Act assigns responsibility under ESA to the Secretary of the Interior, who is always a political appointee governed by the wishes of the elected President of the United States. The Secretary, in turn, delegates this authority to the Director of the U.S. Fish and Wildlife Service, who is usually—definitely not always—a career civil servant who has worked his way up through the ranks to merit the position. This unfortunately has not always been true. Several directors of the F&WS have been political appointees, chosen for their loyalty to the Administration far more than for their concern for wildlife.

Lynn Greenwalt was perhaps the best qualified Director of the U.S. Fish and Wildlife of any man so appointed. He was born on a wildlife refuge, the son of a refuge manager. He worked for the Fish and Wildlife Service during summer vacation from his studies in wildlife management. Deliberately placed on the career ladder (where he definitely belonged), he served in several different disciplines from law enforcement to Federal Aid in Wildlife Restoration, in posts of increasing responsibility from Portland to Atlanta. The same is true of former Director John Gottschalk, a man of wide experience before being tapped for the post of Director of USF&WS. Both Greenwalt and Gottschalk lost the position of Director when the administration changed and the newly elected administration chose their own Director.

In the early days of the ESA, the Director of the F&WS selected a Chief of the Office of Endangered Species. In the early days of the Act, this office was under the direction of Keith Schreiner, career wildlifer and well qualified. He deserves a lot of credit for maintaining the integrity of the ESA against the thousands of pressures which tried to adulterate the provisions of the act. Most of these pressures came from industries that felt the impact of the ESA, and almost all of them were funneled through congressmen who were in the pocket of industry. Most of these pressures took the shape of watering down the ESA by granting individual exemptions from its provisions.

After Keith Schreiner was promoted to be top man in Alaska, the scope and authority of the Endangered Species Office has been slowly and inexorably weakened. The centralized oversight has been removed to the regional offices and then removed again to area offices in the field. This has had the effect of greatly reducing the effectiveness of the Office, and has so diluted authority that it has also diluted responsibility. In the early days, the Recovery Team was the principal unit working to prevent extinction of a particular species. Now Recovery Teams do not even exist for many species—although the species certainly is still endangered. The Office of Endangered Species is presently hard to find on either the national or regional level as it has been "folded into" other positions in the name of economy. In this case, Economy has reduced Effectiveness, and wildlife species have suffered.

Responsibility for marine species was assigned to the Secretary of Commerce who works through the Director of the National Marine Fisheries Service. Far more than the USF&WS, the Department of Commerce is amenable to the commercial interests it is supposed to regulate. This separation of responsibilities between terrestrial and marine species interposes another layer of bureaucracy that must be penetrated to accomplish anything. Surprisingly, this dichotomy has worked fairly well to date.

Similarly, responsibility for endangered plant species has been assigned to the Department of Agriculture. Cooperation between Interior and Agriculture has not been bad. It also has not always been good.

The ESA tries to help endangered species that are threatened by destruction of habitat, over-use or overhunting, disease or predation, or by any other threat.

The procedure to list a species thought to be endangered or threatened is fairly simple, if you are familiar with bureaucratic procedures. Anyone can propose a species for listing. When the proposal is received, the Office of Endangered Species conducts a review of the situation, and contacts knowledgeable individuals. If the evidence warrants this action, the Office of Endangered Species publishes a notice of "proposed rule making" in the Federal Register. The public is then given at least sixty days in which to respond to the proposed rule making. The governor of an affected state is given at least ninety days to make his wishes known—and his wishes usually reflect the feelings of his State Game and Fish Department or State Department of Agriculture. There may also be a public hearing on the proposed rule making.

Sifting all of the evidence and listening to everyone, the F&WS makes a final determination. This determination, published in the Federal Register is usually effective within thirty days of its publication.

Once on the endangered list, the species is now protected by the full force of federal law. How to get off the list? In most cases removal from the list is caused because the species is now considered to be extinct. Most removals mean that we have again failed in our efforts to prevent extinction. There are still a few triumphs when a species recovers to the point where it can be reclassified from Endangered to Threatened. . . . or even have its name removed from the listing entirely.

Then we come to the Critical Habitat Provisions of the ESA. These provisions were enacted by Congress for one purpose. That single purpose was to protect the habitat of an endangered species on federally owned or managed lands. It was never intended that this protection of critical habitat would extend to privately owned land. This act did not create an inviolate sanctuary on any privately owned habitat needed by an endangered species. Destruction of habitat is the single most common reason for a species becoming endangered. For example, the clapper rails of California became endangered by reason of the destruction of coastal marshes to make room for mankind's crowds. But the clapper rail was between a rock and a hard place, for the coastal marshes it needed so badly were not federally owned or managed. Perhaps the most spectacular implementation of these provisions was the case of the snail darter which was thought to exist only in one river in Tennessee. That water was named as "Critical" to the tiny snail darter and the federal law and the federal courts stopped *federal* construction of the Tellico Dam for a while.

There is now a great hullabaloo about critical habitat for the northern spotted owl. Its "critical habitat" seems to be mature conifer forests in the northwestern United States. Protection of this critical habitat may stop lumbering, upon which many people depend for their livelihood. Please note that this protection of habitat by stopping lumbering applies only to the federally owned forests, controlled by the U.S. Forest Service. It does not apply to privately owned timberlands. We discussed this confrontation in Chapter four.

In August of 1976, Keith Schreiner wrote "The determination of critical habitat is a means of helping all Federal agencies meet their responsibilities under the Endangered Species Act of 1973. It is a tool to help save and restore species, not a weapon to hinder economic or social progress." His summation of the meaning of the critical habitat provisions was accurate, but anyone concerned with stopping the extinction of wildlife species must be constantly alert to attempts to circumvent the critical habitat laws. To the great majority of our elected representatives, a phone call from a concerned constituent is reason enough to work for some sort of exemption from the provisions of the Critical Habitat laws. To most of our elected representatives in Congress, these Critical Habitat Provisions should be strictly enforced—in every congressional district except *his* congressional district. When it comes to balancing economic hardship of a constituent against the welfare of an endangered species, almost every single elected representative remembers that wildlife species do not vote, nor do they contribute heavily to election campaign war chests.

If you are concerned about the plight of endangered species, your number one job is to make sure that the provisions of the Critical Habitat legislation are not bypassed by our federal administration.

139

25

CITES
and the
International Picture

Citizens of the United States of America have many misconceptions about what goes on in other countries. We are rightly accused of being too wrapped up in our own importance; too free to give advice without being asked and ignorant of events that transpire in far-off places. Leaders of developing countries constantly complain that they know everything about America, yet America knows nothing about them.

Intellectually, the great mass of our people are isolationists. We tend to think that all good ideas come from America—which simply isn't true. They are certain that America supports a big part of the rest of the world with money—and they think that our "foreign aid" is outrageously costly. But the world outside of our borders is not the backward, poverty-stricken world many of us envision. Let's look at a few facts.

1) Sweden spends more money per capita on foreign aid than we do.

2) Finland sends more money to help African and Asian wildlife programs, per capita, than we do.

3) The largest and most prestigious organization helping endangered species is the International Union for the Conservation of Nature and Natural places (IUCN). While American organizations and agencies are members of this organization, its headquarters is in Gland, Switzerland, and British and French leaders play larger roles than do Americans in determining its policies.

There is a lot of very good work being done by non-U.S. agencies and organizations, for the good of endangered species. We are not alone in the struggle; we have many good partners.

One of the best tools of international cooperation for endangered species is the CITES treaty.

CITES is an acronym standing for Convention of International Trade in Endangered Species. Uncle Sam is a signatory to that treaty, as are more than 70 other nations. In May of 1977, Uncle Sam published regulations designed to enforce the provisions of CITES. These regulations established procedures to control and monitor the export of imperiled species from a country and the import of an imperiled species into a nation that is signatory to CITES. This agency regularly publishes a list of wildlife species which are considered to be endangered. Our own Office of Endangered Species also publishes a list of endangered species. Although these lists overlap about 90%, they are not identical, nor are they the same as the scientific listings put out by the IUCN—in their Red Books of data about endangered species.

Why was CITES necessary? Why was it created? CITES was a very intelligent attempt to preserve endangered species by eliminating the market for individuals of that species. For example, several South American monkeys are endangered. There is almost no market for those monkeys in their native countries. There was a big market in the United States (and to a lesser extent in Europe) for these monkeys as pets. Now the CITES treaty makes it illegal for those monkeys to leave the country of their origin, and it also makes it illegal for those monkeys to be imported into the countries (like the United States) which wanted them for profitable resale as pets. With the profit motive removed, the monkeys were no longer captured in their native habitat and no longer sold in international trade. Illegal trade in these monkeys through smuggling was greatly reduced because the pet fancier could no longer legally buy them, nor could he legally own them. It has worked in most cases in the way it was intended.

In *most cases*, not all cases!

We put our American alligator on the endangered list, even though Louisiana was up to its elbows in alligators and Florida had more than they cared to have. Peripherally, the alligator was endangered—in other words it was greatly decreased in numbers on the outer edges of its range—in Texas and in the Carolinas and Georgia. Because we placed the alligator on the endangered list, the CITES treaty ruled that international trade in almost all crocodilian hides be stopped. After all, once the hide is stripped from the crocodilian, it takes an expert to separate the American alligator hides from the Orinoco caiman hides. This is especially true after they've been salted and dried.

France was not a signatory of CITES at that time. France is the world leader in fashioning elegant shoes, boots, handbags and wallets from crocodilian hides. France suddenly found itself deprived of 90% of the raw hides which it needed to make these elegant products of French *haute* fashion. The French became hopping mad, and with reason. The people of Louisiana became hopping mad, for they were forced to safeguard a crop which appeared to be abundant and were forced to let it go to waste. The net result was even bad for the American alligator, because state agencies stopped expenditures of funds for alligator-benefiting projects. Why manage and develop a resource that you are forbidden to crop?

As a result of State Department pressures on the Department of the Interior, French protests were finally heard by the United States and the 'gator was removed from the endangered list where it should never have been in the first place. Another result was that France then became a signatory to the CITES treaty.

Many of the world's spotted cats are considered to be greatly reduced in numbers. This is surely true of the South American ocelot, margay and jaguar. Africa and Asia have already lost most of their cheetahs. To the best of my knowledge, the leopard has never been shown to be endangered. Yet, for some reason, CITES put the leopard on the endangered list in 1972. This meant that no nation signatory to CITES could legally allow the importation of a leopard skin or trophy.

The first result of this action was obviously to stop sportsmen from going to Africa for the purpose of hunting leopard. On average, a visiting trophy hunter leaves five thousand or more dollars in each African country where he hunts. That supply of foreign exchange was very important to most of the poor African nations. Recognizing the value of this trophy hunting, most African nations were beginning to manage their leopard populations wisely, safeguarding the goose that laid the golden egg.

But when they could not sell the end product—the leopard hunt safari— they immediately lost all interest in safeguarding the leopard. Small African nations stopped anti-poaching efforts, because the leopard was no longer worthy of protection. The moral of this is evident. "Each man kills the thing he loves," and CITES was killing the leopard by overprotection— protection that was never needed. By placing the beautiful cat on the endangered list, we did it no favor. By reducing the monetary value of the leopard, we caused it to be ignored by African wildlife managers.

CITES also provided the enemies of hunting and trapping with a new weapon. The United Kingdom (for unknown reasons) succeeded in placing all members of the order *Felidae* on the endangered list, thus effectively stopping all international trade in all cat skins.

Thousands of bobcat skins are taken each year in America and most of the pelts are exported to Europe, for fashion use. Suddenly it was necessary to have an export permit to ship any bobcat skin over the Atlantic. The U.S. Fish and Wildlife Service, knowing that there was no shortage of bobcats, thought that they could simply issue the necessary permits. Enter the Defenders of Wildlife. They worked through the courts to force the U.S. Fish and Wildlife Service to bring forth proof that there were enough bobcats in America to allow for hunting and trapping them. The Endangered Species

Scientific Authority (ESSA) agreed, and state and federal agencies wasted millions of dollars and months of time in proving what everyone knew, that the bobcat was not endangered.

In many cases when international politics conflicts with the obvious needs of wildlife management, the Washington scene comes down to a battle between the State Department's anxiety to please all foreign interests, and the Department of the Interior's anxiety to further good wildlife management. In almost every case, the State Department has been an automatic winner. Politics over good sense, in most cases.

Although it has its evident drawbacks, CITES has been a very important positive force for good, and Uncle Sam should never consider withdrawing from that treaty. We must further every program which allows us to work with the international community.

What do I mean by "international community"?

Well, for starters, let's see who belongs to the IUCN? Membership varies from year to year for obvious reasons. In 1988 IUCN membership included 117 countries. Individual memberships totalled 592, made up of 59 states, 125 governmental agencies, 357 non-governmental national organizations, 30 non-governmental international agencies, and 21 affiliates. In 1987, IUCN employees were stationed at Gland, Switzerland (59), Bonn, Germany (6), Cambridge, England (24), with another 7 at Kew, Nairobi, Kenya (6), Washington, D.C. (2) and one at each of Harare, Zimbabwe; Dakar, Senegal; and Karachi, Pakistan.

Individuals are not entered into membership, as I understand it, only the agency or organization they serve. Among United States members we find the National Geographic Society, The Smithsonian Institution, and the Wildlife Conservation International. Looking farther down the list we find some surprises. Citibank USA is a member, as are Digital Equipment Corporation, Exxon, RJR Nabisco, the Ford Foundation, The Andrew Mellon Foundation, and others too numerous to mention.

Truly, the IUCN is the overall umbrella agency working for the preservation of endangered species. While Americans play an important part in its work, we do not run it! All of the world is party to this struggle to prevent extinction, willingly or unwillingly. This is one planet, one Spaceship Earth. Thank God we are not alone in the struggle. We are only a part of the struggle.

26

Israel's Endangered Species

I was privileged to tour Israel as a journalist-guest of the Israeli Defense Forces in the year 1977. In three weeks of 18 hour days, we toured the tiny nation from the Golan Heights in the north and the Lebanon Border, through biblical locales all the way into the Negev Desert, and got within eyesight of the Suez Canal. As a wildlifer, I was severely disappointed in what I saw. With the exception of a very few birds and a few rock-rabbits, I saw no wildlife at all.

Israelis make bittersweet jokes about the stretch of rock-strewn history that is their only homeland. One of them told me, "They say we are the chosen people of God. But take a good look; we are the only nation in this part of the world without its own oil supply. Chosen?"

I left Israel thinking that it was a biological desert insofar as birds and mammals were concerned. True, I did see a growing awareness that a wise stewardship of the land is most important in the world. I saw indications that the young-old state of Israel had learned the basic lesson that all life comes from the land, and they were taking care of the land. Irrigation projects doled out their insufficient water supply to water cash crops and food crops that went all over the continent of Europe and were widely purchased—albeit quietly—in many Arabic nations.

Perhaps it was appropriate that one of the world's most endangered birds, the Negev lappet-faced vulture, was making its last stand in Israel. Insofar as anyone knows, there is only one wild breeding pair of these vultures left in the world. The female is larger than the male and can weigh as much as 26 pounds, making it the largest bird in Israel.

At the time Israel became independent, there were 35 nesting pairs of vultures left in the country, by best estimate. They suffered losses to human intrusions of all kinds. In 1975 there were only three pairs known in the wild! Most of the remaining population was captured and brought under Natural Reserves authority. In late 1989 Israeli aviculturists successfuly reared a chick hatched from an egg laid in captivity. Although there are many lappet-faced vultures in zoos around the world, this was thought to be a first. Incidentally, the first egg produced by this captive female was removed to encourage her to lay another. The first egg proved infertile, but the second one was successfully incubated. Perhaps there is hope for the lappet-faced vulture in Israel and eventually—perhaps decades from now—reintroduction into the wild.

Near Ein Gedi, and farther down along the Dead Sea, I saw "Israeli snow", huge sheets of translucent plastic which covered row crops. This plastic trapped the moisture inside, preventing its loss to the fierce sun that shone down across Masada and on into the warm and salty waters of the Dead Sea. It was hard to believe that this furnace-hot, arid land was of any value to wildlife. Centuries ago Masada resisted the might of Imperial Rome, fed by the granaries and cisterns cut into the solid rock. Today shaded water storage and careful use of "drip" irrigation and "root" irrigation produced crops in what had been a sterile desert for a hundred years.

Newly reclaimed land boasted of lush orange groves. The oranges were stamped "Joppa" or "Joffa" to identify their source as they went into international trade. A percentage were not stamped, as they were intended for export into Arabic nations.

Just as products "recognizably Jewish" were not allowed to cross the borders into the hundred times larger Arab states surrounding it, so cooperation between Israel and surrounding states was non-existent in wildlife management matters.

Israel had much to offer in this regard. Money from America and from the prosperous nations of Europe flowed into Israel to finance development plans of all kinds. Israel had a high level of education and produced scientists capable of manning the ramparts for wildlife restoration. But international cooperation seemed impossible.

This tiny nation which earned the admiration of the world by its surgical rescue of the Entebbe hostages in a hostile land many miles from Israel—this same nation was not to be defeated by the hatred of its neighbors. If intrigue was needed, Israel had the necessary intrigue. Example . . .

The World Wildlife Fund started Operation Oryx in 1962, spurred by fears that the white oryx was in imminent danger of extinction. Israel tried to join the endeavor, but was snubbed. The Phoenix, Arizona zoo managed the captive herd of white oryx and that herd prospered. The progeny were given to Arab nations—Jordan and Oman. Israel was still on the outside, looking in. But in 1980, a herd of six white oryx suddenly showed up in Israel! It seems that the Israelis somehow acquired a gorilla, which they traded for the six oryx. The deal was handled by an unnamed zoo. Regardless of how the deal was pulled off, the Israeli herd now has increased to more than 38 animals.

The onager, or wild ass, is a very rare and endangered animal. Israel obtained a herd of onagers and is raising them in the wild, where the last sighting of a wild onager was in the 1930's. Two of the fast running asses crossed the border into Jordan and were promptly shot by Jordanian soldiers.

During the last decade Israel has tried to turn former military training grounds into Natural Reserves—homes for the creatures that roamed this land in Abraham's day. Makhtesh Ramon is an example. Formerly used for low level bombing practice, it is now home to onagers, Nubian ibex, gazelles, jackals and striped hyenas, which had been considered extinct for decades.

In biblical times, the land area that is now Israel was rich in game. Herod was a great hunter and had no trouble finding game when he was in residence on the awe-inspiring fortress of Masada. Nubian ibex roamed near Ein Gedi and scrambled over the rocks where the Essenes hid the Lost Scrolls. But waves of war have washed back and forth through this crossroads country. The Turks cut most of the timber to construct—and fuel— their railroads which crossed Israel. Bedouins overgrazed the land to near devastation. When Israel created the Nature Reserves Authority in 1963— there was a long list of indigenous species considered extinct in Israel. The Asiatic lion was gone, there were no ostriches, ibex, oryx, wild asses or bears; and about 50 smaller species had disappeared. Gazelles were almost extinct.

As this is being written, there are now more than 10,000 gazelles in Israel! Wildlife scholars there tell me that they are not able to exchange information with the wildlife authorities of surrounding countries, even though they share a common interest in the various populations of gazelles. There are now more than 3,000 ibex roaming where they once roamed when Jesus walked the backroads of this most historic of all nations.

How was this accomplished? First of all, it was accomplished by intelligent management of lands. More than an eighth of all of Israel's tiny area is now in Nature Reserve Authority management. 75% of that area is still used by the military for training maneuvers. However, the training is done without great harm to wildlife—because the Army has given overseer authority to the Nature Reserve people.

Israel is currently in a strange position. They have the breeding stock and the facilities to supply "restocking" stock to many of the surrounding nations which have lost many species. Israel could help in the restoration work, but ancient hatreds (on both sides) prevent such mutually-advantageous cooperation.

Given its tiny size—8,000 square miles at most—less than one-fifteenth the size of my native New Mexico—it would seem that Israel is unimportant in the fight against extinction. Its location bespeaks of a greater importance, for it is located at the crossroads between Asia and Africa and at the crossroads of migration for many species of birds.

Its "crossroads" position has made it the battleground of nations and cultures and led to its deforestation and the extinction of its varied wildlife. The fact that it is home to three of the world's great religions has not helped to preserve its natural values. Israel is so important to so many people—this is the fact that gives a glimmer of hope for Near East and Middle East wildlife as it fights for survival.

The tiny state of Israel deserves a hearty *"mazel-tov"* from all of us.

The jackass penguin of South Africa is reduced in numbers by our overfishing of its food stocks, but these birds face an even greater danger from a ship full of oil, sunk in their back yard.

27

Extinction in Africa

It is not surprising that wildlife numbers on the African continent have decreased greatly in the past thirty years. What is surprising is that there are any animals left.

Africa probably was the richest continent in wildlife species and in wildlife numbers. This is also a continent with more than its share of human misery, poverty and disease. With few exceptions, African nations are not doing an adequate job of managing their wildlife resources. Why not?

Most of Africa is now governing itself, after centuries of colonial rule by European nations. With the exception of South Africa, majority is supposed to rule across the Dark Continent. But African majorities are built of ignorant, poverty-stricken, superstitious masses which have not yet consolidated their strength after long wars of liberation from their European rulers. All too often colonial rule has been replaced by despotic dictators whose tyranny is not improvement over colonial status. In actuality, there are only two democracies in the entire continent—24 year old Botswana and one year old Namibia. Former colonies are now ruled by one man dictatorships—such as Qaddafi in Libya, Mugabe and Kuanda in the former wildlife paradises of Zambia and Zimbabwe, and almost every other African nation. There is no history of democracy on the continent and "strong men" have replaced the former tribal chiefs—and rule in much the same way as did the former tribal chiefs.

These new nations have not done a good job of managing their great wealth of wildlife. But before condemning them, remember that it is hard

149

to be altruistic when you have a hard time feeding your family. It is difficult for a poor nation to enforce enlightened rules of wildlife management when many of its people are near starvation. Do you tell a native that it is immoral to kill an elephant for its ivory when that native is looking at a large sum of money offered by the white man who craves ivory knick-knacks? Do you tell a mother that it is illegal to kill an antelope with snares—when that same mother has seen two of her children die in her arms of starvation?

South Africa is doing a far better job of preserving its wildlife legacy than the rest of the continent. But South Africans take no pride in this pre-eminence. In the words of a South African wildlife manager, "We take no pride in being pre-eminent in wildlife preservation because that is the result of being pre-eminent in wildlife destruction. Fueled by the diamonds of Kimberly and the gold of Johannesburg, the South African economy was strong enough to blast wildlife out of its way in its rush to 'development'. We hit rock bottom in wildlife sooner than did the other nations to the north. Because we hit rock bottom first, we began restoration and preservation work first."

Without moralizing and without condemning developing nations—let's look at the situation for African wildlife.

The tsetse fly preserved African big game for centuries, because cattle could not exist in tsetse infected lands. But when the European came with his sprays to eliminate the tsetse, he upset the entire web of life in the sprayed areas. Worst of all, these people made the land habitable for cattle, sheep and goats who ruined great tracts of land by overgrazing.

In addition to the tsetse fly, the absence of transportation preserved African wildlife. Most big game areas were reached only by arduous—even dangerous—journeys on foot. The white man built railroads and roads, removing the shield of distance from wildlife areas.

For centuries past, tribal wars had kept human numbers from mushrooming. With the colonial period, the superior firepower of the European colonials brought a sort of "Pax Africana" to the tribal warfare scene. In addition, colonial governments had a salutary effect upon sanitation and the rudiments of health care were initiated. Native human populations began to mushroom, and human populations doubled and trebled in some African countries. Increasing numbers of humans owned increased numbers of exotic livestock.

To most native Africans, cattle represents wealth. Increasing herds of cattle served little economic purpose but severely damaged the environment by uncontrolled overgrazing.

During the past thirty years, the great herds of big game in Africa have been cut in less than half. Unnoticed and unchronicled, lesser known species have disappeared from the planet. Almost all species of wildlife have been greatly reduced in numbers. Let's take a look at some of the more celebrated cases.

ELEPHANTS, possessors of the largest brains on dry land, have been slaughtered for their tusks, causing a crash in population numbers all across Africa, with the notable exception of the relatively small herds in South Africa where management has come closer to stopping poaching. Kruger National Park in South Africa has a population of 7,700 elephants and is maintaining their numbers at a level consistent with the carrying capacity of the habitat. In most of Africa, poachers kill the huge pachyderms and chop out their ivory, leaving the rest to the vultures and marabou storks. Several nations have waged heroic programs to stop poaching—but this seems to be an war which is impossible to win. Without active support of the general populace, a few wardens cannot protect elephants over huge expanses of jungle and veldt. It is still impossible to surround five hundred poachers with fifty wardens. Punishment has been swift and drastic in many cases, but the poachers continue to exact a terrible toll from elephant stocks. Whose fault is this?

Perhaps we ought to blame the people who buy the ivory trinkets and *objects d'arts*, furnishing a market for the illegal ivory. Most of us hate to agree to that, for it puts the blame on the ultimate user—reminding us of Walt Kelly's Pogo who made the memorable observation, "We have met the enemy and he is us."

It is obvious that we must take the profit out of elephant poaching if we hope to save the elephant. Surprisingly, there seems to be hope on this front. In June of 1989, President Bush announced a total ban on imported ivory, as part of America's observance of World Environment Day. President Bush intended this ban would remain in effect until the Commission on International Trade in Endangered Species (CITES) met later in 1989 to consider such a ban worldwide. 102 nations belong to CITES, but seldom are they able to act in concert. The basis for Bush's action was the Department of the Interior study which had decided that African elephants cannot sustain current poaching levels, which is a bureaucratic way of saying poachers are exterminating the African elephant.

America is the market for about 15% of all ivory, most of that trade coming through Hong Kong. Japan is the largest importer of ivory, but the Japanese have indicated a willingness to go along with the worldwide ban on ivory sales. We should remember that Japan agreed to go along with the worldwide ban on whaling, but Japan is still killing minke whales under the guise of "research". A new development is that China has joined the ivory import ban.

Kenya recently put an exclamation point to the statement that international trade in ivory must be stopped. They publicly burned over a million dollars worth of ivory—taken by antipoaching patrols, proving that they are determined to stop the international trade by drying up the supply. Now, if we can just dry up the demand. Traveling through countries of southern Africa, I found a degree of skepticism about Kenya's grandiose act

151

of burning ivory. Many knowledgeable wildlife men felt that the ivory should have been sold to finance more anti-poaching efforts. Many expressed outright doubt that the Kenyans had not acted out of altruism on this, but had actually been compensated for the destruction of ivory wealth.

South Africa, Botswana, and Zimbabwe oppose a worldwide ban on ivory trading, pointing out that their elephant herds are not being decimated by poaching, and asking that they be allowed to sell legal ivory in world markets. The big problem is that it is impossible to separate legal from illegal ivory in trade. The open loophole for South African ivory would undoubtedly allow illegal ivory to enter world trade without being caught. South Africa does have a sustainable argument here, for we know that regulated cropping of wildlife herds is part of good management. We also know that people protect the source of their income, and South Africans will be less anxious to protect elephants if there is no longer a market for the produce of elephant herds. In the language of a South African position paper on elephants, "The African elephant *Loxodonta africana* is not seriously threatened with extinction and therefore can be utilized in a rational manner." But there are signs that the Republic of South Africa is not above the corruption that has characterized all governments to their north. The amount of ivory legally exported from the Republic of South Africa over the past few years greatly exceeds the amount of ivory legally culled in that country. In other words, South Africa has been guilty of laundering the illegal ivory from other countries.

Is the elephant really in trouble?

In 1980 a detailed survey accounted for 600,000 in eastern and southern savannas and at least 500,000 in western equatorial forested regions. Effective census methods for forest elephants have not yet been perfected, so this census should be considered a minimum figure. Zaire had about 400,000, Tanzania 200,000, Zambia 160,000 and Sudan about 130,000.

There were roughly 1,700,000 elephants in Africa in 1978, and the current population is less than 700,000. More than a million of the world's elephants were killed in that short period. Poaching for ivory is the principal cause of the decline.

Elephants are still found in 31 countries of Africa, and they are in trouble in about 28 of these countries. If international demand for ivory can be stopped entirely, there is hope that we can succeed in saving the elephant. Please—please, don't buy anything made of ivory, now or ever!

At the time CITES enacted the total ban on international trade in Ivory, most South Africans (along with Botswana and Zimbabwe) were incensed. They said that it would only drive the price of illegal ivory to new heights, encouraging more poachers to enter the deadly, high risk game. In the first year of the total ban, there is a mounting tide of evidence that the price of illegal ivory has come DOWN, rather than increased. This is more a result of having a moral stigma attached to buying or wearing ivory, than to the enforcement of the ban.

There has been hardship and unfairness about the ban on ivory trading. The great Kruger National Park in South Africa, arguably the greatest wildlife showcase in the world, has lost a very considerable income from the sale of "culled" ivory. Even the huge Kruger, which is home to 7,700 elephants, finds that the elephant numbers must be kept under control to avoid permanent damage to the habitat. They customarily cull 300-500 elephants per year, thus financing a large part of the park's expenses. I hated to see that income disappear, but felt that the greater good must be served. At last report, Kruger National Park now sells live baby elephants to individuals, thus earning back the lost income. Most of the elephants have been sold to South African landowners who simply like the idea of having an elephant on their land.

To evaluate the loss of elephant numbers, let us put on the record the survey conducted by Dr. Ian Douglas-Hamilton in 1980. His census work was conducted under the funding and auspices of the World Wildlife Fund, the New York Zoological Society and the International Union for the Conservation of Nature. He estimated totals as follows:

Mauritania	150
Mali	1,000
Niger	1,500
Chad	15,000
Sudan	134,000
Ethiopia	900
Somalia	24,300
Senegal	450
Guinea	300
Sierra Leone	400
Liberia	900
Ivory Coast	4,000
Ghana	3,500
Upper Volta	1,700
Nigeria	2,300
Central African Republic	71,000
Cameroon	16,200
Equatorial Guinea	1,300
Gabon	13,400
Congo	10,800
Zaire	371,700
Uganda	2,000
Kenya	65,000
Tanzania	316,300
Rwanda	150

Angola	12,400
Zambia	150,000
Malawi	4,500
Zimbabwe	30,000
Mozambique	54,800
Botswana	20,000
Namibia	2,700
South Africa	7,800

The brutal fact is that the African elephant has been reduced in numbers and has almost disappeared from most of the continent. Only in South Africa is he increasing in numbers and is probably holding his own in Botswana.

Was the CITES ban on selling ivory a wise move? Only time will tell, but early indications are that it was wise. One very articulate South African, who stands to lose a lot of money by reason of the ban, told me that he is willing to go along with it. In his words, "I feel sorry for Kruger Park that will have its operating income greatly curtailed, but they can stockpile the ivory taken in culling operations. In five or ten years, let's re-think the situation. In the meantime, poaching is decreasing."

It is unfortunate that the CITES ban hurts the very countries that were doing a good job of protecting and preserving their elephants. Ivory has been a medium of trade for millennia, and it is likely that such trade will become legal again—after the threat to elephant existence has ended. We presently have about 600,000 wild elephants in the world. In light of this population figure, it seems ridiculous to say that the elephant is an endangered species. But we know that more than half of the world's wild elephants disappeared in the past ten years and that makes elephants endangered in my book.

RHINOS are in greater danger of extinction than are elephants. The black rhino, smaller than the white, has a hooked upper lip which it uses to browse the woody plants which make up most of its diet. The larger white rhino has a square lipped mouth, designed to help it graze on grass, rather than browse on forbs. The black rhino is quicker, more wary, far more apt to be belligerent than the white. As I photographed my first rhinos in Natal's huge preserve known as Hluhluwe, I asked Tim Parker, Assistant Manager of Hluhluwe, "Are these white rhinos?"

"We wouldn't get this close if they were blacks," he replied. Natal's parks play a determinant role in white rhino salvation. With the exception of 24 specimens left of the northern race of white rhinos, all of the white rhinos in existence are descended from stocks maintained in Natal's provincial parks.

In the mists of early morning, a white rhino cow stands between the photographer and her calf. Almost all of the world's remaining population of white rhinos can thank the Natal Provincial parks for its very existence.

There are very few free-ranging rhinos in existence outside of the Republic of South Africa. The decimation of rhinoceros stocks is due directly to illegal poaching. Composed only of hairs, the horn of the rhino is thought to have great medicinal value by many orientals. Many other parts of the rhino are thought to possess medicinal values and the demand for rhino parts in primitive medicine is very strong. In addition, the Yemeni men absolutely have to have a rhino horn handle on their ceremonial dagger. Those daggers are fashion statements in Yemen and no adult male would be caught dead without his rhino horn-handled dagger.

Rhinos grow horns on top of their heads, and that has been their undoing. The northern white rhino, *Ceratotherium simum cottoni* is nearly extinct in the wild. The black rhino *Diceros bicornis* dropped from 65,000 to about 3,800 in seventeen years from 1970 to 1987.

In actual fact, there is a stronger demand for rhino parts than there is for elephant ivory. In some countries of Africa, individual rhinos have been assigned around the clock protection by armed guards, but still their numbers shrink. The poacher is infinitely better armed, and certainly has a stronger motivation—than does the hired guard.

In an attempt to close down trade in rhino horn, the World Wildlife Fund

155

sent Dr. Esmond Martin, vice-chairman of the African Elephant and Rhino Specialist Group to work on the countries which imported rhino horn. He attempted to get South Korea, Brunei, Singapore and Macao to prohibit the import and export of rhino horn. He also attempted to talk North Yemen into enforcing their laws prohibiting importation of rhino products. Since then, all eastern Asian countries have effectively banned legal trade in rhino horn. The word to watch in that sentence is "legal". In addition, North Yemen has agreed to end its trade in rhino horn and to encourage the use of water buffalo horn for ceremonial daggers.

The tremendous profit to be made from poaching rhino horn, and from serving as a middleman in the trade of rhino horn makes it very difficult to secure cooperation from poor countries. CITES is the most important factor working to reduce rhino horn trade, but the comparatively wealthy United Arab Emirates are now about to withdraw from CITES. Burundi, which is not a signatory to CITES, is very active in the international trade in rhino products.

It should also be noted that there is a growing movement on the part of Americans, mostly Texans, to farm the rhino in this country. This is fostered by Game COIN International. The stated purpose is to provide stocks to reinstate the rhino eventually into African lands where it has vanished. This is an extension of the South African program which has furnished rhinos to Swaziland, Mozambique, Botswana, Zambia, Kenya and Zimbabwe, in addition to selling more than a thousand white rhinos to private landowners in South Africa where they are used for conservation, or hunting purposes. Since 1960 more than 3,000 rhinos have been relocated from the Zululand reserves, proving that the rhino is capable of prospering if poaching is stopped. As is so often the case, the best friend a wildlife species has is the hunter who puts his money where his mouth is in an effort to preserve the species.

White rhinos are strictly African. They stand as tall as five feet at the shoulders and can weigh up to 4,500 pounds. This is the least wary of all rhinos, which accounts for the subspecies extinction from Uganda and the Sudan, and accounts for it's prospering when completely protected.

Black rhinos, still strictly African, are a third smaller than the white rhino, but still weigh a ton and three-quarters. They are much more wary and more agressive than the white, and suffer as much from poaching as the bigger white. Like the white, the black rhino sports two horns, one much smaller than the other.

Because poachers want the horn, an experimental program in Namibia is actually removing the white rhino's horn surgically in the hopes that dehorning will save his life. As the horn is composed of hairs, it will grow back, but slowly. Is it realistic to maim the rhino to save the rhino? Most of the wildlifers I talked to in the southern half of Africa said that it was necessary and that they hoped it worked. The only worry was whether or not the "horn-less" mother rhino could do a good job of protecting her calf. First

156

results are in, and it looks like the mother rhino can adequately shelter her calf from predators. Skilled rhino watchers say that the unprotected calf gets his ears bitten off, or at least gnawed by predators if his mother cannot drive them away. So far, rhino calves in Namibia are still in possession of their ears.

Rhinos are not found solely in Africa, so let's take a look at the subspecies in Chapter 28.

MOUNTAIN GORILLAS are in very serious trouble, and their numbers may have already decreased to the point where survival of the race is imperiled. Dian Fossey spent her life, and lost her life, defending the mountain gorilla. If you haven't read her book, *Gorillas in the Mists*, or seen the movie, you should have. These animals, largest members of the same family as man, are gentle giants, feeding entirely on vegetation. They desire only to be left alone on the forested slopes of mountains in Africa's rain forests.

How sad to note that there has been a thriving trade in selling parts of these giant apes. Can you believe that a member of *Homo sapiens* would actually buy an ash tray made out of the hand of a butchered gorilla? Does the human who displays the skull of a gorilla as a conversation piece really rate the "*sapiens*" in his scientific name?

In a search for tourist dollars, the governments of Rwanda, Uganda and Zaire foster "gorilla-sighting" trips into the mountain fastnesses of the mountain gorilla. The gorilla does not need the company of man. We can only hope that the mountain gorilla becomes so valuable as a tourism builder that these governments will succeed in protecting the source of tourism dollars. The international trade in living gorillas is now pretty well regulated, and it is almost impossible to hide a baby gorilla long enough to get that gorilla to a zoo and sell it. Furthermore, zoos have long ago lost the "I don't care where you got it; I'll buy that gorilla" mentality.

The prognosis for the mountain gorilla is very pessimistic. Who to blame? Blame ourselves, for we crowded into the jungle on the slopes of its distant volcanic mountains—crowding the gorilla into more and more contact with our species. Gorillas have no rifles or spears, and must lose any conflict with us. Blame those of us who actually paid money for parts of gorillas, encouraging the poor natives to kill more gorillas. If the mountain gorilla disappears, mankind is to blame.

Zoos paid tremendous sums of money for juvenile gorillas, captured alive by the simple expedient of killing the mother of that juvenile gorilla. But zoos are now aware of the plight of the mountain gorilla and are going into propagation research in a big way. Perhaps the day will come when the mountain gorilla exists only in zoos. Perhaps the day will come when zoo-raised gorillas will be reintroduced into the wild? It has happened with other species.

157

CHEETAHS are the fastest of all carnivores, maybe the fastest runner in the world. Their numbers have been greatly reduced in Africa in the last three decades. In 1980, the research team of George and Lory Frame estimated that there were at least 1,000 cheetahs on the vast Serengeti National Park in Tanzania.

Over the past fifty years cheetahs have practically disappeared from original ranges in Asia, especially in India, and from most of Africa. Surveys indicate that the total cheetah population is being halved every ten years. Reasons given are illegal poaching for sale of pelts, mankind's expanding into their habitat (crowding them out), disappearance of their natural prey and even deliberate extermination in some areas.

Cheetahs prosper in the Serengeti, where the original conditions prevail to a great extent, and where man's numbers are preserving—instead of destroying—the habitat of the cheetah. The prognosis seems clear—cheetahs will continue to exist, but only in token numbers in carefully protected areas, such as the Serengeti National Park.

Anne Van Dyk, of the De Wildt farm in the Transvaal of South Africa, is perhaps the world's greatest authority on cheetah reproduction. For many years the study of cheetah in captivity was a obsession with this lady. She dedicated her ancestral lands to the rearing of cheetahs and had more than 100 on the premises when I visited. She told me that she can produce as many cheetahs as there is a demand for—but that the open plains habitat needed for this sight-hunting speed merchant are disappearing. She said that captive-reared cheetahs quickly adapt to the wild—provided they are re-introduced into an area which does not already house a territorial cheetah. Although fed on raw meat during their captive years, the liberated cheetah learns to hunt and to kill—and learns quickly. Ms. van Dyk says that it is instinctive for the cheetah to chase anything that runs away. Because the cheetah is the fastest mammal in a sprint, it catches the prey and learns to kill quickly. It is a sad commentary on man's habit of crowding out the wild animals that there are no longer habitats into which the cheetah can be reintroduced into the wild—even though cheetahs can be mass-produced in captivity.

Ms. van Dyk says that the answer is to replace the cheetah on the list of huntable game. She told me that with considerable sadness, but with the realistic approach. "If the cheetah can be hunted, it becomes valuable to the landowner, who will then protect it."

JACKASS PENGUINS

The flightless jackass penguin is the central figure in one of the most interesting cases of wildlife extinction on the African continent. There are now 200,000 of these formally feathered birds on the southern tip of the Republic of South Africa. Too numerous to be officially called endangered?

Yes, but their number has dropped from 600,000 to 200,000 in ten years. That makes them endangered in this book.

Disembarking from a boat furnished by the National Parks Board of South Africa, I clambered over the guano-whitened rocks to get near the jackass penguins on Jutten Island. The black and white birds seemed alarmed at my presence for human traffic is severely curtailed on their island sanctuary. But they didn't go into the water and my patience was finally rewarded by being able to photograph several hundred of them. When frightened, they dove into openings in the huge pile of boulders— going to ground instead of going to sea.

Why are the jackass penguins decreasing in numbers? Because man is overharvesting the pilchard population of the waters off the Cape of Good Hope. Man is actually taking the food out of the mouths of the penguins. There is a comparison here with the fact that we in the United States overharvested the small sardine-like fishes off the California coast, with disastrous effects upon the big game species of fishes which used those schools of little fish as their food source.

There is a serious attempt on the part of South Africa to regulate the harvest of pilchard in such a way that the jackass penguin may be allowed enough food to live on. But a far more dangerous threat now faces the flightless penguin.

In 1983 a big oil tanker, the Castillo de Bellver, sank off this coast with a cargo of 250,000 tons of crude oil. The wreck still holds more than 100,000 tons of oil, and the wreck is poised 1,300 feet below the surface of the sea off Saldanha Lagoon. Environmentalists point out that this wreck could break up at any moment and that the resultant spill would be worse than the Exxon Valdez catastrophe in Alaska. Nothing has been done to avert this potential catastrophe and perhaps nothing can be done, warn salvage engineers. The potential disaster would destroy the fishery upon which the jackass penguin depends, would ruin the rock lobster beds between Saldanha and St. Helena Bays. Oil could also destroy life in the Langebaan lagoon, one of the most important marine bird sanctuaries in the entire continent. When I visited this lagoon, it held migrants from as far away as the Russian Arctic.

The future of the jackass penguin is not rosy.

The Percy Fitzpatrick Institute of African Ornithology commissioned a study by eminent ornithologists. That study came up with the opinion that no native bird species in South Africa was endangered. But Ian MacDonald of that Institute told me of other endangerments in the southern half of Africa. The Damara tern, for example, is thought to be reduced to less than 120 breeding pairs! The whitewing flufftail, similar to our Californian species, is decreasing in numbers, due to overgrazing and burning of its grassland habitat.

159

Geometric Tortoise

Probably the most endangered tortoise in the world—with a worldwide count of some 4,000 to 6,000—is being exterminated rapidly from its best habitat in the Cape Province of South Africa. The losses are due to loss of habitat to private development—making room for man to crowd in with his marinas and orchards, condominiums and agriculture. This endangering of a species by coastal development sounds very familiar to us in America, especially in California and in Florida.

It is very difficult to get facts on many endangered species on the African continent, simply because those governments have more immediate crises to deal with, and there is only a fledgling organization similar to our National Wildlife Federation, or Izaak Walton League to assist in gathering data.

Contradictions exist in data already gathered. For example, the Scops Owl, listed as endangered in Kenya was commonly sighted on my birding trips in Botswana's Okavango Delta. Perhaps both observations are correct and the tiny owl may be peripherally endangered in Kenya and still common in Botswana.

Not enough attention has been paid to the important role played by the southern end of the continent in providing wintering homes for much of Europe's and Asia's bird populations. As in all other parts of the world, local concentrations occur—concentrations which are very vulnerable to changes in the habitat. For instance, Schaapen Island is the largest known breeding population of black-backed gulls, also known as Kelp gulls. Ten percent of the world's population of African Black Oyster Catchers breeds on the West Coast National Park of South Africa.

Acquired Immune Deficiency Syndrome (AIDS)

Catastrophic events are happening in Africa which have significance for the future of the continent, indeed for the future of the human race itself. The most important is the explosion in numbers of AIDS sufferers. As I write the final words on this African chapter, the total reported for AIDS cases shows the United States as the worst hit, followed by Brazil and then Nigeria. That statistic shows only that the United States is reporting its AIDS problem accurately. Figures produced by African nations are worthless, as they bear no resemblance to the real picture. For instance, the Congo has not reported on AIDS since December of 1987!

In the second half of 1990, entire villages are disappearing in the belt of African nations stretching from the Ivory and Gold Coasts, across to Kenya and Tanzania and southward to Zambia. These villages are gone because their inhabitants are dead or dying of AIDS!

The reason why this catastrophe has gone mostly unreported is that there exists no governmental agency in all of these countries capable of assessing the real damage. I talked to people reporting the evidence of their own eyes—telling of the death of entire populations of Africans between the ages of 14 and 50–in Angola, in Nigeria and in Zambia. The same situation holds true in all of the central 60% of Africa, according to knowledgeable reporters.

What does this mean to the subject of wildlife extinction? This human suffering has great significance for wildlife, simply because the depopulation of Africa will turn back the clock to a human population of 1900, thus providing room for wildlife that is not present today. Terrible as it is to contemplate, AIDS may provide the "culling" of the human race which wise management would suggest. We have no reason to believe that this great reduction in human populations will be restricted to Africa—far from it. The entire world faces this problem. But the effects of AIDS is being felt today in Africa, and its results will be far-reaching. Nevertheless, the African AIDS epidemic, terrible as it is, is but a minor slip on the steadily growing graph of human population. Please remember that no one is advocating AIDS as a management tool; we are only reporting on what is happening, beyond any human control.

The reduction of the human presence works wonders for wildlife numbers. An example is Mozambique, racked by two decades of civil war. Terror-stricken natives of Mozambique have flocked to the cities, or to neighboring Malawi or South Africa, abandoning the hinterland to guerilla forces. As a result of the reduced human presence, big game herds are flourishing in Mozambique in the total absence of law and order.

After seeking answers from biologists and wildlife managers in seven African nations, and after studying the situation intensively in two nations, I have come to the conclusion that none of us in the United States can even begin to understand the situation in Africa. This leads to the inescapable conclusion that we should stop making decisions for African nations.

Mr. David Varty, a very articulate manager of wildlife on the Londolozi Game Reserve, offered some good advice for Americans: "Don't send us any more research projects," says Mr. Varty. "Those projects have only one

The African wild dog is severely endangered across sub-Saharan Africa. These are photographed on the Okavango Delta, Botswana.

end product—a doctor's degree in wildlife management. The research is not what we need. We know what works; it has been working here for forty years on Londolozi. Don't send us any more money for airplanes and helicopters, guns and rifles to stop poaching. Efforts along this line do not produce a permanent solution. As soon as you grow tired of financing the anti-poaching effort, you stop sending money and the situation is back to square one. What we need to do is to show the African that there is greater economic benefit in protecting the animals than there is in slaughtering them. When we put money in his back pocket (wallet) he becomes a force for good, instead of a poacher."

For four decades wisely managed game reserves have shown that there is more money to be made from tourism than there ever could be from killing or otherwise destroying wildlife in Africa. And the income from tourism repeats itself, while the income from poaching is a one time affair. Tourism is the goose which repeatedly lays the golden eggs for African nations. Only in giving the native a share in the golden eggs of tourism can we hope to arrest the slide into extinction for Africa's wildlife.

Tourism in the great hope for African wildlife. There is far more money to be made in showing the lion to the tourists many times more than there ever could be in killing the lion.

28

Disappearing
Asian Wildlife

Asia is our most populous land mass. China holds one fourth of the world's people, with more than one billion Chinese. India is close behind and bids fair to have a larger population than China in the next decade.

Asia is a land of infinite contrasts, from the icebound parts of Siberia to the steaming tropic jungles of Indonesia. It is a land of many religions—Taoism, Buddhism, Christianity, Mohammedanism, Shinto, Confucianism, Animism are only a few. These religions reflect different attitudes toward wildlife. Asia includes the highest peaks on earth in the Himalayas, and the sea level swamps of Bangladesh. Asian terrain ranges from the dry deserts such as the Gobi to the monsoon rains of the Indian sub-continent.

This great diversity means that no one statement will apply to all of Asia.

This great diversity in habitats is reflected in the biodiversity of Asian wildlife. Let's take a look.

Giant Pandas

The World Wildlife Fund chose the giant panda as the symbol of its efforts to save endangered wildlife. It is very easy to sympathize with the plight of the panda. Its appearance—looking like a black and white big teddy bear—makes it a favorite of many people.

164

Giant pandas live only in China's interior, with about 800 to 1,000 individuals in existence in the Chinese provinces of Szechuan, Gansu and Shaanxi. They inhabit about 11,000 square miles on the densely forested slopes of mountains which reach into the clouds. Their habitat is limited by the presence of ice and snow at higher elevations which limits their food supply and by the steady encroachment of humans who crowd in from below in their own search for land upon which to grow food. A further limiting factor is the panda's dietary preferences. It seems to live entirely on the stems and leaves of various kinds of bamboo—the world's largest grasses.

The giant panda was almost unknown in the western world until 1936, when wealthy Chicago socialite Ruth Harkness paid for the capture of an infant panda—named Su Lin—for the Chicago zoo. In those days zoos were even more competitive than they are today, and the new arrival in Chicago incited the envy of almost every other zoo in the world. As a result, by 1949 a total of 73 giant pandas had gone from China to outside zoos. The price of a live panda rose to great heights.

In the mid 1970's, at least 138 giant pandas were known to have died of starvation in their cloud-shrouded Chinese mountain habitat. Why? Well, it seems that bamboo species all have a common life story. They grow and flourish for a period of from 40 to 100 years, depending upon the species. Then at this maturity age, they flower, distribute their seeds and die back. It takes from 8 to ten years for the new growth bamboo to reach the stage where the pandas can dine on it. This flowering and dying does not take place simultaneously over the entire range of the giant panda, but if it takes place in the dwindling islands of suitable habitat, and there is no place for the panda to flee to, starvation results. This relationship between panda and bamboo probably evolved as a genetic trait among pandas to ensure migration from one site to another, thus broadening the gene pool of each panda population. Forced to seek new feeding areas, they found new mates and new areas to dwell within. When the opportunity to migrate was unfortunately taken away by China's crowding human population, it spelled curtains for the giant panda.

The best friend the giant panda has to date is the World Wildlife Fund. WWF furnished the consultant John McKinnon, who worked with Chinese representative Qiu Minjiang to develop the original plan for setting up the twelve panda preserves which provide hope for the giant panda's survival.

In each of these preserves, human settlement is prohibited; grazing, agriculture and burning are prohibited. This is a sincere effort on the part of the Chinese government, which has even gone so far as to resettle thousands of its own people to make living room for the endangered panda. Chinese villagers have stoutly resisted these resettlements—and this has built hatred for the endangered panda which ousted the people from their ancestral homelands. It is strange but true that the human poor of China are bearing the biggest expense of trying to save the giant panda.

It appears that panda groupings cannot exist solely in their own preserves without a chance to intermingle with other panda groupings. Normal groupings consist of 10 to 50 pandas in one geographical area. Evidently these are minimal groups for reproduction purposes. Experience has shown that a population falling below 20 animals is in grave danger of extinction—because the breeding group doesn't contain enough different individuals to remain viable. The WWF consultants also recommended corridors of suitable habitat, linking known populations of pandas to encourage the migration which seems to be necessary for survival of the species.

There has been some success in captive breeding of the giant panda. Chapultepec Zoo in the polluted air of Mexico City, the world's largest city, has bred four cubs which survived. The travels of panda breeding stock is a story unto itself.

Chia Chia, a lusty young male from the London Zoo, made a much publicized romantic *tour de force* a few years ago. He was flown first to Toledo, Ohio, where 81,000 people bought tickets to see him. Toledo tourism people said that the panda visit would bring in more than 15 million dollars to the city's businesses. After his dalliance with the Toledo female panda, Chia Chia went on to Mexico City where he was expected to breed three young females in that zoo before returning to London. In some cases, zoos have pledged great sums of money to China to help in panda restoration work, in return for the visits of the lordly panda.

When a captive panda does get pregnant, its period of gestation is followed by the press of the entire world. Television cameras watch it almost hourly and a team of obstetricians gathers to facilitate the entry into the world of another panda. In fact, there are more people in attendance upon a pregnant panda than upon a pregnant reigning monarch in Europe.

Given China's drastic effort to curtail its human population, and given the world wide attention to the plight of the panda, it is possible that this interesting "teddy bear" may survive through the next two decades. Much will depend upon the political situation in China, where outmoded governmental and economic forms are struggling to maintain control, suppressing the swelling tide of democracy. So far, the attitude of the government in China toward its pandas has been exemplary. However, the mind-set shown by the massacre of its own people in Tienanmen Square in the spring of 1989 is not the mind-set of a government destined to remain in power. With a change in government, anything is possible for the giant panda—from the very best to the very worst. The prognosis is that the panda will continue to exist in captivity, but its existence in the wild is very much endangered.

As we go to press with this book, word comes from China that two Chinese have been sentenced to death for selling panda skins. Liang Yongzheng and He Guanghai appealed the sentence. The higher court upheld the sentence and the two were executed. They bought one skin for roughly $1,100 dollars and resold for $20,000. That's quite a profit, but not enough to die for. But this does illustrate the point that the world's poor will take great risks to supply "trinkets" for the richer people elsewhere. To my mind it would have been more appropriate to sentence to death the person or persons who bought the panda skins. We must eliminate the demand if we wish to save wildlife species.

The panda is only the symbol of the troubles of Asian wildlife. Now we speak of the plight of other species in Asia, such as the rhinoceros:

Indian rhinos have increased in numbers under protection in the Indian sub-continent. Probably numbering more than 2,000 presently, restocking of suitable coverts is now possible. Although they do not grow the impressive horns which have been the downfall of the African rhino, the Indian is a big one, weighing as much as two tons.

Javan rhinos number less than 100 individuals and are now found only on the Ujung Kulon Nature Reserve, where they have been protected since 1921. One horned, the Javan rhino is another 3,500 pounder.

Sumatran rhinos are the smallest of the race, weighing less than a ton. Their four and a half foot tall bodies are covered with bristly hair, unlike the hairless, armor-plated skins of the other four species. No one knows enough about this smallest rhino to give us an accurate estimate of numbers, but surely there are less than 500 of them scattered across huge areas of the Indonesian Islands, principally on Sumatra.

Orangutans

One of the rarest of all anthropoids, the orangutan of Indonesia has been the subject of much study in recent years—study which points up the precarious position the "people of the forest" find themselves in.

Entirely non-carnivorous, the orang is a secretive large ape of the rain forests, a surprising orange in color, with a very expressive face. Completely harmless to people, the orangutan has been used as food by primitive people in Indonesia and Malaysia for millennia. But it is modern man's activities which endanger the orang. Until the last few years, there was a steady market for young orangutans, usually captured by the simple expedient of killing the mother orang. The youngster, still very dependent upon its dead mother, remained with the body until forcibly pulled away by its captors.

Indonesia has set up a nature preserve on Kalimantan (the Indonesian two thirds of the island of Borneo), and has outlawed the killing or possession of orangs over the entire sprawling archipelago which makes up this, the fourth most populous nation in the world. With legal protection and with the cessation of international trade in wild orangutans, there is an optimistic prognosis for the future of these harmless, comic, orange-coated people of the forest. My closest acquaintance with an orangutan was in the National Zoo in Washington, D.C. Proudly showing four relatives through the zoo, I was last in line passing in front of a seated large male orang. He watched impassively as my four relatives passed in front of him. When I got close, he pursed his lips and shot an amazing quantity of saliva all over my white shirt. Maybe it was something I had written about his kinfolks?

Tigers

The beautiful and fearsome Bengal Tiger is one of earth's largest carnivores and is quite capable of killing and eating man. It is estimated that 40,000 of these beautiful cats roamed the Indian sub-continent in 1900. By 1973, 90% of them were gone!

In 1973, the Indian government and the World Wildlife Fund began a program to protect the tiger. In 1987, India counted more than 8,000 tigers, a one hundred percent increase. Tremendous changes in numbers are possible—both declines and increases show up quickly as mankind changes the ways in which we crowd the Bengal Tiger.

India needs to provide farming land for a half million more people each and every year! The need for farm land hit the tiger with tremendous impact after the partition of the Punjab. Many Indians, desiring to stay under the Indian flag, pressed for opening up new areas, some of which had been the best tiger habitat. A good example is the Kheri District, a combination of swamp lands and rugged mountains—perfect place for the tiger. To secure new cropland, the swamps were drained and the tropical forests were felled. Crowded off of its ancestral lands, the majestic tiger was forced into tiny pockets of habitat which still resembled the original tiger range. One of these enclaves is the Dudhwa National Park. Its 200 square miles protects a lot of tigers, but its small size means that game animals upon which the tiger feeds are scarce. It also ensures that encounters between man and tiger will surely increase. They did, with fatal results for the humans concerned.

One of the most famous of the Indian tiger preserves is the 232,000 acres of Kanha. Another is Ranthambhor National Park, which boasts of 41,000 acres.

Adult male tigers are markedly territorial animals and do not tolerate other males in what they consider their exclusive domain. They either kill the young male who trespasses or drive him out of the safety of the preserve. This greatly increases the chances of a "bent-over" human being taken by a hungry tiger. Researchers have found that the tiger is more apt to attack a "bent-over" human in the mistaken belief that it is a four-legged animal and therefore legitimate prey. An Indian education program stresses the warning that humans should always walk upright and in the middle of the road.

Naturally, there was considerable opposition to the Indian program of protecting the tiger, especially from those who had lost loved ones to the tiger. In the period of 1975–1987, tigers killed at least 600 people, most of them villagers who were working their crops or just cutting grass to feed to their animals. Education programs urged the natives to wear masks of human faces on the back of their heads because the tiger is less apt to attack from the front, preferring to attack its prey from the rear. They have also experimented with a 220 volt electric shock fence to keep the tiger in its preserve and away from humans.

Along with the educational program India has gone along with its positive program of protecting the tiger by providing enough room to live in. Indian government has found it necessary to relocate as many as 6,000 people to make room for the tiger. Tiger areas must be large enough to support a prey population of chital, sambar deer and other species, because the tiger needs forty pounds of red meat per day on the average.

In the last thirty years, sanctuaries and preserves have been established throughout the tigers' range. In 1987 India boasted of 54 national parks and 248 wildlife sanctuaries. An amazing 12% of all forested lands in the huge country has been set aside for wildlife. This amounted to 38,010 square miles—an area larger than our state of Indiana.

There are now 87 prime tiger habitat preserves. The credit for progress along these lines goes to Indian conservationists. One of the most vocal is Arjan Singh, the only Asian to date to receive the World Wildlife Fund Gold Medal. Although his neighbors accused him of purposely feeding humans to tigers, Singh has stuck to his defense of the Dudwha Tiger Preserve.

As we write this, the magnificent Indian Tiger still has a tremendous problem—how to survive in small enclaves without meeting humans. India's people share the problem because tigers still kill and eat people every year. People continue to increase in numbers and "tiger room" continues to shrink as humanity crowds in on the Bengal tiger.

The government pays compensation to victims of tiger killings. Indicative of the comparative value of life, the compensation ranges from $154 per cow to $584 per human. Putting tiger killings in perspective, there are 100 deaths from snakebite in India for every one death blamed on the tiger.

Once there were eight subspecies of tiger in Asia; three are now extinct. Gone into the shades of oblivion are the Caspian tiger (*Panthera tigris virgata*), the Javan tiger (*Panthera tigris sondaica*) and the Balinese tiger

(*Panthera tigris balica*). There are five subspecies still around. In 1985, biologists estimated their numbers as:

Indian tiger (*Panthera tigris tigris*) about 3,000.

Indochinese tiger (*Panthera tigris corbetti*) about 2,000

Sumatran tiger (*Panthera tigris sumatrae*) about 800.

Amur tiger (*Panthera tigris altaica*) down to about 400.

Chinese tiger (*Panthera tigris amoyensis*) no more than 40.

Other researchers put the number of Indian tigers much higher than the 3,000 listed herein.

Prognosis: The Indian tiger will continue to avoid extinction, but will never become numerous in the wild again. The forecast for the other four sub-species is exceedingly dark.

To better understand the plight of many Indian species, let's take a deeper look at India.

At one time this great sub-continent floated free of the Asian continent, borne by its own tectonic plate. It moved slowly northward and finally slammed into the Asian tectonic plate with such force that it jutted skyward into the mightiest mountain range on earth, the Himalayas. India is different, in almost every way, from the rest of the planet.

Like other parts of Asia, India is cursed with an overabundance of people. The ceaseless battle for survival became a battle for food in India, despite the fact that the nation boasts a lot of very fertile land, watered by the monsoons and renewed by the monsoon floods which carry the topsoil of higher elevations down onto the fertile deltas.

But of more importance when we consider the possible extermination of species—religious beliefs in India prevent the taking of animal life. Cows are considered sacred by many Indians and herds of cattle, underfed, diseased but very prolific, roam a large part of the nation with calamitous results. Still, the people of India have not decimated their wildlife stocks to provide food. A good friend of mine, Bill Fitzwater, is an acknowledged expert in the control of commensal rodents (meaning rodents which eat man's food). He was sent to India to lend his expertise in controlling hordes of rats which ate Indian crops while Indian children starved for lack of those crops. Bill told me that his biggest problem was not in devising control methods, but in getting the people to use those control methods—because of their distaste for killing anything.

This nation—the world's largest real democracy—has a good record in trying to preserve wildlife. The pitifully few Asian lions in existence are found in the Gir Forest where they are completely protected. Corbett National Park, named for the famed tiger slayer, now contains more tigers on its 100 square miles than it can support.

Faced with the impossible task of feeding more than 600 million people,

170

hampered by superstitious beliefs which forbid killing of cows and even rats—lacking governmental funds—India is doing battle for its endangered species, fighting valiantly for their existence. Excellent projects funded by the International Union for the Conservation of Nature (IUCN) and/or the World Wildlife Fund are producing results. Yet it seems certain that the world will lose many species in India. Among the many endangered species are:

Markhor (common in many zoos world wide)
Snow Leopard
Ladakh Urial
Long-tailed Macaque
Blackbuck (common on many American shooting preserves)
Great Indian Bustard
Kashmir stag
Nilgiri tahr
Gaur (huge, buffalo-like animal hit hard by cattle diseases)
Golden Langur (one of the world's most beautiful monkeys)
Siberian white crane (about which more later)
Musk deer (a deer with canine teeth like tusks)
Western tragopan and many other pheasant-like birds.

There are many other endangered species in India; some of them still not even classified by biologists. Many other Indian species have gone into oblivion without man ever having known that they existed. But India's government is trying—against big odds and facing immense obstacles. Increased public awareness is their best hope—that and the establishment of reserves for particular species whose range is restricted.

Let's consider the plight of the Siberian white crane.

America's whooping crane is arguably the most publicized of all endangered species, but there are many other cranes in trouble around this tight little planet, and they all deserve our help.

The black-necked crane is endangered in Cuba and the West Indies, the hooded crane has problems maintaining its existence in Japan and the USSR. The red-crowned crane is one of the troubled birds in China, Korea, Japan and Asiatic Russia, while the Mississippi sandhill crane is on the endangered list in our own country. The Siberian white crane is one of the world's rarest birds along its dangerous migration path from Russia to India, China and Iran. Add the endangered white-naped crane from Mongolia and we find that our whooper is far from being alone in his dangerous spot.

Through the International Crane Foundation (ICF) of Baraboo, Wisconsin, we were able to communicate with Sergei Smirenski, of the Moscow State University, who studies the plight of the Siberian White Crane at the Oka State Nature Reserve in the USSR. George Archibald, Director of the ICF, was the first to propose a joint US-USSR study of the Siberian crane.

171

Sergei Smirenski reminds us that both the Patuxent Wildlife Research Center in Maryland and the Oka Nature Reserve have had success with artificial propagation of the big white birds—the Siberian and the Whooping—miles apart, but together in time of danger.

With their history of captive propagation, both American and Russian scientists have gained valuable information about such matters as preserving genetic diversity along with housing and feeding of the big birds. Both countries are now working at the task of reintroducing their captive flocks into the wild. The cross-fostering effort previously described in chapter three succeeded in producing more individual cranes, but the results haven't yet translated into a "breeding" population in the wild.

Smirenski points to the many similarities between Siberian and Whooping crane troubles. Both birds fly long dangerous migration paths from breeding grounds to known wintering grounds, and both species have aroused the interest of their governments. Canada and the US have long cooperated internationally in the effort to save the whooper. The Siberian crane is now protected by agreements between the USSR, Iran, and India and there is hope that China will soon join as a signatory. The Chinese people cherish the crane as a bird which brings good luck and there is much local sentiment in favor of the white cranes.

Both species face considerable pressure on their available habitat with Siberian reserves being actively explored for possible oil and gas drilling, and the whooping crane being affected by oil production at and near the Aransas National Wildlife Refuge. You should know that the oil and gas industry has been very cooperative in the vicinity of Aransas, even helping to finance purchase of the refuge in the first place.

In both species, eggs have been collected and used to raise a captive flock. Both species have benefited from experiments to provide cross-fostering in the wild. As a last unhappy similarity, both flocks have suffered disease outbreaks.

According to Smerinski, the Siberian crane poses a more difficult problem because of its longer migration route and the fact that this route passes through regions where meat for food is scarce and where education levels are very low. For example, Pushtun natives in Pakistan have been guilty of using decoys so successfully that they have killed as much as ten percent of the entire flock during migration.

Less is known about the breeding grounds of the Siberian crane than is known about the whooper. One population which winters in Iran flies north to a completely unknown breeding area—which reminds us that it is not too many years ago that the breeding grounds of the whooper were still undiscovered. Two thousand of the world's estimated population of 2,500 Siberian cranes winter in China, and the breeding ground of this large segment of the population is still unknown.

Undiscovered breeding grounds are obviously protected from humans.

Smirenski also points out another danger to the Siberian which is not a problem for the Whooper. Migrating herds of caribou may destroy the nests of the Siberian crane in Russian territory when spring is late, simply by stepping on the eggs while passing *en masse.*

Long before Gorbachev popularized the word "glasnost" into American English, there was good cooperation between scientists in the lands of the two super powers. The ICF propagation facility in Baraboo, Wisconsin will receive some of the captive flock produced at Patuxent, Maryland, in the U.S. Fish and Wildlife propagation center. This will further distribute the genes of the whooping crane, ensuring that all will not be lost by one natural catastrophe. In the meantime, let's learn all we can about the world's cranes. Not only our whooper, but seven other lordly cranes are in such short supply that their future is in doubt.

If we lose one of them, we will be lessened by that loss.

29

Central America: Biodiversity at Stake

by Chris Wille

In the tropical rainforests which once formed a verdant green belt around the planet's midsection, the discussion of endangered species turns to the loss of biodiversity. The plant and animal life in the rainforest is so rich and the destruction of these areas is so rapid that biologists do not have the luxury of focusing on one symbolic species: a whooping crane or California condor.

The rate of species extinction now under way because of tropical deforestation rivals any such period in the Earth's history, including the catastrophic die-offs more than 65 million years ago that claimed the dinosaurs. Nobody knows what effect this radical reduction will have on the biosphere. The Earth, of course, will survive. The question is: what will happen to the five billion and more human beings who depend on the present ecosystem balance?

Tropical Deforestation: A Rent in the Fabric of Life

Tropical forests cover only seven percent of the Earth's surface, yet they contain at least half of all plant and animal species. Slightly less than half of the pre-Industrial Age rainforests are now gone. The surviving pieces are mostly in Latin America (57%), Southeast Asia and some Pacific islands (25%), and West Central Africa (18%). (In recent years, the term "rainforest" has been used generically to mean all tropical forests, even though some of these forests are quite dry and even deciduous.)

These jungles are being logged, cleared for cattle pasture, burned acre by acre to make way for small food plots, flooded by hydroelectric dams, and otherwise destroyed at an appalling rate. It is difficult to quantify the loss, but there is general agreement that at least 27,000 square miles (an area the size of West Virginia) of tropical forest is destroyed each year. At this rate, nearly all of the remaining tropical forests will be vanquished or seriously degraded within a human lifetime.

Tropical forests are the richest ecosystems on Earth. Harvard biologist Dr. E.O. Wilson discovered 43 species of ants on a single tree in Peru, about equal to the entire ant fauna of the British Isles. There are about 700 different tree species in North America; botanists found more than that on ten selected one-hectare plots in Borneo. Tiny Costa Rica has more bird species than all of North America. In Western Ecuador, there are (or were—since 1960, 95% of western Ecuador's forest has been razed) at least 15,000 species of plants; by comparison, Europe, with an area 31 times greater, has 13,000 plant species.

Dire Calculations

We know much about the surface of the moon and the interior landscape of molecules, but, according to E.O. Wilson, "We do not know the true number of species on Earth, even to the nearest order of magnitude." Wilson, who is a Pulitzer Prize winning writer as well as an esteemed scientist, and others have struggled with this remarkable hole in our basic understanding of life on Earth. How can we comprehend what we are losing if we don't even know what we have?

About 1.4 million species of all kinds of organisms have been collected, given scientific names, and described for posterity. Wilson and others believe that there are at least 5 million species out there. Taxonomists at work in tropical forests are finding so many new creatures—mostly insects— that the total number of species may be as high as 30 million.

Extinction is a natural process. Looking back over millions of years, scientists calculate that a species disappeared every year or so. Rare cataclysmic events such as an asteroid strike caused mass extinctions. British biologist Dr. Norman Myers calculates that tropical deforestation in just two countries, Brazil and Madagascar, over the past 35 years has eliminated or doomed as many as 50,000 species. Myers and Wilson agree that the current extinction rate in all tropical forests probably exceeds 10,000 species a year. This is thousands of times greater than the natural "background" rate of extinction.

The agents of this destruction are strikingly visible in Central America, an area with fantastic biodiversity and daunting conservation challenges.

Central America: An Isthmus in Turmoil

Central America is a narrow but remarkably diverse land bridge joining two huge continental ecosystems. It is the meeting place for species from the north and south. Central America is a designation of convenience; there is no such regional identity. The rubric covers seven countries: Belize, Costa Rica, El Salvador, Guatemala, Honduras, Nicaragua, and Panama.

From its widest point, 300 miles across, the isthmus tapers down to the narrow waist of Panama, where only 40 miles of land separate two seas. The area is mountainous, with peaks topping 12,000 feet. This geographic variation, combined with precipitation patterns ranging from 15 to 295 inches of rain per year, accounts for the wide variety of habitats, from coral reefs and mangrove swamps at sea level to cloud forests, high montane forests and alpine vegetation. Costa Rica alone has 12 life zones. Central America is one of the richest repositories of genetic wealth in the world.

The area is beset by intractable, interlocking problems which including poverty, extraordinary population growth, social unrest, war, uncertain economies with the millstone of external debt, inefficient and destructive land-use practices, and governments so enmeshed in short-term crises that they are unable to confront the readily apparent degradation of the area's natural resources.

In Central America, as in most other tropical forest areas, land distribution is uneven and often inequitable. Poor, landless campesinos are forced to clear forests in order to grow even subsistence crops. This practice is widely encouraged by governments, who will give title to land only after it has been "improved." The standard method of "improving" forest is to cut it. But the peasant farmer discovers a cruel paradox: The soils supporting the luxurious green mantle of the rainforest are often too poor to sustain crops. The best farmlands, the alluvial floodplains and other black-soil lowlands, are already occupied—often by large foreign-owned plantations of coffee, bananas, sugar cane, or oil palms. So millions of so-called "shifting cultivators" cut and burn a piece of forest, farm in the ashes for a few years, and then move on to slash and burn another area.

Less than 40% of Central America's original forest remains today, replaced in large part by eroding "wet deserts," scruffy cow pasture, and marginal farms. More than half of El Salvador's arable land is badly eroded, and farmlands throughout the region are producing far below their potential.

176

Forestry experts know that the whole area is facing a grave and imminent wood shortage. Even in Costa Rica, with its stable government and conservationist image, reforestation lags far behind cutting levels. Loggers and other users take an estimated 150,000 acres per year. Costa Rica is already importing wood from Chile and, foresters say, by the year 2000, the country will have no primary forests left outside of its park system.

There is a region-wide crisis in Central America: natural resources, from the coral reefs to the cloud forests, are being "mined" to meet present day needs. The effects on wild plants and animals is easily foreseen. The people of the area face the same consequences. Central Americans have a close and dependent relationship to the land. According to H. Jeffrey Leonard, who did a landmark study on Central America for the International Institute for Environment and Development: "The well-being of the majority of the populations of all seven countries of greater Central America still depends heavily upon the renewable natural resource systems of the region— the sustenance from subsistence agriculture; the revenues from timber, livestock, and commercial crops; the fruits of the bountiful coastal waters; the employment from natural resource processing industries; and the tangible goods supplied by the region's resources, including hydroelectric power, firewood, lumber, and supplies of potable water."

While the task of conserving Central America's natural resources and salvaging some of the area's spectacular wildlands is formidable, a fortunate symbiosis exists: The necessary steps toward ensuring a future for both human and wildlife communities are the same—helping one benefits the other. In recent years, Central American governments, assisted by international aid and conservation organizations, have intensified efforts to improve natural resource stewardship. Valiant attempts are being made to increase reforestation, regulate resource extraction, control pollution, diversify agriculture, modernize natural resource management policy, and develop reserves that protect habitats while meeting the needs of local people.

Environmentalists have recognized that conservation programs must include grassroots economic development, and business entrepreneurs are beginning to understand that development, in order to be sustainable, must proceed with prudent attention toward preserving the natural resource base.

The Costa Rica Story

None of the seven countries in Central America fairly represents the entire region, but Costa Rica is an interesting and illustrative case. This small country (19,575 square miles, half the size of Kentucky) is well known to international conservationists. Costa Rica abolished its army in 1948 and invested the savings in education, health, and infrastructure. With its long history of political stability and astonishing natural diversity, Costa Rica has become something of an international laboratory for conservation.

Arriving with the early coffee merchants in the mid 1800s, European biologists began exploring and studying the fabulously rich Costa Rica wildlands. They took most of their collections home with them, but local interest and natural history institutions slowly took root. Tropical field research flourished, with increasing participation from Costa Ricans. The park service was established in 1970 and, largely through the efforts of two remarkable conservationists—Mario A. Boza and Alvaro F. Ugalde—the nation's renowned system of protected areas was born. With steady advances in local academia, professional biologists and fully qualified tropical ecologists are now able to get the training they need without leaving Costa Rica's narrow confines.

The government of Oscar Arias Sanchez, who was president of Costa Rica from 1986 to 1990, won widespread acclaim (and assistance) for its progressive natural resource policies. Upon his inauguration, Arias created a cabinet position and named Dr. Alvaro Umaña Quesada the first minister of natural resources, energy and mines. Umaña, a capable and courageous administrator, made great strides. The country has established an excellent, if underfunded, system of 28 parks and wildlife reserves.

Costa Rica is buffeted by age-old cultural and economic forces that make conservation problematic. For example, the birth rate and deforestation rate in Costa Rica are among the highest in the world. Still, many conservationists around the world hope that Costa Rica, which has been an exemplary bastion of peace and democracy in a continually turbulent region, will prove that far-sighted husbandry of natural resources is also an attainable ideal.

Taking Stock of Species

The best known conservation project in Costa Rica is the ambitious effort to restore a tract of dry tropical forest—a forest type that was once widespread but is now rarer even than true rainforest. The originator and relentless force behind this scheme is Dr. Daniel Janzen, a University of Pennsylvania biologist. Janzen, widely regarded as the dean of tropical field biology, has been studying ecological relationships in Costa Rica for more than two decades. The promising restoration project was named Guanacaste National Park in 1989.

Janzen has said that there are three stages to conservation: "Save it; figure out what you've saved; and then put it to work for society."

With Janzen's encouragement, Costa Rica has embarked on a bold venture to figure out what it has saved. In 1989, the government, with funding from the United States, Sweden, and private foundations, broke ground for a national biodiversity institute (*Instituto Nacional de Biodiversidad*). The mission of the institute, according to its director Dr. Rodrigo Gámez Lobo, is nothing less than to inventory Costa Rica's flora and fauna. No small task: Costa Rica probably has more than a half million species. Dr. Gámez likes to point out that Costa Rica, with less than one-hundredth of the Earth's land surface, hosts 5% of the planet's species.

The institute will consolidate many of the collections of Costa Rican plants and animals now held in other facilities around the world. Even if all these collections were brought under one roof, they would represent only a small portion of the country's living resources. So the institute is training a small army of collectors to scour the countryside. Already, these "parataxonomists" have found hundreds of new species—mostly insects and plants.

The Nature Conservancy, a respected nonprofit landsaving organization, has established Conservation Data Centers throughout the United States. Using sophisticated survey techniques, these centers gather and catalogue information about species diversity, abundance, habitat requirements and a host of other data sets essential to informed conservation decision-making. Since 1982, the Nature Conservancy has been sharing this technology with Latin America countries. There are now Conservation Data Centers in Bolivia, Brazil, Columbia, Costa Rica, Guatemala, the Netherlands Antilles, Panama, Paraguay, Puerto Rico, Peru, and Venezuela.

The Costa Rican data center has been brought under the wing of the new biodiversity institute. With information on tens of thousands of species, the computerized data bank is the cerebral axis of the fledgling institution. It will organize the countless bits of data on nearly countless species and make it available for use in conservation and development planning and natural areas management.

According to the data center's director, Rita María Alfaro R., special attention is given to threatened and endangered species. The center also strives to collect useful information about "species of economic importance," such as medicinal or ornamental plants, potential new crop species, and animals that are hunted or collected for food or commerce.

One Costa Rican law protects rare animals and orchids; another shields endangered trees. Endangered Costa Rican plants are given some relief from international trade pressure by the CITES treaty. Threatened and endangered species are listed by the Costa Rican government in a process similar to the one employed by the United States. Yet enforcement efforts are thin and little has been done to identify and preserve critical habitats.

At the end of 1989, the data center's computer had information on 37 endangered or threatened amphibians (out of 162 species recorded in Costa Rica); 37 reptiles (216); 114 birds (848); 22 mammals (205); 1,500 plants (9,000); and 45 trees (1,000). Scientists estimate that there are

3,000 plant and 200 tree species yet to be described. There is little information on the population status of marine and freshwater fish, fungi, insects, or lower life forms.

As usual, species that require large ranges or specialized habitats are at the greatest risk. Nearly all of the large spectacular species—suffering from habitat loss, hunting, and other human pressures—are endangered to varying degrees: the various species of cats, monkeys, peccaries, hawk-eagles, and macaws as well as the manatee, giant anteater, tapir, harpy eagle, crocodile, and so on. But in Costa Rica, as in the other tropical forest areas, thousands of less showy species will vanish into oblivion before they are even discovered.

Species Profile: The Baird's Tapir

The Monteverde Cloud Forest Preserve sits high astraddle the Continental Divide in a northwestern province of Costa Rica. It is managed by a private research center, the Organization for Tropical Studies. A common tourist destination, Monteverde's most famous resident is the resplendent quetzal. Ornithologists argue over whether or not the quetzal is endangered in Costa Rica; it almost certainly is endangered in most of the rest of its Central American range.

The Monteverde Conservation League conducts local community outreach programs and solicits funds to enlarge and manage the preserve. When choosing a mascot, the league considered the quetzal but selected, instead, the Baird's tapir. Why? Because, according to long-time Monteverde resident Wilford Guindon, the tapir is a perfect symbol of tropical wilderness. Guindon, who is head of the league's park protection program, has spent innumerable days hiking in the cloudforest. Yet he has sighted tapirs on so few occasions that each is a treasured memory.

Tapirs require large ranges of nearly pristine habitat and are intolerant of human disturbance. These qualities make them an apt symbol for a rainforest conservation group; they are also the animal's downfall.

Tapirs are one of the oldest living mammals, living representatives of the "megafauna" that roamed the Americas from 10 to 60 thousand years ago. Before the arrival of humans, tapirs were widespread in North America. At the time of the Spanish Conquest, tapirs were common from southern Mexico through Middle America to the West Coast of Columbia and Venezuela. Where habitat remains, they are still found in this range, but because they are so secretive, sightings are uncommon. A different species hangs on in forested pockets of Indochina. All tapirs are endangered.

The tapir is the largest indigenous terrestrial mammal in Central America; adults weigh up to 600 pounds. They have a long and dexterous upper lip, suggestive of an elephant's trunk; odd, splayed feet on stocky legs; thick, leathery hides; poor vision; excellent senses of hearing and smell; and a diet of leaves, twigs, and fruit.

Tapirs reproduce slowly, bearing one young after a gestation period of more than a year. They are non-aggressive, relying on their camouflage and ability to sneak silently away from predators. Big cats such as jaguars and cougars share the same range as tapirs (and have the same preference for large undisturbed areas). Undoubtedly, cats, where they survive, prey on young tapirs; but hunters, loggers, and cattle ranchers present a far greater threat.

Although they once ranged through varied habitats from coastal mangrove swamps up to the steep mountain slopes to about 11,000 feet, tapirs are now relegated to ever-diminishing fragments of tropical forest and, even in these redoubts, they are persecuted with dogs and guns.

Central American countries, in the face of grinding poverty, runaway population growth, stumbling economies, social and political unrest and even war are struggling to save large viable tracts of their tropical forest heritage. If a country can properly manage an area—for wildlife **AND** people—large enough to support tapirs, it will have saved untold other species, many unknown to science. Thus, the tapirs of Monteverde and elsewhere in Central America are symbols of hope: While they survive, we humans know that we still have time to learn how to live in harmony with the tropical forest. We still have time to save Nature's most extravagant creation for future generations to use and enjoy.

—Chris Wille is co-director of the Tropical Conservation Newsbureau, a project of the Rainforest Alliance, and is the international field editor for *Audubon* magazine.

❀   ❀   ❀   ❀

Estimated Number of Species in Costa Rica

Plants	10,000
Fungi	2,500
Vertebrates	1,500
Insects	300,000
Aquatic	75,000
Arachnids	50,000
Nematodes	10,000
Bacteria, etc.	50,000

(Source: *Instituto Nacional de Biodiversidad*)

BIBLIOGRAPHY

Caufield, C. 1985 *In the Rainforest* Alfred A. Knopf

Janzen, D.H., ed. 1982 *Costa Rica Natural History.* University of Chicago Press

Leonard, H.J. 1987 *Natural Resources and Economic Development in Central America* International Institute for Environment and Development/Earthscan

Myers, N. 1985 *The Primary Source: Tropical Forests and Our Future* W.W. Norton and Company

Stiles, F.G. and Skutch, A.F. 1989 *A Guide to the Birds of Costa Rica* Comstock Publishing Associates/Cornell University Press

Terwilliger, V.J. 1978 "Natural History of Baird's Tapir on Barro Colorado Island, Panama Canal Zone" Biotropica 10(3):211–220

Vaughan, C. 1983 "A Report on Dense Forest Habitat for Endangered Wildlife Species in Costa Rica" Costa Rica National University/U.S. Department of the Interior

Wilson, E.O., ed. 1988 *Biodiversity* National Academy Press

30

South America

On my first trip into the backwoods of South America, I went by boat up Colombia's Rio Cauca, into Lago La Raya and on into the Rio Caribona. There far from civilization, I had the most wonderful experience which an avid birdwatcher could dream of having. I discovered a new world, filled with new-to-me birds of all sizes, shapes, colors and habits. In the course of one morning in a boat moving silently up the river I saw at least 100 species of birds I had never seen before!

I fished in the Rio Caribona and caught *mojarra, picuda and dorado*—fish I had never seen before. As we prepared fillets of the delicious fish for broiling beside the stream, a terrifying roaring came from the jungle a few yards away. Instinctively, I whirled around and prepared to do battle with the only weapon I had, a flimsy flyrod. My Colombian guides almost dissolved in laughter. The horrible roaring came from fairly harmless howler monkeys. I'd heard them only once before, at Palenque in Mexico. As I stood on a rocky shoal casting for more *picuda*, I was enveloped in a great swarm of small, pink butterflies. They settled on me, my tackle, the shoal and the nearby bushes in a lovely pink blanket covering several hectares. After about ten minutes the entire flock got airborne again and disappeared down river. During that afternoon, I swear that I saw at least fifty different species of butterfly—none of which I'd ever seen before. My host on that memorable trip was Kjell von Sneidern, a commercial outfitter born in Colombia, despite the very "un-Spanish" family name. His father came from Sweden to study birds and became so wrapped up in his ornithological studies that he never did return to Sweden. As an ornithologist, he was already in a temporal heaven.

South America has many species found nowhere else. But all is not well in the jungles of tropic Central and South America. The biggest enemy of wildlife in South America must be the deforestation that is going on in an attempt to provide more food to feed the burgeoning population. Brazil has suffered the most, because Brazil possessed most of the lush green drainage of the mighty Amazon, biggest river on earth.

In 1872, English naturalist Henry Walter Bates visited the 4,000 miles of Amazon drainages and listed some 14,172 species of life forms—8,000 of them had never been discovered previously.

More wildlife habitat is lost each day in South America than we can create in a year in North America. Slash and burn cultivation invades the sylvan jungles which once sheltered marmosets and tapirs, jaguars and resplendent-feathered birds of rare species. Although jungle growth is lush, jungle soils are usually thin and impoverished. The problem is the heavy rainfall which leaches nutrients out of the soil as fast as they can be put in the soil. A couple of years of raising row crops and the slash and burn farmer has exhausted his soil and must move on. Sadly, most of the wildlife species that once called this jungle "home" cannot move away—they simply disappear.

A hundred species of parakeets, parrots and macaws used to display their gaudy colors in South American treetops. Many still do, but the collectors who sell these beautiful species to pet dealers have wreaked havoc with their numbers. Many are listed as endangered, but it is certain that intensified research would find another hundred endangered species. Parrots entering the USA illegally are confiscated by Customs and wildlife agents. One species, the Thick-billed, was once native to Arizona. Through intelligent use of the confiscated birds, the thick-bills have been re-introduced to that state and seem to be doing well.

Andean condors are listed as endangered from Colombia all the way down to southern Chile. This is of special importance to us in our efforts to rescue the California condor. Our recovery teams are studying artificial propagation and release into the wild of this condor, seeking guidance for the same procedures with the California condor, arguably the rarest bird in the world. Their primary concern is with the California condor's future, but the Andean condors in the research program will be released into the wild in Colombia in late 1991, in an attempt to re-establish this condor in that country.

Brazil fears for the future of its two species of cotinga, and with good reason. Two species of curassow, the razor-billed and the red-billed, are becoming rarer every month in Brazil. South America, which lists 100 different species of hummingbird for every one species that visits us, has listed the hookbilled hermit—a true hummingbird—among those endangered. Three colorful macaws, the glaucous, indigo and little blue, are endangered in Brazil, as is the golden parakeet, the ochre-marked parakeet; three parrots—the red-browed, red-capped and the red-spectacled.

Extinction looms for many species in South America and not only in Brazil. The giant armadillo is disappearing from Venezuela and Guyana and is scarce all the way down to Argentina. The Andean cat and the tiger cat are both endangered—even the chinchilla in Bolivia. The marsh deer and the pampas deer are both listed as endangered now. Two other deer, known locally as *huemuls,* are also endangered. Never seen a huemul? Better hurry if you want to see one. Even the Amazon manatee is in danger. See chapter 12 for more on the manatees. Marmosets, among the most beautiful and interesting of all mammals, are in danger throughout their South American homelands, as are the wooly spider monkeys of Brazil. The golden lion tamarin, one of the most beautiful of mammals, has seen its population drop to less than 400 survivors in the southeastern corner of Brazil. Threatened by logging, grazing and forest destruction, it seems that the golden lion will be exterminated—due to the unwise opening of the rain forest to agriculture. But—can we really chide the *Brasilenos* for trying to feed their human population, which is among the fastest growing in the world?

One of the rarest of all wildfowl, the white-winged guan still survives —we hope—in dwindling forest habitat in northern Peru. This guan has been over-hunted in recent years. With its habitat becoming scarce, it can no longer withstand hunting pressures which would have gone unnoticed in good habitat.

South America is an incredibly varied continent, ranging from the icy-cold of the towering Andes Mountains down to the sweltering swamps of Venezuela and Surinam. Inhabited only by primitive Indian tribes until Columbus spoiled this Eden by showing the way to its treasures of gold and silver. South America presented a tremendous variety of wildlife until white men started to exploit its riches. The valley of the Amazon offered two million square miles of rainforest when the white man came. How much of it is still undisturbed?

Dictatorships and economic mismanagement have impoverished almost all of South American peoples. Like great parts of Africa and Asia, South America is a land where the next meal is the biggest worry for millions. In this kind of environment, it is difficult for anyone to worry about another species. They have enough worries about their own species. To add to the troubles caused by the great difference in standard of living between the very rich and the very poor—South America is the source of a lot of the drugs which have flooded the USA in the past decade. Cocaine, made in the jungles of Bolivia, Colombia, Brazil, Ecuador, Venezuela and Peru, tempts people of the impoverished nations with unbelievable amounts of money. Drug growing has made great pieces of South America off limits to all but the most foolhardy. Who is to blame? We are; because we buy the damned stuff.

The greatest enemy to South America is the destruction of its rainforests. The day is near now when all the world will be looking for oxygen-producing plants to help overcome the dangers of polluted air. South America poses the greatest potential for preserving jungle—but humanity is losing the battle, and in losing we are speeding up the slide into extinction of many endangered species.

The prognosis for most of South and Central America's endangered species of wildlife is not good. And the worst part of it is that many hundreds of other species—many of them still unstudied—are qualified to join the ranks of the endangered. We simply do not know enough about South America and its wildlife to hazard a guess of how many. But it appears that the mindless, unplanned destruction of the rainforest is a crime of the first magnitude—a crime against wildlife all over the hemisphere.

This destruction of tropical ran forests all over the world is one of man's greatest mistakes, a mistake which is fast coming back to haunt us.

Let's take a closer look at just one species which has suffered from the elimination of the tremendous rainforests of South America—the golden lion tamarin. This is one of the most beautiful mammals to be found anywhere. Scientists refer to it as *Leontopithecus r. rosalia* and say that it is the largest of the *callitrichids*. Its name comes from the "mane" of gold colored hair which frames the almost bare face of this rare and beautiful mammal.

Golden lion tamarins were once found in good numbers in the coastal forests of southeastern Brazil, especially in the states of Rio de Janeiro and Espirito Santo. One century ago, it had limitless miles of montane forest to call home, and it thrived in no danger of elimination as a species. They were traditionally trapped and kept as pets in this part of Brazil. This was a downward pressure which the species easily withstood, because its habitat was good. They were often sold in intercontinental commerce, and this seemingly posed no problem.

But the impoverished people of the crowded big city slums clamored for land and a chance at life, and the rush to "reclaim" the rainforest began. First came the big timber companies harvesting the wealth of jungle woods by clearcutting the rainforest. After the timbering interests had removed the big logs, the *campesino* came with his axe and fire. Slash and burn cultivation enabled the hard working *Brasileno* to wrest a living from the thin soils of the rainforest for only one or two years. With soil nutrients leached out by the heavy rains, and with no rainforest to constantly put back a supply of nutrients, the thin soils were soon exhausted and unable to provide even a subsistence crop for the farmer. At first this was not recognized as a problem. After all, Brazil was one of the biggest countries in the world and its western reaches of Amazonian jungle seemed endless. But the crowding hordes of people moved westward and southward from the big cities of overcrowded Brazil like the march of army ants, and they destroyed much of the rainforest in a few decades.

Slash and burn cultivation was accompanied by abortive attempts to ranch cattle on the land that had previously been rainforest. Today there are millions of hectares which support ranching on a minimum level—with very few cattle to the square mile. This grazing—overgrazing—prevents the land from reverting to forest. Impoverished people cut wood for heating and cooking, adding to the troubles of Brazil.

Back to the golden lion tamarin, where international traffic in the species was stopped by law in the late 1960's. There were a few strikes against the species in its fight for survival. There was a lot of aggression in individual animals. Surprisingly, most of this aggression was exhibited against sexually immature females, often by their mothers. Perhaps this was an inborn mechanism for forcing young females to move out of their immediate family—although scientists still argue this point.

In addition, there was a genetic defect in the wild population when it got down to dangerous population numbers. This was a diaphragmatic hernia, which appeared in many individuals.

Because the tamarin had been raised in captivity—by zoos—for many years, and because zoos had taken advantage of the Stud Book developed by Marvin Jones in 1973—there was better genetic diversity in the captive population than in the wild population!

By 1981, the survival of the captive population seemed to be secure—but the wild population had decreased to less than 100 individuals! The very existence of this wild population was precarious, for it was confined almost entirely to the Pocos das Antas Federal Biological Preserve in the state of Rio de Janeiro. What happened to the glorious coastal rain forest? In addition to disastrous lumbering and farming and ranching practices in the interior, the beaches themselves were lost to construction of condominiums for the wealthy. The home of the golden lion tamarin was lost to the crowds of wealthy who wanted a beach front home!

In 1983, there were more than 370 golden lion tamarins in the well managed captive population. Since that date, the emphasis has been on slowing the rate of growth of the captive population and trying to preserve the last of the wild population.

Reintroductions into the wild have achieved only minimal success. Most pen-reared tamarins have to learn to find food in the wild. In fact, many of them fear freedom and stay close to familiar cage structures even when free to move into suitable wild habitat. Yet there has been at least one case of successful mating and reproduction in the wild, resulting from the releases.

Present population in the wild is just an estimate, and not a very encouraging estimate. Perhaps as many as 250 wild golden tamarins exist in the government preserves of Poco das Antas and Campos Novos, and maybe another 100 remain in isolated pockets in the wild.

The contribution of zoos to the survival effort for the golden lion tamarin cannot be overstated. The gene pool is safe, and it is well managed. Research at the National Zoo in Washington and at the San Diego Zoo has been noteworthy, and great acclaim should be given to the pioneering work of Brazilians like Adelmar Coimbra-Filho, in the establishment of the safe havens provided for the beautiful animal.

Suffice it to say that the golden lion tamarin will not become extinct as a species. However, it is problematical that the golden lion tamarin will survive as a **WILD** species.

For that reason the tamarin is symbolic of the entire picture in South America. Gene pools must be preserved and managed against the unlikely day when the human population of South America solves its problems and stops crowding out the wonderful wildlife it once possessed.

The prognosis for the golden lion tamarin—as for many other South American species in captive propagation—seems fairly safe. Regretably, the prognosis for the wild populations in South America is not so promising.

31

Extinction Down Under

Australia and New Zealand are a separate world unto themselves, isolated by more than time and distance. The wildlife includes many endangered species, species which are genetically programed without defensive abilities.

New Zealand repeats the history of the Galapagos Islands and of Hawaii, but on a larger scale. Isolated environments allowed species to speed up the evolutionary process, to develop new subspecies to fit new environmental niches. If there were no carnivores present, birds and mammals did not develop escape patterns to protect themselves from predators. Why learn to avoid a meat-eater if there are no meat eaters?

Bird species that found no need to fly evolved into flightless subspecies, as in the Kiwi of New Zealand, or the flightless Cape Barren geese of Australia's isolated beaches. Evolution produced some species so far removed from any known parent stock that even the scientific community refused to believe their existence—as for example, the duck-billed platypus. This egg-laying mammal sports a fur coat, a duck bill, webbed feet, and a propensity for finding its home niche in and under the water. When the first stuffed specimen arrived in England, authorities refused to believe their eyes and reported that it was a hoax, a taxidermist's production. Here, as in many other animals of Down Under, truth proved stranger than fiction.

Australia's most famed mammals are the marsupial kangaroos. Four species are listed as endangered by the United States: the eastern gray, the western gray, the red kangaroo and the Tasmanian forester 'roo. These are the famed marsupials that bounce along on their hind legs, balancing themselves with long heavy tails. They are herbivores and take the green stuff that the Australian rancher wants for his livestock. As a result, some species of 'roos are widely hunted and killed. Most hunting is done by riflemen, shooting with the aid of powerful headlights.

Six species of wallaby, close marsupial relatives of the kangaroos, are listed as endangered: the banded hare wallaby, the brindled nail-tailed wallaby, the crescent nail-tailed wallaby, the Parma wallaby, the Western hare wallaby, and the yellow-footed rock wallaby.

The cuddly, lovable koala, symbol of Qantas Airlines, is not endangered, despite popular belief that it is.

Other endangered species in Australia include mammals:

Five bandicoots, the barred, desert, lesser rabbit, the pig-footed and the rabbit bandicoot.

The dibbler (*Antechinus apecalis*)

Three more marsupials, the eastern jerboa marsupial, the large desert mouse marsupial and the long-tailed marsupial mouse.

Nine mice species: two different Australian native mice, Fields and Goulds, the New Holland mouse, and four mice of the *Pseudomys*, very different one from the other, known as Shark Bay, Shortridges, Smoky, and western.

Then there's the eastern native cat (*Dasyurus viverrinus*) and the numbat, also called the banded anteater, which subsists almost entirely on termites; two planigales, two possums (marsupials like our North American possums); the Quokka (*Setonix brachyurus*); seven different rats; and the hairy-nosed wombat.

Australia boasts an immense variety of beautiful birds, and some of them are endangered also. As of 1990, bird species battling extinction include a flycatcher called the Eyrean Grasswren (*Amytornis goyderi*); the helmeted honeyeater (*Meliphaga cassidix*); five parakeets and two parrots; the Lord Howe wood rail (*Tricholimnas sylvestris*); the scarlet-breasted robin, actually a flycatcher, (*Petroica multicolor multicolor*) which is limited to Norfolk Island off the coast of Australia; the noisy scrub bird (*Atrichornis clamosus*); the Plain wanderer (*Pedionomous torquatus*); and the western whipbird (*Psophodes nigrogularis*).

Only one Australian reptile is include in our list of endangered species: the Short-necked turtle (*Pseudemydura umbrina*), while New Zealand lists the tuatara (*Sphenodon punctatus*). New Zealand also lists only one amphibian, the Stephen Island frog (*Leiopelma hamiltoni*).

New Zealand's bird life offers several very interesting endangered species. The complete list includes:

New Zealand bushwren (*Xenicus longipes*).

The Kakapo (*Strigops habroptilus*) about which more later.

190

The Kokako also called wattlebird (*Callaeas cinerea*).
The Forbes parakeet (*Cyanoramphus auriceps forbesi*).
The New Zealand shore plover (*Thinornis novaseelandiae*).
Auckland Island rail (*Rallus pectoralis muelleri*).
The Chatham Island Robin (*Petroica traversi*).
Campbell Island flightless teal (*Anas aucklandica nesiotis*).
New Zealand thrush (*Turnagra capensis*).

But a mere listing does not tell us much about the varied and fascinating bird life of New Zealand. During my short stay on these two lovely big islands, I must admit that I fell in love with Ao-teo-roa, land of the long white cloud. New Zealand's excellent fighting forces like to call themselves "kiwis," and one scurrilous doggerel of the Pacific War years referred to the New Zealand expeditionary forces as "Peter Frazier's ten thousand thieving kiwis." in reference to the New Zealanders ability to make "moonlight requisitions" of needed military supplies from other commands. I spent considerable time trying to spot a kiwi (the bird not the soldier) but without success. This strange bird seems to be covered with long thin hairs, instead of with feathers. It is almost entirely nocturnal and is flightless, so its numbers were greatly decreased when European settlers brought dogs and cats with them.

But a far more interesting story is that of the kakapo. Consider if you will, that the kakapo is the world's largest parrot, that it cannot fly, that it has a very strong odor, that it is the only parrot family bird that utilizes dancing grounds or "leks" to call the female within range, that it has no fear of dogs or cats, and that it breeds only about every four years. You have a species headed for extinction.

The kakapo had no enemies until the seafaring Maori people brought the Polynesian dog with them. When European settlers came along much later, the range of the kakapo had already shrunk alarmingly. Introduced dogs and cats, along with rats which preyed on the nest of the kakapo, seemed to seal the doom of this big parrot.

Although there are many theories, no one knows for sure what triggers the "booming" call to reproduction every four years. It seems to be tied in with an abundance of food available to the kakapo. Remember that this big parrot does not fly. He walks up the steep sides of the rocky mountains of New Zealand, clearing out a path to his dancing spot. This spot is usually chosen so as to have a vertical rock behind it, to increase the acoustic values of his call. Meticulously he cleans all twigs and errant stones out of the path which leads up to his booming area. Remember that he is the only parrot which uses this type of courtship.

Once satisfied that all is in order, the male develops an air sac which can be puffed out like a bellows. Then the male emits five or six booming sounds, like the measured beating of a drum. This attracts the female to the *boudoir*, where copulation takes place. Remember that this bird is nocturnal and all this takes place in the dark.

When encountered by man or predator, the kakapo has only one defense. It tries to hide itself under a log or rock and then holds perfectly still—for it knows no other form of defence.

New Zealand biologists and members of the Royal Forest and Bird Protection Society are working hard to save the kakapo from extinction. Seemingly the best tool is translocation—moving the endangered birds into locales where predators are absent. In 1986, kakapo populations were only known on Stewart Island, where fewer than fifty existed—and there they were at the mercy of prowling cats, 21 transplants on Little Barrier Island. None of the kakapo had begun breeding as of that date. Remember that they boom and breed only about once in four years. Researchers feel that only about six kakapo remained in the Fjordland area in 1986, although they had once populated every corner of New Zealand. Another strike against the kakapo is that only the female tends the eggs and rears the young, while the kakapo male goes on his solitary way in the dark.

On the bright side, the kakapo is thought to live as long as fifty years. Biologists have succeeded in applying radio telemetry techniques to these shy, nocturnal birds. This allows the scientists allowing them to study the birds' movements and confirm their theories that they are completely herbivorous—to the extent of raiding gardens to eat cabbage.

Most of what is known about the kakapo today was learned by one Richard Henry, early conservationist and very accurate observer. His biography, *Richard Henry of Resolution Island* has been published in New Zealand.

Another New Zealand bird is worthy of discussion. The kea, a big parrot which flies very well, thank you. It has chosen the high alpine country of the South Island for its home. When farmers moved into the southern half of New Zealand, they immediately accused the kea of killing sheep. Considering the small size of the bird and the large size of even a lamb, the accusation seems ridiculous. Yet it is known that the kea—a bird unmatched for curiosity and daring—can harm sheep with its beak (both halves of which are movable) and that this wounding can be the cause of death if infection sets in. However, the kea feeds on carrion. When a farmer saw a kea perched atop a dead sheep, he immediately assumed (wrongly) that the kea had killed the sheep. This situation is similar to America's view of the coyote—a scavenger wrongly blamed for many livestock kills. After seven years of supervising predator control programs for the U.S. Fish and Wildlife Service, I know that coyotes kill livestock. However, most of the livestock eaten by coyotes were not killed by those coyotes. A bounty was paid for the killing of keas and more than 150,000 of them have been killed prior to 1986. This bird is only protected in national parks and monuments, and can be legally killed in agricultural areas "if it is causing harm." As a result of this bounty system, the kea has been reduced in numbers to between 1,000 and 5,000 individuals.

The kea is a polygamous, omnivorous parrot which lays its two to four eggs between July and January, usually in nests located between large rocks on the ground. Although still too numerous to be listed as endangered, it surely deserves better treatment than it gets at this time. It is still legal to keep kea in captivity, under a permit issued by the Ministry of Agriculture. Distressingly, captive keas are kept to act as decoys, luring their wild brethren down into rifle range. One of the most interesting of native birds in New Zealand, the kea needs help to arrest its slide into oblivion—condemned for crimes it couldn't have committed.

New Zealand also fights to prevent extinction of the black robin. With the known population of this species down to the range of 12 or 13 individuals, biologists began to cross-foster the birds. This involved taking eggs from the black robin nest and placing them in the nests of a common bird, known as the tit in New Zealand. By removing the eggs of the first and even the second clutches, they induced the black robin female to lay three clutches in a year. Although the black robin has been seriously endangered for about a century, it now appears likely that it may be brought back from the brink, mainly due to the process of cross-fostering. Genetic inbreeding doesn't seem to have caused problems, yet, although scientists warn that the gene pool is very narrow and genetic problems may show up at any time. So serious is this inbreeding that one female—"Old Blue"—is the mother of six and the grandmother of eleven black robins. The entire population was about 20 at the time old age prompted a honorable retirement for Old Blue.

In both Australia and New Zealand, the introduction of exotic mammals has been the direct cause of the loss of many indigenous species. A spectacular case is that of the introduced (from North America) elk or wapiti onto the South Island of New Zealand. This browsing animal removed much of the available food of the takahe. The elk are being stocked into many coverts formerly occupied by the takahe, with disastrous results. The biologists want these translocations of elk curtailed, because of the deleterious effect upon the takahe, a valued indigenous species. The shooting fraternity wants the elk introduced, to improve their hunting and their wallets. Hard feelings have been caused between fans of the takahe and the fans of the wapiti. Indeed, there have been occasions of elk-lovers killing wild takahe, so as to prevent that bird's presence being the reason for a halt in elk stocking.

Rabbits introduced into Australia had catastrophic results leading to the purposeful spreading of the dangerous disease Infectious Myxomatosis, with disastrous results. Indigenous species that have never had a need to protect themselves against predators are easily killed by the introduced

193

predator. Examples are everywhere—but perhaps Hawaii and New Zealand are the worst examples, with Australia running a close third.

The obvious moral is: Exotic animal species are better left exotics. Any introduction of exotics should be exhaustively studied for many years before being undertaken.

32

Zoos and Wildlife Parks

Way back in 1961 I was sent to the San Antonio (Texas) Zoo to advise Fred Stark, famed Superintendent of that institution, on ways to reduce the infestation of rats which plagued his zoo. As I strolled about the grounds with him, I suggested that we use zinc phosphide to poison the rats. Smiling, Fred turned the next corner and asked, "Will this big bird eat a dead rat?"

That big bird was one of the rarest birds on earth, a whooping crane. I had to tell Mr. Stark that I was pretty sure that a whooper might take a dead rat as part of his menu. I also had to admit that the rat might cause the death of the rarest bird on earth. We silently agreed that there'd not be a poisoning program.

At that time, there were three whooping cranes penned up in zoos—in San Antonio and New Orleans. Those birds were lonely, useless reminders of a species that once was. In a zoo setting, they could do nothing to help the survival of their clan. Because of the work of pioneers like Fred Stark, we learned how to keep the rare cranes alive in captivity. State of the art aviculture had not progressed much past that point—at least where cranes were concerned. But that was thirty years ago.

Today, aviculturists at the San Diego Wild Animal Park and at the Los Angeles Zoo have been entrusted with the care and reproduction of the California condor, the rarest bird on earth. Modern zoos are scientific institutions of the highest caliber. They were given the job of reproducing the condor for the simple reason that they were the best qualified to reproduce

195

this rare bird. Their early success in 1989 testifies to the wisdom of this decision. This is not an isolated instance.

When the Wyoming people began to reproduce blackfooted ferrets with success, they knew that they dared not leave all their ferrets in one place for fear that disease or natural catastrophe might wipe out this only known gene pool of ferrets. They studied the field and then chose two zoos—in Omaha, Nebraska, and in Front Royal, Virginia. We are now propagating ferrets in three widely separated locations. Why in two zoos? Because the zoos were the best qualified.

Anyone who has read *Gorillas in the Mist,* Dian Fossey's tragic story of the mountain gorilla, will remember that zoos were villains in that piece. Zoos bought mountain gorillas without asking where they came from, or whether or not adult gorillas had to be killed to capture the baby gorilla. Those days seem to be gone.

No longer is a zoo a place where we pen up the last remaining specimen of a species—pen it up and put it on display so that people can say, "I once saw a cheetah" or "This is the last red lechwe in existence and I saw it." Far from it. Today's zoological parks have made great strides. Consider . . .

In Florida's zoological parks, scientists have learned how to better the chances of the manatee by inducing it to reproduce. They used a better, vitamin-loaded, diet and the manatees took on parenthood chores.

In Albuquerque, the Rio Grande Zoo propagated several ibex species, and their offspring was introduced into the wild—now there are more of the Persian red goats in the wild in New Mexico than there are in Saudi Arabian coverts. From the same source, New Mexico introduced the Barbary sheep into the wild where it is prospering, providing a worthy opponent for hunters, and preserving the species which is declining rapidly in its North African niches.

Zoo-trained aviculturists have developed many techniques for increasing the numbers of a bird species. Removing eggs and placing them in the incubator—if done properly—causes the parent bird to lay another egg to replace it. The result, known as double-clutching, often doubles the number of viable eggs hatched by that institution, and a 100% increase in numbers of young.

Trained aviculturists have developed "cross-fostering" to a science. They've substituted the egg of the whooping crane for an egg of a greater sandhill crane, thus causing the wild parent to rear a foster chick. This procedure produces more fledgling young. But there are problems with this foster-parenting. The young birds thus reared do not seem to have the inclination to mate. Probably because they think of themselves as greater sandhill cranes, rather than as whooping cranes, they do not have the advantage of watching adult birds in courtship and mating.

Another problem of artificial propagation is that the newly hatched bird seems to have a tendency to "imprint" on the first thing it sees after hatch-

197

ing. Patuxent's Wildlife Research Center found that newly hatched whoopers thought they were the offspring of their keepers—in other words, they thought they were humans and wanted to follow the person around, learning all the wrong things. This problem is being overcome by raising the birds in isolation from people, and by using robots or puppets to do the feeding chores, causing the young birds to imprint on the puppet which resembles a whooping crane adult, or a condor's head, as the case may be.

Scientists have resorted to desperate methods to preserve the last chances of the "nearest to extinction" species. The sperm of rare males has been frozen in liquid nitrogen to preserve it against the day when it can be used. Artificial insemination has been used successfully in dozens of species from the very smallest to the very largest.

Zoos now keep genealogical records on their animals, thus developing a family tree which can be used to scientifically "mate" animals with reduced danger of inbreeding. It is commonplace for a gorilla to travel by airline thousands of miles to see if he or she is compatible with another gorilla. Pandas enjoy the same care and treatment, and the whole world waits and watches to see if they mate. Once we thought that "Familiarity breeds contempt." But we also know that familiarity attempts breeding, and the zoo performs a needed chore in just getting male and female together in the first place. This is often fraught with peril. If either male or female doesn't like the idea, a savage struggle may ensue, and one or both of the animals may be killed. Zoo "know how" prevents this from happening, in most cases.

For more of an "in depth" look at the contribution made by zoos, let's examine the program of the San Diego Wild Animal Park. They've set up the Center for Reproduction of Endangered Species (CRES), to perform wonders in increasing chances for reproduction of a rare species. Some of their work . . . comparative physiologist Dr. John Phillips is studying wild populations of wild monitor lizards in an effort to determine why female monitors seem to shut down their estrus cycle in captivity. The importance of this work cannot be overstated, because the monitors of Asia and Indonesia, the Bengal monitor is officially endangered; so are the Desert monitors of North Africa, the huge Komodo monitor of Indonesia and the Yellow monitor of Asia's drier climes.

At CRES, scientists are gathering DNA fingerprints of the big Galapagos tortoise to establish blood lines that will improve reproductive success of these big tortoises. The job is complicated by the fact that more than one male may father one clutch of eggs.

Strangely enough, Asian elephants do not reproduce readily in captivity, despite the fact that they have been reared in captivity for centuries. It was easier to catch a baby Asian elephant in the jungle and bring it in for taming and training, so Asian peoples did just that. Only 56 normal births have been recorded by zoos in North America—but 27 of these have taken place in this decade of the Eighties. Study of elephant reproduction is made difficult by the fact that females come into heat only three times per year and then it takes 22 months for the mating to result in a calf. CRES is having success. Right now three Asian elephants at the CRES are pregnant.

CRES scientists are anticipating further losses in the fauna of the South American rainforests, and are analyzing chromosomes of several South American primates. It is hoped that this will enable zoos everywhere to do a better job of managing their primate collections. Cell samples from zoos around the world regularly arrive at CRES for analysis, and the results aid zoos everywhere. Perhaps the day will come when zoo collections of South American primates will be the source for stocks reintroduced into the wilds of South America. Already Andean condors, used in research at CRES, have been reintroduced into the wilds of South America—to replace a species extinct in what was once its range.

CRES scientists have had success with using semen which has been frozen and then thawed out. Cryopreservation (preservation by freezing) has been studied at CRES since 1985 and promises to provide another tool to be used against extinction. CRES scientists recognize that some species simply require privacy to reproduce successfully. As I write this, CRES is providing a "honeymoon suite" for drills, an endangered species of West African baboon. One of the rarest of all animals, this drill is represented by only 18 individuals in captivity. The species may be extinct in the wild. If it is extinct, the study of these captive animals may lead to increased reproduction in zoos and possible re-introduction into the wild, if conditions for survival in the wild are improved.

In the short years since CRES was established, it has made great contributions to the chances for survival of cheetahs, Indian rhinoceros, Chinese monal, and Przewalski's horse. Dr. Donald Lindburg heads the Behavioral Study division of CRES, which studies the reproductive cycles of any species whose reproductive rate in captivity is lower than that observed in the wild. This division attempts to find the reasons, and to gain an improved reproductive rate.

Dr. Valentine Lance and his colleagues at CRES study the endocrinology of captive species to answer many questions about hormonal imbalances, about time of ovulation, and many other mystifying events. By studying the sex steroid hormones in the droppings of rare birds, they have effectively learned how to pair birds for best chances of successful mating.

Dr. Oliver Ryder heads the CRES genetics study. Its greatest value in the future may be in its development of a "frozen zoo" in which the ova and semen of species are stored against the day when they will be needed. More than 1,500 different frozen semen specimens are now catalogued and stored for future use. Genetic studies of such different species as condors, orangutans, okapis and Asiatic wild asses, along with chromosomal studies of the Sumatran rhinoceros and the Kirks dik-dik, are providing a reference library which is being consulted by zoologists all around the world.

Disease is always a threat to any captive population, and CRES devotes considerable time and effort to finding ways to make captive animals healthier. Comparative physiology gets a lot of attention here at CRES. This study has resulted in improving conditions for survival among captive species, and has greatly influenced captive reproductive success, as with the green iguana, an endangered species in Central America.

American humans are going through a re-evaluation of the problems connected with "surrogate" motherhood, wherein one woman carries the embryo of another woman, gives birth to it and then surrenders the new-born child to the genetic mother. The same method is being used when the female of an endangered species is unable to carry her own fetus to fruition. At CRES, scientists are studying this plan, whereby mouflon ewes would carry the fetus of the rare Afghan urial.

Some of the advanced work in animal reproduction carried on by CRES may seem like "Dr. Strangelove" type of science fiction, but the results are not fictional and the future of many endangered species is brighter because of their work. Although CRES of the San Diego Wild Animal Park is surely the most publicized of such programs in the United States, it is by no means the only one. Similar—although less ambitious—programs are underway in several European countries.

The International Species Information System (ISIS)

Located at 12101 Johnny Cake Ridge Road, Apple Valley, MN 55124-8199, ISIS is a computer-based information system for wild animal species in captivity. This pooled database now includes information on more than 106,000 living vertebrate specimens, plus a greater number of their ancestors, in more than 335 zoological institutions in 34 countries.

Basic biological information such as age, sex, parentage, place of birth, and circumstance of death is collected and used for many different kinds of reports and analyses of the status of captive populations. An optional subsystem pools basic normal laboratory data such as chemistry and hematology to help in disease detection in exotic animals.

Why go to all the trouble of collecting all of this data? Many wildlife species have become extinct in the wild and their only remaining populations are in zoos. The European bison became extinct in the wild, but was successfully propagated in captivity and then re-introduced back into the wild. Same goes for the Arabian Oryx. Przerwalski's horse, extinct in the wild, is currently being propagated in zoos and will someday be reintroduced into the wild.

In other chapters we've discussed in detail the plight of the California condor and of the Blackfooted ferret. Both of these species became extinct (we believe) in the wild and the sole remaining population was successfully propagated in zoos.

To be long-term stable and of maximum conservation value, captive populations need good specimen records assembled and available, on which genetic and demographic management can be based. To best allocate captive habitat space among threatened species, one needs to know total captive holdings of all related taxa.

Assembly of the needed database also offers short-term convenience and advantages to captive species managers. ISIS publishes registries of "who has what" and short summaries of the 2500 and more registered species. This is invaluable in finding a needed specimen, as well as for finding people with expertise in dealing with a particular species.

To oversimplify the valued contribution of ISIS: Let's just say that your zoo finds itself with a mature female of an endangered species and would like to breed that mature female to the male of the same species. ISIS can quickly tell whether or not such an appropriate male exists in captivity—what his blood lines are, whether or not he is related (closely or distantly) to the mature female. In many cases, this information is absolutely essential for the prevention of extinction of captive species. ISIS serves a very important function in the world of zoological parks.

SPECIES SURVIVAL PLANS

Just as biologists have prepared "Recovery Plans" for the prevention of extinction in wild species, so do zoo scientists prepare Species Survival Plans for endangered species which are kept in captivity around the world. This work is sponsored by the American Association of Zoological Parks and Aquariums (AAZPA), and much of its work is headed up by Dr. Thomas Foose of the Minnesota Zoological Park.

Currently, the following taxa are designated for SSP's:

Snails	Black Lemur	Clouded Leopard
Puerto Rican Crested Toad	Golden Lion Tamarin	Snow Leopard
Chinese alligator	Ruffed Lemur	Tiger
Radiated Tortoise	Gorilla	Asian elephant
Lion-tailed macaque	Asian lion	Drill
Cheetah	Aruba R-snake	Orangutan
Indian Rhino	Dumerils boa	Bonobo

Sumatran rhino
Humboldt penguin
Andean condor
California condor
Hooded crane
Red-crowned crane
Okapi
Guam rail
Micronesian kingfisher
Arabian Oryx
St. Vincents' Parrot

Black rhino
Maned wolf
Red wolf
Red panda
Spectacled bear
Barasingha
White-naped crane
Palm cockatoo
Bali Mynah
Scimitar-horned oryx
Blackfooted ferret.

Asian otter
White rhino
Asian wild horse
Grevy's zebra
Chacoan peccary
Wattled crane
Gaur
Thickbilled parrot
Addax
Chimpanzee

Each Species Survival Plan has a Species Coordinator, who updates the program as individuals are born or die, and as more information is gathered on his (or her) individual species. The results are obvious. For example, an SSP arranged an exchange of a male okapi between the Oklahoma City zoo and the Dallas zoo. This exchange produced a healthy calf for the female okapi in Dallas. According to officials of the SSP committee, the end of this century will find about 80% of the world's human population living in the poorest, least developed countries where about 80% of the world's remaining wildlife populations now dwell. By the year 2,000 SSP reports estimate that Africa's population will increase by 104% and South America's population will increase by 96%. Biologists estimate that this population increase and the resulting demands upon the total biota will result in the extinction of as much as 20% of the world's living plants and animals. SSP points out quite logically that many of these species, otherwise slated for extinction, could be preserved genetically in zoos. Realizing the problems that arise with very small relict popultions of mammals and birds, the SSP plans to do its work scientifically to prevent or mitigate problems of inbreeding and consequent loss of diversity.

Within the confines of this book on WILDlife extinction, it is my opinion that the preservation of a "specimen" population of any wild animal is laudable, but that it only prolongs the agony. If we cannot have the species in the wild ever again, then there is little value in preserving the captive population. I agree that we must protect any species as long as we can. But the fact remains that human population increases must be stopped—and reversed, if we are to preserve a species from extinction—preserve it in such a way that it can exist in the wild. We must stop crowding out wildlife species. There is no other permanent solution.

33

Is Hunting to Blame?

Predators have hunted prey and eaten prey species since the first proto-
zoan ancestor dined on a simple one-celled organism. Predators are not
bad, in and of themselves. They are doing what comes naturally.

Remember that predatory species have hunted and eaten prey species
for millions of years, and we do not blame them for causing the extinction of
a species. Indeed, we do not feel that they DID cause the extinction of a
species. In most cases, alteration of the habitat was more influential in causing extinction than was hunting.

Enter the most effective predator of all—us! Pogo spoke the immortal
line, "We have met the enemy and he is us!" No one ever said it better.

In all the history of this troubled planet, no one predator has been so supreme as man has become in this modern day. Not even the sabre-toothed
tiger—not even *Tyrannosaurus rex*. They never had the complete and total
power to eliminate another species if they so wished. Modern man, unfortunately, does have that power.

By lowering the water level in desert ponds, man can eliminate several
species of pupfish. By shutting off a scant water supply, man can exterminate a species of isopod. By permitting poachers to hunt elephants, man has
the power to eliminate that wonderful species—whose brain is larger than
our almost-unused brain. Man hunted the passenger pigeon and the passenger pigeon—whose flocks darkened the skies little over a century
ago—is gone.

Government encouraged hunters decimated the great herds of plains buffalo, aided and abetted by the United States Army for the purpose of making the Indian tribes, original occupants of this continent, completely dependent upon the white man. Without this source of food and sinew and leather, the Indian was helpless and moved meekly into reservation life, a conquered race of people.

But wait a minute! There is another side to this coin. The hunter is also the best friend that most wildlife ever had. In the United States, it was the hunter who taxed himself through the Pittman-Robertson Act and the Dingell-Johnson Act to pay for the wildlife restoration programs which have been the saving of many species. By the purchase of "duck stamps," the American hunter provided the funds which bought more than 300 national wildlife refuge areas—areas which are staving off the extinction of many species. Please don't tell me that hunters worked only to provide wildlife for their hunting pleasure. The Aransas NWR provides a home for whooping cranes, a species which will never be huntable. Even those refuges which are designed to help huntable species also help non-hunted species. Refuges which consist of wetland homes for ducks and geese also shelter red-winged blackbirds, bitterns, egrets, wrens and chickadees, along with turtles and fishes of many species.

It has now become routine for hunters to pay for wildlife improvement projects. However, those who criticize hunting seldom put their money where their mouth is. How many birdwatchers—and I am one—can honestly say that they pay for anything which helps wildlife?

Man is inherently selfish. Show man where he can benefit by helping wildlife and you'll usually enlist his support. We've already mentioned the fact that the sport hunter willingly spends to help wildlife species which he can then hunt for sport and food. But whether he hunts or not, the help he provided is there and can be measured.

Let's take a look at the relationship between the human hunter and the African leopard. Shortly after the end of the colonial period, when African nations were assuming control of their own destinies, one of these nations banned all hunting of the leopard in their nation. This had several immediate effects. Most important of all, the leopard now stopped bringing in money to the people; so the leopard was bereft of economic value. It became only a predator that killed cattle and sheep and goats and occasionally a pet dog. There was no longer any reason for the penniless native to preserve the leopard. No longer were there jobs provided by safari hunters. No longer did the nation benefit by the thousands of dollars spent by each hunter in pursuit of the spotted cat. The leopard now had no friends, and its numbers declined faster than they ever had under controlled hunting.

The fact that people will support wildlife if it is to their benefit has led to the obvious. Zimbabwe now enlists the support and the help of the native population through their "Operation Campfire." This operation earns the help and respect of the native, by paying him his share of the proceeds of sport hunting.

South Africa has developed a system whereby the native population which inhabits the game ranges with the rhino, the elephant, the lion and the leopard, are compensated for the sport hunting of "their" game animals. In cases where the game animal is edible, the natives are given most of the meat, or are able to buy it at very low prices. Pelts are turned over to native cooperatives which prepare them for sale as souvenirs to hunter and non-hunting tourist alike. As a result, South Africa has earned an enviable record as a protector of wildlife. This, coupled with the best enforcement on the continent, has made South Africa the leader in wildlife management. Given suitable habitat for the hunted species, regulated sport hunting seldom has hurt a species. Loss of habitat is a far greater danger to every species than is legal hunting.

Sixty years ago illegal hunting of waterfowl—especially ducks—was very prevalent in our country. The species could withstand this mortality—simply because the habitat was good and the reproductive potential of ducks in good habitat is wonderfully high. There was very little stigma attached to illegal duck hunting. When I began work as a federal game law enforcement agent, I hauled three southwestern Missouri hunters into court with a bushel basket full of illegal ducks and three snow geese. This was in the spring, and spring hunting had been outlawed by law for years. They pled guilty. The judge gave them a scolding, but no punishment. Then, to add insult to injury, he told me to return the illegally taken waterfowl to the miscreants and—this is a direct quote—"Don't bother this court with such unimportant stuff."

That judge was right, although not in accordance with the law. The mortality caused by illegal hunting was not important to the survival of waterfowl. And Missouri was not alone in holding this view of the "importance" of wildlife laws.

Let's move up to the recent past. Federal biologists introduced their theory of "compensatory mortality." They claimed that waterfowl had a very short life span in any event. What the hunter took had no effect upon the total population next year. To prove their theory, they decided to keep regulations the same for at least five years—to make sure that hunter take had no effect upon the population.

This theory might have been effective if there were still great expanses of habitat on the breeding grounds, and if normal rainfall conditions prevailed. But this best of all worlds did not occur. Drainage of wetlands needed by waterfowl continued at an alarming pace, and five years of drought on the breeding grounds did almost as much damage as the dragline and the drainage tile. Duck populations took a disastrous slide—a slide from which they may never recover.

Today we can graph all of the pertinent indicators—wintering ground

205

counts of ducks and geese, aerial counts of breeding pairs, June pothole in-dices, on-the-ground brood survival counts, hunters kill—and every single line on that graph points downward at a steep angle. In other words, if pres-ent conditions continue and present hunting pressure continues there is only one possible conclusion—ducks are doomed to extinction.

This probably will not happen, but waterfowling as a sport seems doomed. It is now obvious that the federal government should have closed the duck season entirely back in 1987 when the decline was documented beyond any question. Closure was never seriously considered. Why not?

Because no one in charge had the guts to stand up and take the heat which surely would have resulted!

I haven't shot a duck in four years, because I would be ashamed to take even one out of the limited supply. I hasten to add that I've shot my share of Canada geese during those same four years, for the good reason that geese numbers are not declining.

Why have geese not suffered as ducks have suffered? Because they are more tolerant of man's proximity on their wintering grounds, because their nesting habitat has been relatively unchanged compared to ducks' breeding areas, and because they have benefited from a more intelligent control of mortality. For example, quota systems have been established for the har-vesting of geese in Illinois—traditional wintering area for half a million geese, and hunting stops when that quota has been reached. Interestingly, quota numbers have been raised several times, showing that the population is definitely not being hurt by that quota harvest. But, at the same time, sev-eral species of ducks which were suffering badly still remain as legal targets in that same area—with no special consideration given. Canvasbacks have almost disappeared from that area, yet it is still legal to kill canvasbacks there, without a quota!

Many factors are at work here with the duck hunting fraternity. There has been a steady decline in numbers of duck hunters, despite an increase in total human population. This is a a simple case of diminishing returns. When the anticipated legal take is so low that the hunter doesn't want to go hunting, he simply doesn't go. But waterfowling traditions are strongly en-trenched in many of us, and we go hunting simply because hunting is a part of our lives.

Faced with decreased goose population in the Eastern Shore area of Maryland, the daily bag was reduced to one Canada goose. But the same group of men journeyed to the same shooting blinds and went through the same ritual—shot their one goose per hunter, then adjourned to the club house to talk about goose hunts of days gone by. If the harvest is reduced to one goose per year, many hunters will still go through the ritual—one of the rites of autumn. Dedication to the sport of waterfowling is imprinted in thousands of sportsmen. This is important, because it leads to the surpris-ing conclusion that hunters will do almost anything to perpetuate their sport. This dedication explains why sport hunters are willing to pay great sums of money for wildlife.

Hunters work and spend to perpetuate their hunting. Oscar Wilde had it right when he wrote, "Each man kills the thing he loves."

Now let's carry my duck hunting prognosis to the logical end. If any species of duck becomes extinct in the wild, will the hunter be to blame? The far greater blame must rest on the destruction of habitat, but the hunter must share some of the blame.

The duck hunters of America are far ahead of their "leaders" in one regard. They ARE willing to accept any limitation on their sport, accept any increased costs, to assure the continuation of the species. If the U.S. Fish and Wildlife Service, for which I worked many years, would come forward and say, "It is apparent that the continent's duck population cannot withstand continued hunting—and we must close the duck season for at least three years", a great majority of the sportsmen of the nation would stagger under the shock; but then they would go along with the necessary closure. They would also continue to put money into DUCKS UNLIMITED, the private sector organization which does so much to improve waterfowl habitat in Canada and in the States.

The soldiers are willing, but the generals are too lily-livered to take the heat of closing a season. If we lose even one species of duck, a great part of the blame can be laid on the U.S. Fish and Wildlife Service for being too timid to do what they know is required.

Another part of the blame can be placed on another unit of the U.S. Government. Legislation set up programs to protect dwindling waterfowl areas, and they work. But, when the farmer who has been paid for this cooperation in the program comes upon a year in which hay is in short supply, the Department of Agriculture allows those farmers to mow the hay on the waterfowl areas—thus eliminating them as effective duck habitat. This is another evidence of lack of guts, the guts needed to enforce a contract—the guts needed to withstand political pressure.

In North Dakota, federal money is supposed to be withheld from farmers who drain wetlands—after an agreed upon date. However, weak-kneed officials have looked the other way in hundreds of cases and have even gone so far as to say that "thinking about possibly draining in the future" is the same as "having begun a drainage project" before signing the contract not to drain. Their flouting of the law certifies that they consider the law of the land to be for purposes of welfare payment to the landowner, rather than as constructive effort to help waterfowl.

This has proved particularly irritating to me, as a native North Dakotan who remembers the waterfowl production paradise that was there when I was a boy. Less than one tenth of that duck factory still exists. Is this the fault of "hunting"? Certainly not. It IS the fault of misguided management of a resource, and the fault of greedy farmers and weak-kneed bureaucrats.

Sport hunting will not become extinct, of that I am sure. But sport hunting, on every continent, and in every habitat, will increasingly be more regulated, more formalized and more costly.

Surprisingly, the hunter is ready for these changes. If the leadership of the state and federal agencies would just catch up to the hunters they regulate, we could get on with intelligent management.

There's hope on the horizon. The North American Waterfowl Management Program (NAWMP), a blueprint for progress in waterfowl, written by Canadians and Americans from the United States, was signed into law! For the first time, the entire continent was involved in a program which set very modest goals for waterfowl numbers—and then, unbelievably, set out the steps which must be taken to reach those goals. At last!

Canada jumped in right away with sizable governmental appropriations and the actual start of construction on waterfowl programs in the prairie provinces. Uncle Sam dragged his feet to the extent that most of us thought it was another case of big talk but no action. Pressure from sportsmen's organizations in the U.S. forced the reluctant Reagan Administration to appoint Harvey K. Nelson, career waterfowl scientist as the leader of NAWMP on our side of the border. Things began happening. There was a lot of action looking toward getting the moneys needed—and that total is astronomical when totalled up for the next fifteen years.

The North American Wildlife Foundation, under Chip Collins, made excellent strides in money-raising. Ducks Unlimited seemed reluctant to dive in wholeheartedly at first, but came around and began working with NAWMP with their usual vigor. They are helping with NAWMP in addition to continuing their own heroic efforts to save wetlands in Canada. At last the machinery was in place to allow our "leaders" to catch up with the rank and file of sportsmen-hunters-conservationists.

In February of 1990, another milestone was reached when the President signed into law the North American Wetland Conservation Act, which provides some eleven million annually for purposes of the NAWMP. One million dollars of this annual amount is to come from fines levied against violators of the Migratory Bird Treaty Act; the other ten million comes from the interest on the Wildlife Restoration Fund. Of great importance is the fact that the legislation directs the Secretary of the Interior to provide matching funds for wetland projects in both Canada and Mexico—the first time the U.S. Government has addressed wetlands and waterfowl loss outside of our own borders. Remember that Canadians are spending many times as much, per capita, as we are in this effort to preserve waterfowl. Finally, our "leaders" will allow us to spend our own money for the things we care deeply about!

Did you buy a Duck Stamp last year? If not, why not?

First of all, remember that this is a Migratory Bird Hunting and **CONSERVATION** Stamp. In addition to complying with the federal law that you must have a stamp in your possession before hunting migratory waterfowl, the stamp makes an invaluable contribution to waterfowl conservation. Remember also that a refuge purchased with Duck Stamp money may also protect moose, and cactus wrens, egrets and eagles.

Duck Stamp sales have declined quite a bit during the past five years, mirroring the decline in waterfowl numbers and the curtailing of hunting opportunity. In 1983-84, 1,867,998 stamps were sold at $7.50 each, in 84-85 1,913,375 stamps were sold at $7.50, in 1985-86 the figure was 1,779,928 were sold at $7.50; in 1986-87 1,793,383 stamps were sold at $7.50. Then the price of the Duck Stamp went up to ten dollars and the numbers of ducks went still farther down the road to oblivion. As a result, 1987-88 sales of the ten dollar stamp dropped to 1,659,608 and in 1988-1989, preliminary figures show that the sales were down to 1,377,298 stamps at ten bucks each. Preliminary figures for the first two quarters of the 1988-1989 Duck Stamp show that only 1,125,173 stamps were sold. Remember that is for half a year, but the first half of the year usually sees the great bulk of sales, because waterfowl seasons open in the first quarter of that year.

Duck Stamps have provided the money to purchase the National Wildlife Refuge System in the last fifty years. If you want to work for wildlife, please buy a stamp, even though you don't hunt. If you are a hunter, you ought to buy two stamps. Sign one and carry it with your license. Keep the second one clean and unwrinkled and its value to collectors will enable you to sell it ten years later for three times what you paid for it. In other words, purchase of a Duck Stamp is a wonderful investment for the waterfowl and a good investment for you. How can you lose?

Besides buying a Duck Stamp, there are other ways in which the individual hunter can contribute to the future of waterfowl. The most obvious is that of Voluntary Restraint. Don't feel that you have to kill a "limit" every time you go hunting. Most of us know that we go hunting for the privilege of being out there in the fresh air, of enjoying good companionship, and trying our best to outwit a duck with decoys and duck calls. Anglers often release their catch to swim away and fight again another day. Hunters should pass up the temptation to kill a limit and voluntarily restrict themselves to less than the limit. The bird you didn't shoot may return to Canada next spring and raise a brood of twelve young ones, thus making a real contribution to the continent's waterfowl population.

34

Are They Really Gone?

Who was it? Pollyanna? Someone in literature who said, "I'll worry about it tomorrow. I don't want to talk about it today."

Then there was a close relative of mine who reported that his doctor had told him that he had diabetes. He finished his account by saying, "I'm not going to do that again."

"Not going to do what again?" I asked.

"Not going to a doctor again. I don't want to hear that stuff," he replied.

There is a lot of that attitude in all of us. We don't want to hear bad news, so we shut it out.

Many of us refuse to believe that wildlife species we have known are now extinct. We don't *want* to believe that it is true; therefore we do not believe that it is true. This obviously doesn't help the species survival at all.

Are they really gone?

Sometimes our refusal to accept reality can become a statement of fact. For example, in the case of the blackfooted ferret, I stated in 1981 that the blackfoot was extinct in the wild. No one argued with me. But the ferret was not extinct in the wild—a colony was found near Meteetsee, Wyoming and today the ferret population is increasing by leaps and bounds.

It happens all the time. In 1851, biologists identified a tiny pupfish in Leon Springs, Texas. Due to irrigation pumping which lowered the water levels in its only known habitat, it suffered a great decrease in numbers. By 1900 it was pronounced extinct. But as the famed comic remarked, "Stories of my death have been greatly exaggerated." For 65 years it remained on

210

the list of species which had been exterminated after having been known as a living species. Then biologists discovered the Leon Springs pupfish in the Diamond Y Springs, nine miles north of Fort Stockton. The dead had arisen—the lost had been found, and there was cause for rejoicing. Even today, the Leon Springs variety is one of six endangered pupfish species which hang onto a precarious existence in widely scattered, highly specialized habitats.

No passenger pigeons have been seen for a century; no Leon Springs pupfish had been seen for nearly a century, then the pupfish resurfaced. Does this mean that the passenger pigoen might not be extinct? Certainly not. It was much too visible to be overlooked, while it is easy to overlook a pupfish.

Even large species may be overlooked for a long time. The Sinai leopard had been thought to be extinct for three quarters of a century when it was rediscovered in 1975.

In 1981, we wrote that the ferret was gone, and now it is back. We now write that the dusky seaside sparrow is gone. Will we have happy news in the future? Is the sparrow really gone? Or will another colony be discovered somewhere else in the vast expanses of Florida? The odds are very much against that happening.

When population numbers get really low, that species may be doomed to extinction although it is still visible. The gene pool may be so narrow that it is either a case of line inbreeding, or no breeding at all. When we discuss inbreeding, we recognize that it is a complicated subject. We can generally state that inbreeding exaggerates common traits—for good or for bad. It exaggerates weaknesses found in a remnant species. In 1941 we almost wrote off the whooping crane because the wild population was down to 21 individuals. Many scientists thought that the whoopers' gene pool was too narrow to allow for survival of the species. When a congenital weakness of the leg joint turned up, some of those scientists thought that this was an inbreeding exaggeration, maybe the fault which would doom the species. It turned out that different incubation methods—turning the eggs more often—almost eliminated that problem. Now the whooper population is counted in the hundreds instead of the dozens. Is the whooper safe? Definitely not, for that narrow gene pool might yet spell extinction for the species. Are they gone? Absolutely not, and there is hope that they will never be gone. But sometimes extinction processes reach the point of no return, even though a seemingly healthy population still exists.

Perhaps this is what is happening with the Attwater's prairie chicken, whose numbers seem to fall, inexorably—year after year—despite heroic efforts to arrest the slide into extinction. As we wrote in the chapter about this Texas Gulf Coast chicken, there are many reasons for its population losses, but it still might be possible that the extinction process has already reached the point of no return. We surely hope not.

If the population of a species of great whales is reduced to the point where a lonely male cannot find a lonely female in breeding season, the future extinction of that species is guaranteed. However, if an isolated male does meet with an female of breeding age another calf will surely be born. This means that the species will exist as long as that new calf is alive. If it lives to be seventy years old, it will delay extinction for seventy years. Yet the doom of its ancestors may have already been sealed when the calf was born. When the numbers of a species are reduced to the point where they cannot reproduce themselves every breeding cycle; then that species is foredoomed to extinction.

Genes once lost can never be reformulated. Despite our great advances in "chromosome engineering" and other esoteric sciences, we cannot retrieve or synthesize a species once it has been lost. Certainly we wrote off the coelecanth, a particularly unlovely fish known only from fossil remains. It was thought to be extinct for many centuries, perhaps even for a million years. Then a fisherman pulled a live one up from the depths off of South Africa! We presently know there is a population of coelecanths in the southern Indian and Atlantic Oceans, and we even study this living fossil. Surely that which had been lost is now found.

Between September of 1986 and 1989, Dr. Jerome Jackson of Mississippi State University tried to locate the endangered ivorybilled woodpecker in its former range in the southeastern United States. His work was funded by the Endangered Species Act. He looked intensively in eight states, and played a recording of ivorybill sounds into the pine woods. He got repeated replies to the recording in both 1987 and 1988, but did not sight a single individual ivorybill. Scientists who just plain hate to give up are planning to continue the search for two more years. It would be wonderful if they did locate a breeding pair of ivorybilled woodpeckers, but don't bet on it.

Some times we classify a species as endangered simply because we did not locate its populations. This was true of the trumpeter swan, proposed for listing as endangered in the United States. Then British Columbian authorities pointed out the existence of a healthy, large population in that beautiful province and the trumpeter is not listed as endangered. The drill of Equatorial East Africa is very rare; perhaps it is extinct in the wild. It is being reared in captivity under the assumption that the wild population is doomed—or already extinct. But the drill may turn up in other parts of its jungle range, for it is hard to census animals there and interest in the plight of endangered species is slight. Yet don't count on it.

But the coelecanth, the Sinai leopard, the blackfooted ferret have all taught us a lesson. Don't be too quick to proclaim the extinction of a species. Let's wait a century to be sure—or in the case of the coelecanth, let's wait a million years.

35

Captive Propagation

When we are discussing endangered species and we refer to captive propagation, we are usually describing a last ditch attempt to save a gene pool that is either A) extinct in the wild or B) so reduced in numbers that it cannot continue to exist as a species without scientific help.

In this book we have discussed at some length several different species being propagated in captivity. The whooping crane, symbol of our struggle against extinction, is a wonderful example. We have continued the existence of a wild population at all times. The strange quirk of the crane's reproductive process is that the birds lay two eggs, but usually only succeed in rearing one chick. This made it possible for us to steal the second egg and incubate it artificially. As a result, we kept a growing wild flock and added a second captive flock.

The captive flock has been used as a source of re-introduction, new birds for the old flock. The co-existence of the wild flock has eased the problem of reintroduction to the wild.

With the whooper we found several problems. One was that the newly hatched whoopers imprinted on their keepers, and grew up psychologically confused—thinking perhaps that they were young humans instead of young cranes. Another problem was that the young birds lacked the example of mature adults when it came to courtship, mating and nest-building. We cross-fostered another flock of whoopers at Grays Lake NWR, wintering on the Bosque del Apache. Their parents were sandhill cranes. Whether caused by imprinting on sandhills or not, the resultant whooper flock has so far shown

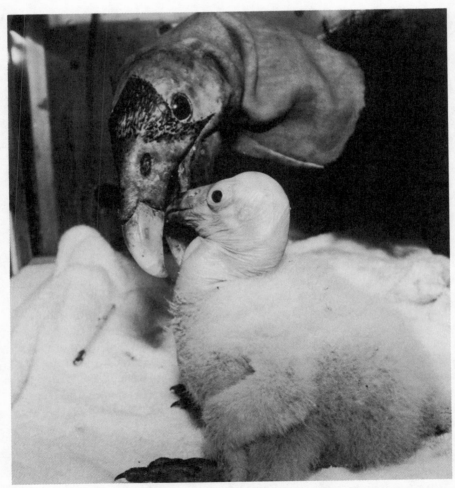

A puppet head resembling an adult condor is used to feed the condor chick.

itself to be completely without a clue when it comes to reproduction. But captive propagation of whooping cranes has succeeded beyond our hopes, and we now have enough cranes to allow us to separate populations, to give one group to the International Crane Foundation in Baraboo, Wisconsin, and to furnish the seed stock for the creation of a non-migratory flock in Florida. Chalk up a big plus for captive propagation.

Captive propagation of blackfooted ferrets has been even more successful, due to the higher reproductive potential of the ferret. But will pen-raised ferrets know how to kill their prey? Will they know how to avoid golden eagles and other predators?

When a species is maintained in a controlled environment and exhaustively studied, we learn many things that we could not possibly learn by monitoring a wild population. Manatees in captivity didn't seem to reproduce, until a researcher tried improving their diet—adding vitamins and minerals. Voilà! The manatees' reproductive rate increased markedly.

Because Cornell University researchers were good observers of their needs, captive peregrines reproduced very well, and the peregrine has been returned to the wild in many places—truly a success story. Perhaps this is the prime purpose of captive propagation—to preserve a gene pool, to nourish the resulting population and to re-introduce it into the wild. This business of being a caretaker for the gene pool has worked very well in most instances, and failed miserably in a few. Where captive propagation has failed the usual reason was that we started too late. When we finally took the dusky seaside sparrow into captivity, all we had were males. That very nearly happened with the California condor, before all the legal obstacles were cleared. There were perilously few condors to place in a captive propagation program in the first place. It will be several decades before we know whether or not we have succeeded in preserving the condor.

Modern science is now working wonders in the field of captive propagation. Artificial insemination is now fairly commonplace for many endangered animals, removing the problem of incompatibility. Relying on the natural affinity of male for female has led us into some grand failures. For example, when a bull gorilla rejects a mate led into his boudoir, the results may be fatal to the female. The same can be said for several of the larger carnivores—where love-making can be terrifying, even fatal.

Artificial insemination led to collection of both egg and sperm from individuals and cryogenically preserving them against future needs. Thus, it is now possible to use semen from a long dead male to inseminate females of his species as much as ten years after his death.

Injection of hormones to bring on ovulation has been standard practice in commercial fish raising ventures for generations. Now it is being used to increase the receptivity of the female, to increase the chances of natural insemination. Manipulation of temperatures and manipulation of light intensities can be used to fool the individual of a species into thinking that the normal time for reproduction has arrived. In this way we have been able to produce two litters (or broods) in a year, when normal reproduction would only produce one.

In the case of extremely rare species, it has been possible to fertilize the egg from the rare species with the sperm from that same rare species—and then implant the resulting embryo into the uterus of a related species. In this way, common beef cattle have been used as surrogate mothers to produce purebred young of some of the rarer wild oxen.

As previously noted, stud books have been established to record the ancestry of every individual of a species kept in captivity around the world. This very significant improvement has made the entire zoo population of the world part of a planned parenthood system which guarantees genetic diversity when possible. Zoos can actually breed for resistance to disease, or to correct abnormalities which have crept into the captive population.

But there are those who say that captivity is the same as extinction for a species which was wild. In our discussion of the California condor, we discussed the difference between the bird sitting on a perch in an aviary, feeding on meat brought to him by his captors, and the wild-flying bird, soaring majestically over the California mountains, finding his own food and fighting his own battles. Esthetically, they are very different; genetically they are identical. But if we keep our eye on the doughnut and not on the hole—if we keep in mind that captive propagation is only a way station in the fight for survival and that the final goal is the establishment of a wild population—then captive propagation is not only desirable, but absolutely necessary.

When should we take the entire remaining population into artificial propagation? When extinction is the only possible outcome in the wild. This is what we did with the California condor and with the red wolf. The experiment is still going on; we do not have the final result yet. Perhaps we will never have the results—but I feel that we must continue trying.

Sometimes we really had nothing to say about the matter. For example, Przewalski's horse was prospering in several zoos when it was determined that the horse seemed to be extinct in the wild. If it is true that the entire world's population of this horse is in zoos, we certainly have a duty to propagate it. Do we also have a duty to re-introduce it into the wild? Can the pen-reared Przewalski's horse make a living in the wild? Could it survive on the barren steppes and wind-swept plains which are its ancestral habitat? I think we have a duty to find out.

Some orangutans reared in captivity in Borneo had great difficulty returning to the wild when turned loose. Some researchers felt that this was due to the young orangs not having learned the art of foraging from their parents. Others felt that the orangutan had simply learned something in captivity. He had learned to rely on handouts from the release station, so why hunt up your own grub?

216

I remember a case many years ago when an enterprising rascal bought two ancient jaguars from a zoo, then advertised jaguar hunting in Texas. He got his "sportsmen" hunters in the vicinity; then he turned one of the old cats loose. With great excitement, his hound pack tracked the jaguar and treed it against a big boulder, where the so-called sportsmen shot it. That jaguar had been born in a zoo. It had absolutely no inkling of what being wild means. It didn't even try to fight off the dogs, nor did it try to escape. That sorry spectacle is the very epitome of what captivity can do to a wild animal. Captivity can remove all of the wildness, all of the natural defenses which the wild species has in abundance. If we do that to an animal, we are worse than murderers.

By becoming so completely dominant among our fellow animals on this planet, man has assumed a fearful responsibility. Are we our brother animal's keeper? We most assuredly are. Finally we are beginning to learn how to make the right decisions with regards to captivity for our animal brothers. The fate of many species lies in our hands. Are we wise enough?

36

The Role of Federal Agencies

In the United States of America, governmental agencies play a leading role in the fight against extinction of wildlife species. Implementation of the Endangered Species Act, the Critical Habitat regulations, and of our part of the CITES treaty all call for leadership from the U.S. Fish and Wildlife Service.

Most of the Recovery Team leaders doing the actual work in the trenches are employees of State or Federal wildlife agencies. This is easily explained, for only a full time wildlifer has the funds, travel authority, and the time to do such a job.

A very large part of the United States of America is under federal management, a grand total of 673,971,056 acres. This includes only the big four land managing agencies, not the smaller ones such as the Army, Department of Energy, etc. The Bureau of Land Management controls 336,391,462 acres; the U.S. Forest Service 189,407,923 acres; the National Park Service supervises 62,234,090 acres; while the U.S. Fish and Wildlife Service manages 85,937,581 acres of public domain. The very size of the federal stewardship forces us to examine it—because wildlife depends entirely upon habitat and these 673,971,056 acres represent a tremendous area of different habitats. To put this in perspective, the 674 million acres of America managed by these four agencies is forty times the total area of the state of Texas and seventeen times the acreage of Alaska, our biggest state!

Before examining the performance record of some of the federal agencies, permit me to express a personal opinion. The work of earlier leaders of governmental agencies was of critical importance in starting some of the more ambitious programs for endangered species of wildlife. Leaders like Ding Darling were few, but they were of great importance for they fought for the rights of wildlife and fought the good fight for their cause. In later years, we don't seem to have such charismatic leaders—leaders who fight for the natural resource all of the time. Presidents have put stringent controls on their cabinet officers and those cabinet officers have increasingly dictated to the directors of federal agencies—with tragic results for wildlife. For example, it is senseless to blame the Director of the U.S. Fish and Wildlife Service for not heroically standing up for what he knows is right. When he was appointed, he was told that he must be a "team player." That means that once the Administration has decided on a budget message to send to Congress, he must not challenge that budget. To do so is to be a traitor to his department and his president. There is not much incentive for a conscientious leader to become a hero. If he is a hero, he becomes a hero out of a job. Once fired, he can do precious little for wildlife. But it does go against the grain to listen to a Director of a wildlife agency testifying to Congressional committees, saying that his budget request is "enough to allow him to meet his objectives," when he knows that that budget under discussion is a sell out, one which will make it impossible to reach the objectives of wildlife management. The most effective leaders in recent years have been those leaders who just *accidentally* get asked the right questions by congressional committee members, questions that point out the inadequacy of the budget request, without the leader being a traitor to his President.

During the eight years of Ronald Reagans' presidency, wildlife interests were set back at least two decades. In almost every case where the needs of wildlife conflicted with the wishes of commercial interests, wildlife lost out to decisions coming down from the top. President Bush backed himself into a corner with his infamous "read my lips, no new taxes" statement. Calling himself the "environmental president" without calling for funds to implement environmental initiatives is political expediency and sheer hypocrisy.

Clean air requirements were weakened or ignored by Administration decisions in the 1980's. Important wildlife positions were either filled by incompetent political contributors or—even worse—were left unfilled under the pretense of saving money. Administration of the vitally important Environmental Protection Agency was left to "revolving door" employees of big industry, or was performed to benefit industry rather than the environment. Enforcement of pollution control regulations was noticeable mainly by its absence.

Field operations for endangered species were hamstrung by not filling positions and by de-emphasis of the programs and lowering of the status of employees operating such programs. Often this was done under the guise of "economy," such as the de-emphasis of the endangered species program in the U.S. Fish and Wildlife Service by the subterfuge of "decentralization" of authority in the programs. Authority—and accountability—was transferred out to the field instead of being coordinated in the Regional offices. "Out of sight—out of mind—and too often, out of operation."

National Parks and the National Wildlife Refuges

There are more than 300 national wildlife refuges now, the result of a steady building process that began under President Theodore Roosevelt and greatly accelerated by President Franklin Delano Roosevelt in the dust storm—cum depression—years when land was purchased for a song. Sportsmen hunters pushed through legislation which provided for the Duck Stamp and duck stamp dollars bought many refuges and enlarged many others. Why are wildlife refuges of importance to our story of endangered species?

It is fairly certain that there would be no Key Deer without the Key Deer National Wildlife Refuge. The whooping crane would not have made its first struggling steps up the ladder from extinction without the Aransas National Wildlife Refuge which protected its ancestral wintering grounds from the hands of coastal developers.

The Hawaiian Islands refuge protects the Laysan duck and other endangered species. The Attwater's Prairie Chicken National Wildlife Refuge protects habitat needed by this severely endangered species. The list goes on and on. Many national refuges were authorized strictly to protect one endangered species—but have prospered to protect other species as well, for all wild life is interconnected. Sonoran pronghorns run free on the furnace-hot, dry rock expanse of the Cabeza Prieta Game Range in Arizona, and also share their range with desert bighorn sheep, with white winged doves, and with hundreds of species of desert dwelling birds, mammals, and reptiles.

In New Mexico, the Bosque del Apache NWR protects the wintering habitat of most of the continents *greater* sandhill cranes, and supports the second flock of whooping cranes, along with 30,000 wintering snow geese and countless other species of wildlife. Those whoopers which winter at the Bosque spend their summers at Grays Lake NWR in Idaho. On their migration to and from Grays Lake, they stop over and rest at Monte Vista and Alamosa NWR's in Colorado. Their entire life is tied to the refuge system. The more famous flock of whoopers which winters on Aransas NWR comes from its summer home in Canada's Wood Buffalo Provincial Park, and visits a dozen refuges along the migration route.

Most species of ducks and geese are not YET endangered, and that is partially due to the existence of the great chain of wildlife refuges which protect them from ill-advised drainage projects and from the encroachment of condominiums and shopping malls. It is no coincidence that upwards of a quarter of a million Canada geese spend their winters on Horseshoe Lake, on Horicon marsh, on Crab Orchard or Brigantine or Blackwater. National Wildlife Refuges are the single most important factor in waterfowl's struggle for survival.

Some refuges are production areas—before the salt water fought its way back in, Bear River NWR on the edges of Great Salt Lake was a wonderful duck and goose factory. It is presently worthless as a breeding area because of the salt water. Perhaps some day we will again see the fresh water push the salt back and allow Bear River to again become a production area. Lower Souris NWR in North Dakota is also an important waterfowl producer among a hundred others.

Wildlife Refuges and National Parks are both managed by the Department of the Interior but they have diametrically opposed objectives.

NWR's allow sport hunting and sport fishing for many species. In fact, all refuges allow hunting unless it is not good wildlife management to do so. On the other hand, the National Park Service does not allow sport hunting on any NPS areas, unless forced to do so. In a very few cases, hunting is allowed on the NPS area because the enabling legislation that set up that area wisely provided for sport hunting. For example, the Grand Teton National Park allows elk hunting because enabling legislation forced it to do so. This sport hunting has enabled the NPS to avoid repeating the ghastly spectacle of park rangers shooting hundreds of surplus elk—as has happened in nearby Yellowstone National Park.

Philosophically, the NPS feels that it has a duty to keep an area in a completely natural state. I remember when park employees in the Theodore Roosevelt National Park were told that they couldn't plant a tiny garden behind their homes because radishes and cucumbers were not "native" to the area. In most cases, I applauded this "over strict" interpretation of the park mission. Then I remember that this same park secretly poisoned prairie dogs in the park, because the dogs were ruining the range by overpopulation. Removal of excess prairie dogs was wise management; my only objection was to the hypocritical secrecy.

The NPS seeks to maintain a natural area in a natural state. On the other hand, the NWR system feels that they should intensively manage every inch of a refuge—if that management will provide more food, more habitat for their wildlife charges.

Another factual difference is that the NPS manages its areas for the good of the American people. The NWR's are best managed when they ignore the needs of humans and manage the refuge for the good of wildlife. On a properly run refuge, people are only *tolerated* on an area whose purpose is wildlife.

Manipulation of the environment is considered good wildlife management on a refuge, including controlled burning, levee construction, and planting of feed crops. The NPS considers such actions to be heresy. This great nation of ours has room—and need—for both philosophies.

Even larger than the holdings of the National Parks or the holdings of the refuge system, the Bureau of Land Management supervises great areas of land spread over all of the West. For most of its existence, the BLM paid scant attention to the needs of wildlife. This, thankfully, has changed markedly.

Much of the land administered by BLM was land which people had failed to cultivate. When they failed—for lack of rainfall, for lack of fertile soil, for climatic reasons—the land reverted to the government—to the BLM. For many decades, the BLM functioned as the office which leased land to ranchers, at ridiculously low prices. Some savant was heard to say that the rancher in our west had his snout in the public trough for so long that he deemed it a God-given right. Certainly it is true that the livestock interests benefited greatly by having their "pasture" costs subsidized by the BLM's unrealistic grazing fees. A few were so brazen that they contracted with the BLM to rent pasturage at the rate of (for example only) $2.00 per AUM. An AUM is an animal unit per month. At that rate, 100 head of cattle would pay $200 per month for the grazing privilege on that particular piece of land. Then that same rancher turned around and sub-leased his grazing privilege to another at the going rate, which might be as high as $6.00. This "subsidy" was then pocketed by the permitee, of course.

Several Directors of BLM have tried to raise the AUM to match the going market price. In each case, the influential ranchers' lobby in our western states rose up in "righteous" wrath and lobbied their congressional representative to safeguard their "God-given right." The senators and representatives then rose up in the halls of congress amid dire predictions that an increase in the AUM would drive ranchers out of business, and—too terrible to contemplate—this would raise the price of a beef steak to the American public. All of which was hogwash, of course, but it served the purpose and the subsidy continued in the form of an unrealistic price for the AUM.

The price of an AUM is not of great concern to wildlifers. Far more important when discussing the BLM's stewardship is the question of overgrazing of public lands. This overgrazing has ruined some public lands to the point where they needed fifty years to recover from the abuse. This is slowly being remedied, and I must give the modern day BLM kudos for trying. The National Wildlife Federation, the Izaak Walton League and the Wildlife Management Institute have all been instrumental in keeping BLM grazing permits under close scrutiny. Lonnie Williamson of the Wildlife

Management Institute has been the most eloquent and telling voice raised in favor of realistic pricing for AUMs, and for limits on grazing.

When BLM's activities showed some movement toward wise land use, livestock interests in the west formulated a daring raid on the public lands. Mislabeled the "Sagebrush Rebellion," this was a blatant land grab, which would have turned management of large tracts of your land over to livestock interests controlling state legislatures. The timing of the land grab was excellent, as it came during the time when Ronald Reagan was preaching a doctrine of "de-federalization" of almost everything. But you cannot get away with deals cut in the back room any more—not deals that blatant. Watchdog organizations rose up to put the pitiless glare of publicity on this ill-advised land grab and it was defeated.

In the 1990's BLM will be in the spotlight to an even greater extent. One problem which has attracted more than its share of "loonies" is the problem of wild horses and wild asses overgrazing public lands, causing soil erosion and severely damaging habitat of endangered native species. The obvious solution of shooting the wild horses and asses where they are was much too sensible for publicity hungry opponents. It must be remembered that the agency which tolerates the overgrazing of feral burros may be condemning to death the indigenous population of desert bighorn, of example. Sincere people like "Wild Horse Annie" and self-seeking publicity hounds got together and aroused public opinion—uninformed public opinion—to postpone the solution of the problem through ridiculously expensive programs to trap and "adopt out" horses and asses off the public domain. These programs appease public concern for humane treatment of animals, but they only guarantee that the same problem will be there twenty years farther down the line. How BLM handles such potentially explosive public relations problems will be critical in the years to come. Overgrazing of the public lands is still one of the greatest dangers to wildlife.

The Forest Service

Overgrazing and ridiculously low AUMs have been problems which the BLM shared with the United States Forest Service. The Forest Service has made better progress than has BLM in remedying these wrongs. But the Forest Service has an even worse public image—and deserves it. For a century, the Forest Service has seen itself as an arm of government intended to facilitate the mining of our public land forests by helping commercial interests.

There are thousands of cases where the USFS has spent ten dollars in building a logging road for every dollar realized from sale of the timber on that logging area. This, of course, is another blatant subsidy of logging interests. Of greater importance, the FS has been guilty of subordinating other uses of the national forest to the one over-riding use of cutting down the trees to enrich private companies. You'll find more on this subject in the chapter about spotted owls.

The most telling accusations against the Forest Service have come from its own employees, workers who point the finger at unwise cutting practices which cause erosion, at unrealistically low prices paid to you and me for the sale of our timber, and of unwise decisions to cut certain tracts. At times the only possible purpose served by a timber sale is the enrichment of a private company which cuts the logs.

It is almost impossible to over-estimate the worth of recreational use on the national forests. It is almost impossible to over-estimate the value to wildlife of the national forest lands. Protection of water sheds which provide our nation's drinking water is one of the greatest values of the national forest system.

Where would the red-cockaded woodpecker be without the national forests? Will the northern spotted owl benefit from wise handling of the national forests of the northwest? Will the slowly rebounding populations of Kirtland's warblers benefit from wise management of forests in Michigan? Will the endangered species of trout—the Gila and the Apache among others—benefit from wise management of trout streams in the national forests?

The USFS refers to our national forests as "lands of many uses." Every concerned wildlifer agrees with that principle. But in past history the only "use" of the national forests that took priority was the growing of trees. Careful surveillance is necessary to make sure that the other uses receive due consideration—surely the national forests are sources of drinking water, homes to wildlife, preventers of erosion and places for healthful recreation—not just lumber factories. **YOU** are the best person to ensure that all uses are considered, for it is **YOUR** forest land.

37

You Can Help!

YOU can help endangered species!

If you are seriously interested in doing your bit to help prevent the disappearance of species of wildlife, here are the first grass-roots steps you can take:

(1) Get better informed. How? I'd suggest as the very first step that you subscribe to *Audubon* Magazine. This expertly edited and illustrated magazine is one of the most beautiful publications in existence today. More important, it does a good job of presenting information on the plight of various species of wildlife—factually, and without apparent bias. Other excellent sources of up-to-date information are the tabloid type magazine (*Outdoor America*) published by the Izaak Walton League, and the two beautiful magazines (*National Wildlife* and *International Wildlife*) published by the National Wildlife Federation. These publications come with membership coupons, and you should become a member.

(2) Join! Join your local affiliate of the National Wildlife Federation, the Izaak Walton League or the Audubon Society. Make your own choice, or join all three—to become acquainted with local issues about endangered species, to enjoy the fellowship of others sharing your concerns and to exert your considerable influence on lawmakers. If you think that you can't split your energies three ways, try each one out for a short period of time—a couple of monthly meetings—and decide which group best matches your interests.

(3) Get to work! If you are receiving any one of the three publications

mentioned above, you won't lack for jobs to do. Set goals for yourself. For example, set yourself a quota of—say—five letters per week to your congressional representatives telling them what you think about matters concerning wildlife.

How else can you get to work for endangered species? Are you the type that can stand up and talk to school groups? Tell them about the plight of wildlife species. Most school teachers welcome the help of anyone who is well-informed about a wildlife subject. Find out which organizations will supply you with slide shows or film strips, or video cassettes to help you make presentations to school groups. Children are the concerned citizens of tomorrow and there is no arena of activity that will pay bigger dividends than helping to educate our children about wildlife.

(4) Specialize! Because the endangered species field is too big for any one person or organization to handle completely, it is wise to pick a special cause and go to work on it. Such specialization will not necessarily limit your attention to the whole general field. Rather, such specialization will allow you to focus your energies at one point where you feel most involved, or most dedicated.

For example, you may feel most concerned with the plight of tropical birds of the rain forest. If this is true, write to the World Wildlife Fund and get into that fray. If you are motivated by the continuing struggle of the whooping crane, you'll owe a big debt of gratitude to the National Audubon Society and you might wish to further your interest by joining the **WHOOPING CRANE CONSERVATION ASSOCIATION**, address is 3000 Meadowlark Drive, Sierra Vista, AZ 85635.

If your interest lies in the big game animals of the world—elephants, rhinoceros, tigers, elands, and so forth, you will find that the most active workers for the preservation of these species are the hunters of the world. Don't be afraid of joining such organizations as Game Coin International, or the Safari Club. These people are hunters, but they are also lovers of wildlife and they put their money where their mouth is for the future good of the game they love to hunt.

There no longer is a definite polarization between those who love wildlife and those who love to hunt wildlife. The National Audubon Society, once mistakenly thought of as a bunch of little old ladies in tennis shoes who loved dickey birds and opposed hunting, now represents an impartial group of people who have recognized that the wise management of some species often includes hunting as a management tool. The Audubon Society will adamantly oppose hunting when and where they consider it to be wrong for the species concerned. They are just as firmly committed to hunting when and where it is a part of good management. Their position is based on facts, careful study and consideration of all sides of an issue.

(5) Spread the word! Work to get your family, your friends, your fellow workers—everyone—concerned with the issues that concern you. Many

people are interested in the plight of endangered species but do not take the first step in entering the battle unless someone asks them to come on in, the water's fine.

(6) Be careful. Don't let your emotions run away with your common sense. Some enthusiasts suffer from a fairly common fault—they saddle up and ride off in all directions before deciding where it is that they want to go. Study the situation before you make up your mind. Examples? Don't oppose all cutting of forests, because second growth timber—new growth that follows logging—is almost always better habitat for deer, elk, moose, turkeys, grouse, than was the old growth timber. Overage, unharvested forests are fire hazards, which cause great loss of wild life. But it is wise to oppose clear-cutting, which eliminates all of the timber over a big area, for that clear-cutting often (not always) leads to soil erosion, siltation of streams and other hazards to wildlife. Learn why varied stands of timber—hardwoods and conifers mixed together—are far better habitats for wildlife than are monoculture stands of one species, all the same size and the same species of tree.

Don't automatically oppose the opening of a refuge to deer hunters—not until you've studied the situation, and learned the reasons for the hunting proposal. Maybe the deer are stunted and starving from overpopulation and need to have their numbers reduced.

To sum up point 6, be sure you know what you are talking about before you join a stampede on any wildlife cause. Think it over and then don't be afraid to resist the pressures of your friends and associates. You may differ from them because you are better informed.

(7) Cash. If you are faced with the enviable prospect of having to find ways to spend your money, by all means contact the NATURE CONSERVANCY, 1815 North Lynn Street, Arlington, VA 22209. They do a magnificent job of identifying pieces of land which ought to be kept inviolate for wildlife and buying them. They've done a very good job of spending funds for wildlife. I am so convinced of the wisdom of their approach, that I'm giving them this unpaid advertisement—by quoting their printed advertisement:

"In the age of the dinosaur, the earth lost a single species every thousand years. Today, we lose one every single day. At this horrifying rate, by the year 2,000, one of every five species now on the face of the earth will have disappeared.

"At The Nature Conservancy, it is our sole purpose to prevent this cataclysm. And it can, indeed, be prevented.

"Some 30 years ago, we came to a rather simple conclusion; that the surest, most efficient way to preserve natural land was not to beg for it, but to buy it.

"And buy it we have. To date, we have privately secured more than 3 million acres. (That's more land than Delaware and Rhode Island combined).

227

We're protecting wetlands in the Carolinas, prairies in the Dakotas, deserts in the Southwest, islands off the coast of New England, rain forests in Latin America. With 1100 preserves, we've created the largest private sanctuary in the world today. And literally every single day, we protect just about 1,000 acres more.

"We are not dreamers. We are pragmatists. We recognize that the destruction of each species brings us closer to the extinction of our own. We've also come to understand that in allowing one species to vanish, we may be losing forever the cure to a disease or the solution to a famine.

"But faster than we can buy up the land, man is encroaching upon it, polluting it, eliminating it. Which is why we need your help.

"Buying back the earth takes lots of money. And most of our support comes from our members. If you have $10, $20 or $50 to give to become a member of The Nature Conservancy, you'd be advancing our cause dramatically.

"Buying back the earth is ultimately the job of each of us—the people of the earth. Dollar by dollar, acre by acre!"

As you see, I strongly support The Nature Conservancy.

We are in a war to save endangered species—so far it is a losing war. If you want to enlist—and you should—here is a listing of various armies active in the field. Pick yours and go to work!

The top three:

Izaak Walton League of America, 1400 Wilson Boulevard, Level B, Arlington, Virginia 22209, about 50,000 members, all concerned with wildlife matters. Publishes a good periodical, *Outdoor America,* to keep you informed. Look in the phone book, there probably is a chapter near you.

National Wildlife Federation, 1400 Sixteenth St. N.W. Washington, D.C. 20036-2266, with more than five million members, this is the world's largest conservation-oriented organization. Membership includes your choice of two excellent magazines, or you can pay for both. Perhaps the strongest voice affecting wildlife legislation, simply because of its huge membership —and huge voting clout. The NWF has affiliates in every state, perhaps a chapter in your town.

National Audubon Society, 950 Third Avenue, N.Y. 10022, with more than a half million members, the Audubon Society is one of the oldest and most respected of all wildlife organizations. Very much dedicated to the plight of endangered species, the NAS publishes the most beautiful magazine in America (my opinion) which does a good job of counseling on wildlife management and wildlife legislative matters. There's probably a local chapter in your town.

Other, more specialized, organizations deserve your support. We've listed many of them here for your consideration. Editorial comments are only the opinion of the author.

AMERICAN CETACEAN SOCIETY, POB 2639, San Pedro, California 90731. Main interest is with the cetaceans, whales and porpoises, but also interested in all marine problems.

AUDUBON NATURALIST SOCIETY OF THE CENTRAL ATLANTIC STATES, 8940 Jones Mill Road, Chevy Chase, MD 20815, membership is mainly made up of residents of the Washington, D.C. area. Operates a 40 acre wooded sanctuary right in the middle of the megalopolis which Washington has become. I've enjoyed meeting with these good people; you probably would, too. They claim a membership of 9,000 and the organization is 90 years old; so they must be doing something right.

BARRY B. BROOKS FOUNDATION, 1401 Carr, Memphis, TN 38104, was started by the big game hunter, sportsman, conservationist, philanthropist for which it is named. A man who earned his fortune buying and selling cotton, Barry Brooks traveled the world in search of the finest in big game trophies.

His last will and testament left his collection of trophies to found the Barry B. Brooks Foundation, and stipulated that the foundation was to work for the good of wildlife.

When the North American Waterfowl Management Program seemed to be languishing in the stodgy halls of the Interior Department, the BBBF convened a couple of seminars—financing the expenses of several hundred waterfowl managers. Their discussions led directly to a quickening of the pace and to the staffing and funding of the NAWMP. They have been active in many phases of wildlife work—from funding seminars to building observation trails for high school students studying waterfowl management. The BBBF has also been helpful to me in researching this book.

BAT CONSERVATION INTERNATIONAL, POB 162603, Austin, TX, 78716 Why would anyone want to join a bat society? Read chapter 22 of this book. 6,500 members already know the reason for joining this group.

CANVASBACK SOCIETY, POB 101, Gates Mills, OH 44040. Dedicated to the well being of the canvasback duck—not presently listed as an endangered species, but one which has seen its numbers greatly diminished in the last thirty years. Have you noticed fewer "cans" lately? Maybe you ought to join.

CARIBBEAN CONSERVATION CORPORATION, POB 2866, Gainesville, Florida, 32602. Concerned with the conservation of marine turtles . . . Active in turtle research—and there is a dire need for facts on several endangered sea turtles.

CHELONIA INSTITUTE, POB 9174, Arlington, VA 22209. Concerned with the plight of endangered sea turtles. The strange name is taken from the scientific name of the green sea turtle.

DESERT FISHES COUNCIL, 407 W. Line St. Bishop, CA 93514, composed mostly of professionals in the field, the DFC concerns itself with the study and management of the desert fishes, which includes many endangered species.

DUCKS UNLIMITED, One Waterfowl Way, Long Grove, Illinois 60047. is not strictly speaking an organization devoted to saving endangered species. However, it is a very effective force for good on the continental waterfowl scene, raising money in the United States and spending most of it in Canada, where the majority of our waterfowl are hatched. Strictly a private agency, DU is superbly organized in every state of our Union and works closely with DU Canada to further mutual aims. DU is one of the most effective moving forces behind preservation of waterfowl. The habitat they've created or preserved is home to countless other species as well as to waterfowl species. With the implementation of the North American Waterfowl Management Plan, Ducks Unlimited takes on an even greater role in the struggle to preserve waterfowl and the sport of waterfowling. If you are a duck or goose hunter, you should belong in Ducks Unlimited.

ELSA WILD ANIMAL APPEAL, POB 4572, North Hollywood, CA 91607, founded by "Born Free" author, Joy Adamson, is dedicated to the protection of endangered species. Has branches in Kenya, the UK, Japan and Canada.

FRIENDS OF AFRICA IN AMERICA, 330 S. Broadway, Tarrytown, NY 10591, a non-profit organization promoting support for wildlife, mainly in East Africa.

GAME CONSERVATION INTERNATIONAL (Game Coin) POB 17444, San Antonio, TX 78217, an organization of HUNTER-conservationists that participates in wildlife conservation projects relating to protection of habitat, anti-poaching programs and translocation of game animals.

GREENPEACE, USA, 1436 U Street NW, Washington D. C. 20009, A non-profit organization dedicated to "preserving the earth and the life it supports". This is a radical group, the ones who try to stop whalers by interposing rubber boats and their own bodies between harpoon and whale. I admire most of their aims, but am very doubtful about the methods they use to attain those ends. To my mind, Greenpeace workers have more courage than brains. Personally, I prefer to work through more orthodox methods. But if 'action' is what you crave, this might be the group for you. However, be warned that they splinter their efforts into many other fields such as anti-nuclear and anti-war projects.

INTERNATIONAL UNION FOR CONSERVATION OF NATURE AND NATURAL RESOURCES, Avenue du Mont-Blanc, CH-1196 Gland, Switzerland (022.64 71 81). Known usually as the IUCN, this is a tremendous organization, with worldwide projects and worldwide membership. It has only 634 voting members in 120 countries and 61 states. This is not an organization that would welcome your membership, but it is a very important group concerned with the protection of endangered species and with the preservation of tropical rain forests. One of their most important activities is the publication of the Red Data Books, which describe in detail the threatened and endangered species worldwide.

NORTH AMERICAN WOLF SOCIETY, 6461 Troy Pike, Versailles, KY 40383. If you are concerned with the reintroduction of the red wolf into the Southeast, or the reintroduction of the timber wolf into Minnesota or Montana, this is the group for you.

PEREGRINE FUND, INC, 5666 West Flying Hawk Lane, Boise, Idaho, 83709. Interested in all raptors, not just the endangered peregrine, this non-profit, tax exempt group publishes the "Peregrine Newsletter."

RARE, INC. 19th and the Parkway, Philadelphia, PA 19103, is the conservation education affiliate of the WWF. Supported by contributions from the public, it does significant good work for endangered species.

SAFARI CLUB INTERNATIONAL, 4800 West Gates Pass Road, Tucson, AZ 85745, Organized to promote good fellowship and good sportsmanship among sportsman conservationists. The Safari Club also operates the Safari Club Conservation Fund, which sponsors educational programs and research programs which affect endangered species.

SIERRA CLUB, 730 Polk Street, San Francisco, CA 94109, with nearly half a million members, this is an activist group, founded by John Muir way back in 1892. Endangered species is only one of many programs of the Sierra Club. Through the Sierra Club Foundation, they channel donations into worthwhile wildlife projects. There's probably a Sierra Club local in your area.

TRUMPETER SWAN SOCIETY, 3800 County Road 24, Maple Plain, MN 55359. Although the trumpeter swan is no longer listed as endangered, there is still a society dedicated to the welfare of this beautiful bird.

WHALE CENTER, 3929 Piedmont Avenue, Oakland, CA 94611. Active in educating the public to the plight of endangered whales, claims credit for achieving the moratorium on commercial whaling.

WILDLIFE MANAGEMENT INSTITUTE, Suite 725, 1101 14th St. N.W. Washington, D.C. headed by President Laurence R. Jahn and Vice President Lonnie L. Williamson, the WMI is a highly respected membership organization which has an excellent record in fighting for wildlife species. Ask to be put on the mailing list for their *Outdoor News Bulletin.*

WORLD WILDLIFE FUND, 1250 24th Street N.W. Washington, D.C. is the largest USA organization working worldwide to protect endangered species, especially in the tropical rain forests of Central and South America, Africa and Asia. Membership is more than half a million.

XERCES SOCIETY, 10 SW Ash Street, Portland OR 97204, is the organization for you if you are interested in endangered species of insects, especially butterflies. They publish a membership magazine called *"Wings."*

ZERO POPULATION GROWTH, 1601 Connecticut Avenue, Washington, D.C. 20009. It might seem to you that this organization is out of place in a book about endangered species. Yet as I pointed out in the very first chapter, humanity is crowding many endangered species out of existence. Anything that can slow or stop the exploding mushroom of human populations is a big help to "crowded out" wildlife. Without a slowing or negative growth in human population increases, no program will have any hope of success. Too many humans put too much pressure on too many species of wildlife, crowding them out of existence.

I am sure that there are other organizations worthy of your consideration. Some of them I am prejudiced against because it seems to me that they exist mainly to raise funds with which to pay their salaried staff—with very little left over to spend on endangered species programs. Others have failed to make my list because they use unethical tactics, including outright lying and misrepresentation of facts to gain their objectives. I am not one who believes that the "ends justify the means." Sooner or later, unethical actions come back to haunt their practitioner. I'd rather fight fair, believing that it's best in the long run.

But, this is only one man's opinion. If you wish to work through an organization which I have omitted, go right ahead and good luck to you! The National Wildlife Federation sells an annual "Conservation Directory" which contains about 300 pages of "organizations, agencies, and officials concerned with natural resource use and management."

Appendix I

Endangered Species' Heroes

Many people have fought to protect endangered species of wildlife—sometimes they succeeded; many times they failed. But they fought the good fight. Some of them were in the international spotlight, and their feats have been told many times. Others, just as important, did their level best—unsung, almost unheard of.

It would obviously be impossible for any one man—or any one hundred men—to accurately list those who deserve the title of Hero Against Wildlife Extinction. Remembering that fools rush in where wise men fear to tread, I rush in to nominate a few of the heroes who have fought the good fight during my lifetime. Alphabetically, of course, for no one could rank them:

ALLEN, Robert, whom you read about in the chapter on whooping cranes, was sent to the Texas Gulf Coast by the National Audubon Society to work in favor of the endangered cranes. With his writings, Robert Allen proved that the pen is mightier than the sword and brought the plight of the cranes to the collective national attention and hastened the day when the crane could increase its number to the point where we have hope for its future.

BUECHNER, Helmut K., one of the earliest American Fulbright researchers sent to Africa to provide scientific research into wildlife management problems in 1957.

BUSS, Irven, one of the earliest American Fulbright researchers who went to Uganda in the late 1950's to bring scientific research to the management of African big game.

BYELICH, John, of the Michigan Department of Natural Resources, was the first Recovery Team Leader appointed to help the Kirtland's warbler. His recovery team took prompt action in getting suitable habitat set aside for the rare bird. At a time when prompt action probably meant the difference, he took prompt action.

CHAPMAN, Frank, was an investment banker until he got interested in the plight of the egrets that were being killed for their plumes. He quit his job to fight full time for the birds' interests and became the first editor of the magazine *Bird Lore,* which became the forerunner of *Audubon* Magazine.

COIMBRA-FILHO, Adelmar, is not a household name in this country, but he is a respected ecologist and zoologist in Brazil, where he led an long and frustrating struggle in behalf of the golden lion tamarin, one of the most beautiful and most endangered of all wildlife species. If this species survives against almost insuperable odds in the disappearing rain forests of this huge country, Coimbra-Filho deserves a lot of the credit.

DARLING, J.N. (Ding) was selected by President Franklin D. Roosevelt to head

233

the Bureau of Sport Fisheries and Wildlife at the bottom of the dirty thirties, when drought and erosion threatened continental waterfowl populations with extinction. He had been a political cartoonist for the Des Moines (Iowa) Register, and he dipped a pen in acid when he portrayed those who despoil the environment. He was an inspirational leader and his work led to the enlarged National Wildlife Refuge System which benefits wildlife today. If ducks survive as wild species, Ding Darling will smile in his grave. There's a national wildlife refuge named for him, but if this was an ideal world, at least 100 refuges would be named for him.

DOUGLAS-HAMILTON, Dr. Ian, for several decades has been vitally concerned with the plight of the African elephant, and his censusing of the elephant across the Dark Continent was the cause of increased concern for this menaced species. A respected scientist, Douglas-Hamilton is one of Africa's best.

ETNIER, Dr. David, must go down in history as the man who stirred up the tempest in the TVA teapot when he discovered a new fish, the snail darter, while snorkeling in the Tennessee River. Because this tiny fish was thought to exist nowhere else, that part of the Tennessee River was deemed to be critical habitat for the snail darter. Under federal law, the existence of the snail darter stopped the construction of the huge Tellico dam. The dam-builders went to court to overturn this ruling. Circuit and Appelate courts reversed one another depending upon the amount of pressure brought to bear on them by the dam builders and the environmentalists. Finally the Supreme Court ruled in favor of the snail darter. Work was stopped on the Tellico Dam, until the Congress passed into law legislation which stated that the Tellico Dam was exempted from the provisions of the Endangered Species Act. If Dr. Etnier knew what he was stirring up when he described the new fish—the snail darter—he deserves our thanks for forcing the courts to rule on the merits of the law, not on the wishes of so-called developers.

FOSSEY, Dian, was the young woman who gave her life to the struggle to save the mountain gorilla. She spent her boundless energy and her youthful strength on the cloud-shrouded slopes of the Virunga mountains where her beloved gorillas lived. Whether or not she succeeded is for the next ten years to decide. But her fight cost her her health and finally her life, a martyr to the cause she served. The book she wrote and the book written about her did much to enlist humanity in the struggle to save the big apes.

GALDIKAS, Dr. Birute M.F. is recognized as the world's outstanding authority on the endangered orangutan. She started her field work in Borneo in 1971 and is still hard at it. In addition to her orang work, she teaches at Simon Frazier University in British Columbia one term out of each year, and is the president of the Orangutan Foundation, based in Los Angeles. Her research has uncovered facts about the social interaction of these large apes, once thought to be almost completely solitary. She has been instrumental in getting habitat set aside for the use of the endangered orangutans and has been very important in publicizing the precarious situation of this far-off, little understood cousin of man.

GOODALL, Jane, the biologist whose in-depth study of the chimpanzee on its home territory has yielded so much new information applicable to all primates— including man. The chimpanzee, which is related to us in so many ways, is in danger of extinction in its African home. Certainly the chimpanzee benefited from her work. In addition, her work and the work of Dian Fossey, has done much to increase American interest in African wildlife. This in turn has made it much easier to raise money in wealthy countries for the benefit of wildlife in poverty-stricken countries like many of those in Africa.

GOTTSCHALK, John S. had a long and distinguished career in wildlife management. He was Regional Director for USF&WS in Boston, then National Director of

F&WS, and then headed the International Association of Game and Fish Commissioners. In each of these positions he made an impact for endangered species legislation.

GRZIMEK, Professor Bernhard, Director of the Frankfort (Germany) Zoological Society, throughout a long career an enthusiastic, articulate author and television personality and philanthropic champion of African wildlife. Due to his efforts, German money was very important in establishment of the first African College of Wildlife Management.

HENRY, Richard, a pioneer conservationist in far-off New Zealand. Long before most nations were even thinking about management of wildlife, let alone preservation of endangered species, Richard Henry did the first "base-line" research about the kakapo, the kea and many other birds in the rich and incredibly different bird life of New Zealand. His early observations have proved to be strikingly accurate and have been confirmed by modern scientific investigation.

HINES, Robert, is a talented artist whose work has illustrated countless books about wildlife species. As a staff artist for the U.S. Fish and Wildlife Service, he painted the portraits of almost every endangered species. His art taught millions of people what wildlife species looked like, even when they had never seen that particular species. He helped educate a nation to the plight of endangered species. I am proud to add that lovely pictures of many endangered species in this book are the work of my long-time friend and friend of wildlife, Bob Hines.

JONES, Carl, world-famed biologist who performed miracles in bringing back from extinction's edge the Mauritius kestrel and the pink pigeon on the far-off island of Mauritius.

KIMBALL, Thomas, was the director of the Colorado State Game Department and the Arizona Game and Fish Department before taking on the job of leading the National Wildlife Federation on a full time basis as its Executive Vice President. A man of unquestioned personal integrity, he was effective in lobbying for endangered species in the congress of the United States. Carefully cultivating his connections on the wildlife scene in the nation's capitol, Tom Kimball rose to the stature of elder statesman in the eyes of many in congress. He was always asked to testify on wildlife matters before committees of the congress, a chore he took on gladly and performed admirably.

KINLOCH, Major Bruce, Chief Game Warden of Uganda and of Tanganyika, founder of the first African College of Wildlife Management. An authority on elephant control, a pragmatic man who realized that big game numbers had to be controlled for their own good. His life story is the story of wildlife management in Uganda and Tanzania.

LEDGER, John, is the head of the Endangered Wildlife Trust in The Republic of South Africa. He also serves as editor of the magazine named for an extinct species, *Quagga*. His is a strong and respected voice for endangered species.

LEVY, brothers Seymour and Jim, sportsmen and conservationists of Tucson, Arizona. After it was thought that the masked bobwhite was extinct throughout its range, they found its feathers in the nest of a cactus wren in Old Mexico. Encouraged by this find, they searched and found the few remaining bobwhites in Old Mexico and began trying to propagate them in captivity. They also kept up a steady pressure on the U.S. Fish and Wildlife Service and got what they wanted when the FWS started a recovery program for the masked bobwhite.

LONGHURST, William, one of the early American Fulbright researchers sent to Africa in 1957 to provide a scientific basis for managing Africa's big game.

LOUTHIT, Blythe and biologist husband in Namibia, originated the idea of dehorning rhinos to make them less attractive to poachers. But Blythe has worked many years in documenting the story of Namibia's rhinos, making an important contribution to that animal's welfare.

MAYFIELD, Harold, was one of the first (1942) to get interested in the plight of the Kirtland's warbler in Michigan. In 1953, he and his volunteer helpers made the first complete census of this rare species. His work in keeping census figures on the bird has been of great help in the warbler's struggle for survival. His definitive study of the Kirtland's Warbler earned him the highest honor in American ornithology, the Brewster Medal of the American Ornithologists Union. Although only an amateur ornithologist who never had even one college course in the subject, he made five trips to the Arctic and is perhaps the world's foremost authority on the red phalarope.

PENFOLD, Joe, was western regional representative of the Izaak Walton League when he had an idea which led ultimately to the creation of the Outdoor Recreation Resources Review Commission. President Eisenhower appointed Joe Penfold to lead the ORRRC. The work of the ORRRC led directly, or indirectly, to such landmark pieces of federal legislation as the Endangered Species Act, the Wilderness Act, and the Land and Water Conservation Fund act.

PETRIDES, George, one of the early American Fulbright researchers who went to Africa in the late 1950's to bring scientific methodology to African big game research.

QUICK, Horace, one of the early American Fulbright researchers who played such an important part in putting African wildlife management on a scientific basis.

SCHALLER, George, is perhaps accurately described as the "biologists' biologist." His work on great whales, on African lions, and most recently his work on the giant panda of China, have all earned the admiration and respect of his peers. In the case of the panda, his recommendations were accepted by the Chinese government and—if the giant panda is saved from extinction—it will be because the plan he set forth was followed.

SCHREINER, Keith, now retired from the post of Director for Alaska of the U.S. Fish and Wildlife Service, was one of the first chiefs of the Endangered Species division of that service. Keith is a friend of mine from back in 1950, and I know him as a stubborn man, who will hold tight to his beliefs, and not bend easily. In the office of Chief, Endangered Species, he stuck to his guns in administering the law equitably and intelligently despite great pressures to bend a little. Because Keith stuck to his guns, many endangered species are better off than before.

SINGH, Arjan, is perhaps the best friend the endangered Bengal tiger ever had. He fought long and vigorously for the establishment of tiger preserves—tiny enclaves in the disappearing forest and jungle of India. These enclaves, fostered by the Indian government at his prodding, have been the salvation of this most beautiful of the world's felines. Despite threats on his life, and despite the loss of human beings eaten by his beloved tigers, Singh continued his fight. To date, he is the only Asian recognized by the World Wildlife Fund with its top decoration.

SWANK, Dr. Wendell, respected biologist and one of the first American Fulbright researchers sent to Africa to assist in management of big game herds in 1957. With the other Fulbright "scholars" he began the practice of scientific research on a regular basis. In 1990, he is working with the Department of Wildlife and Fisheries Sciences, Texas A & M University.

TOMLINSON, Roy, was the Spanish speaking biologist assigned to locate wild populations of the masked bobwhite, way back in the early days of 1970. Roy found relict populations, got permission from the Mexican authorities to trap some for propagation in Patuxent, and found suitable habitat for their eventual reintroduction in Arizona. He worked with the masked bobwhite for ten years and

236

still maintains an interest in the small quail. Without his early work, it is doubtful that there would be any masked bobwhite alive today.

TRAIN, Russell, dedicated hunter-conservationist, helped form the African Wildlife Leadership Foundation and became its president. He was once Under Secretary of the Interior in America, and first Chairman of the Council on Environmental Quality. A strong, reasoned and respected voice for wildlife management.

TUTTLE, Dr. Merlin, is now assuredly the world's top authority on bats. He has discovered new species, developed new methods of high speed photography to film the fast action of flying and feeding bats. His writings, especially in the National Geographic, have done much to acquaint the world with the fascinating life history of many species of bat. In addition, he has done much to help banish the ridiculous fear of bats which is shared by many Americans. He has been the scientific consultant for documentary films about bats in Africa and Asia, ensuring the accuracy of such films.

VAN DYK, Anne, is perhaps the world's number one authority on the cheetah. When authorities took away her illegally held pet cheetahs, the youthful Anne campaigned for years and finally got a permit to keep cheetahs. Many years later, she is now the owner of the DeWildt Cheetah Breeding Station in South Africa. She is the first to rear cheetahs in captivity. She has it down to a science and says she can raise as many cheetahs as needed for restocking former cheetah habitats.

WILLIAMS, Ted—no, we don't mean the splendid splinter of baseball fame. We mean one of the best outdoor writers to come along in many a year. His blistering exposés of incompetence, insensitivity, and bungling ineptitude—as it harms wildlife—have irritated thousands of exploiters, but the results have stirred up much help for endangered wildlife. He helped place the blame for the Exxon Valdez oil spill in Alaska's pristine Prince William Sound. He is an environmental reporter with a conscience, and with a wonderful talent for expressing his outrage in words.

Appendix II

These are the Endangered

This is the listing of endangered wildlife species, as published by the U.S. Fish and Wildlife Service's Office of Endangered Species:

Mammals

Anoa, lowland	*Bubalus depressicornis*	Indonesia
Anoa, mountain	*Bubalus quarlesi*	Indonesia
Antelope, giant sable	*Hippotragus niger variani*	Angola
Argali	*Ovis ammon hodgsoni*	China
Armadillo, giant	*Priodontes maximus*	S. America
Armadillo, pink	*Chiamyphorus truncatus*	Argentina
Ass, African wild	*Equus africanus*	Africa
Ass, Asian wild	*Equus hemionus*	Asia
Avahi	*Avahi lichanotus*	Malagasy
Aye-aye	*Daubentonia madagarascensis*	Malagasy
Babirusa	*Babyrousa babyrussa*	Indonesia
Bandicoot, barred	*Perameles bougainville*	Australia
Bandicoot, desert	*Perameles eremiana*	Australia
Bandicoot, lesser rabbit	*Macrotis leucura*	Australia
Bandicoot, pig-footed	*Chaeropus ecaudatus*	Australia
Bandicoot, rabbit	*Macrotis lagotis*	Australia
Banteng	*Bos javenicus*	Asia
Bat, Bulmer's fruit	*Aproteles bulmerae*	New Guinea
Bat, bumblebee	*Craseonycteris thonglongyai*	Thailand
Bat, grey	*Myotis grisescens*	USA
Bat, Hawaiian hoary	*Lasiurus cinereus semotus*	USA, Hawaii
Bat, Indiana	*Myotis sodalis*	USA
Bat, little Mariana fruit	*Pteropus tokudae*	Guam
Bat, Mariana fruit	*Pteropus marianus marianus*	Guam
Bat, Mexican long-nosed	*Leptonycteris nivalis*	USA, Central America

Bat, Ozark big-eared	*Plecotus townsendii ingens*	USA
Bat, Rodrigues fruit	*Pteropus rodricensis*	Indian Ocean
Bat, Sanborns	*Leptonycteris sanborn*	N.America
Bat, Singapore	*Hipposideros ridleyi*	Malaysia
Bat, Virginia big ear	*Plecotus townsendii v.*	USA
Bear, Baluchistan	*Ursus thibetanus g.*	Pakistan, & Iran
Beaver	*Castor fiber birulai*	Mongolia
Bison, wood	*Bison b. athabascae*	Canada
Bobcat	*Felis rufus escuinapae*	Mexico
Bontebok	*Damaliscus dorcas d.*	South Africa
Camel, bactrian	*Camelus bactrianus*	Mongolia
Caribou, woodland	*Rangifer tarandus c.*	N. America
Cat, Andean	*Felis jacobita*	S. America
Cat, blackfooted	*Felis nigripes*	South Africa
Cat, flat-headed	*Felis planiceps*	Indonesia & Malaysia
Cat, iriomote	*Felis iriomotensis*	Ryukyu
Cat, leopard	*Felis bengalensis b.*	India, SE Asia
Cat, marbled	*Felis marmorata*	Asia & Indonesia
Cat, Pakistan sand	*Felis margarita scheffeli*	Pakistan
Cat, golden	*Felis temmincki*	Indonesia & Asia
Cat, tiger	*Felis tigrinus*	C.&S. America
Chamois, Appenine	*Rupicapra r. ornata*	Italy
Cheetah	*Acinonyx jubatus*	Africa
Chinchilla	*C. brevicauda boliviana*	Bolivia
Civet, Malabar	*Vivera megaspilla civetina*	India
Cochito (porpoise)	*Phoecoena sinus*	Mexico
Cougar, eastern	*Felis concolor cougari*	Florida
Deer, Bactrian	*Cervus elaphus bactrianus*	USSR & Afghanistan
Deer, barbary	*Cervus elaphus barbarus*	NW Africa
Deer, Bawean	*Cervus porcinus kuhli*	Indonesia
Deer, Cedros mule	*Odocoileus h. cedrosensis*	Mexico
Deer, Columbian w. tail	*Odocoileus v. leucurus*	USA
Deer, Corsican red	*Cervus e. corsicanus*	Corsica & Sardinia
Deer, Eld's	*Cervus eldi*	India & SE
Deer, Formosan sika	*Cervus nippon taiouanus*	Taiwan
Deer, hog	*Cervus porcinus annamiticus*	Thailand, Indonesia
Deer, key	*Odocoileus h. clavium*	Florida
Deer, marsh	*Blastocerus dichotomus*	S.America
Deer, McNeills	*Cervus elaphus macneilli*	China
Deer, musk	*Moschus spp.*	Asia
Deer, China sika	*Cervus nippon mandarinus*	China
Deer, pampas	*Ozotoceros bezoarticus*	S. America
Deer, Persian fallow	*Dama dama mesopotomica*	Iraq, Iran
Deer, Philippine	*Cervus p. calamaniensis*	Philippines
Deer, Ryukyu sika	*Cervus nippon keramae*	Ryukyus
Deer, shansi sika	*Cervus n. grassianus*	China
Deer, China sika	*Cervus n. kopchi*	China
Deer, swamp	*Cervus duvaceli*	Asia
Deer, Visayan	*Cervus alfredi*	Philippines
Deer, yarkand	*Cervus elaphus yarkandensis*	China
Dhole	*Cuon alpinus*	Asia
Dibbler	*Antechinus apicalis*	Australia

Dog, African wild	*Lycaon pictus*	Africa
Drill	*Papio leucophaeus*	Africa
Dugong	*Dugong dugon*	Asia
Duiker, Jentink's	*Cephalophus jentinki*	Africa
Eland, western giant	*Taurotragus d. derbianus*	Africa
Elephant, Asian	*Elaphus maximus*	SE Asia
Ferret, blackfoot	*Mustela nigripes*	USA
Fox, northern swift	*Vulpes velox hebes*	USA
Fox, San Joaquin kit	*Vulpes macrotis mutica*	California
Fox, Simien	*Canis simensis*	Ethiopia
Gazelle, Arabian	*Gazella gazella*	Arabia
Gazelle, Clarks	*Ammodorcas clarkii*	Somalia, Ethiopia
Gazelle, Cuviers	*Gazellacuvieri*	NW Africa
Gazelle, Mhorr	*Gazella dama mhorr*	Morocco
Gazelle, Moroccan	*Gazella dorcas massaesyla*	NW Africa
Gazelle, Petzeln's	*Gazella dorcas petzelni*	Somalia
Gazelle, Rio de Oro	*Gazella dama lozanoi*	W. Sahara
Gazelle, sand	*Gazella subgutturosa marica*	Arabia
Gazella, Saudian	*Gazella dorcas saudiya*	Near East
Gazelle, slender horn	*Gazella leptoceros*	N. Africa
Gibbons	*Hylobates spp.*	Asia
Goat, markhor	*Capra aegagrus*	SW Asia
Goral	*Nemorhaedus goral*	East Asia
Gorilla	*Gorilla gorilla*	Africa
Hare, hispid	*Caprolagus hispidus*	Asia
Hartebeest, Swayne's	*Alcelaphus b. swaynii*	Africa
Hartebeest, Tora	*Alcelaphus b. tora*	NE Africa
Hog, pigmy	*Sus sylvanius*	Asia
Horse, Przewalski's	*Equus przewalskii*	Mongolia
Huemul, North Andean	*Hippocamelus antisensis*	S. America
Huemul, S. Andean	*Hippocamelus bisulcus*	S. America
Hutia, Cabrera's	*Capromys angelcabrerai*	Cuba
Hutia, dwarf	*Capromys nana*	Cuba
Hutia, big eared	*Capromys auritus*	Cuba
Hutia, little earth	*Capromys sanfelipensis*	Cuba
Hyena, barbary	*Hyaena hyaena barbara*	N. Africa
Hyena, brown	*Hyaena brunnea*	S. Africa
Ibex, pyrenean	*Capra pyrenaica pyrenaica*	Spain
Ibex, Walia	*Capra walie*	Ethiopia
Impala, blackfaced	*Aepyceros melampus petersi*	S. Africa
Indri	*Indri indri spp*	Malagasy
Jaguar	*Panthera onca*	Central & S. America
Jaguarundi	*Felis yaguarundi spp.*	C. America
Kangaroo, Tasman Forester	*Macropus G. tasmaniensis*	Tasmania
Kouprey	*Bos sauveli*	SE Asia
Langur, capped	*esbytis pileata*	India Bangladesh Burma
Langur, Duoc	*Pygathrix nemaeus*	SE Asia
Langur, entellus	*Presbytis entellus*	Asia

Langur, François	*Presbytis francoisi*	China
		Indochina
Langur, golden	*Presbytis geei*	Asia
Langur, Pagi Island	*Nassalis concolor*	Indonesia
Lemurs	*Lemuridae spp.*	Malagasy
Leopard, clouded	*Neofelis nebulosa*	Asia & Taiwan
Leopard, snow	*Panthera uncia*	C. Asia
Linsang, spotted	*Prionodon pardicolor*	Asia
Lion, Asiatic	*Panthera leo persica*	Asia
Lynx, Spanish	*Felis pardina*	Portugal & Spain
Macaque, lion-tailed	*Macaca silenus*	India
Manatee, Amazonian	*Trichecus inunguis*	S. America
Manatee, West Indian	*Trichecus manatus*	Florida & Carribean
Mandrill	*Papio sphinx*	W. Africa
Mangabey, Tana R.	*Cercocebus galeritus*	Kenya
Mangabey, white-collared	*Cercocebus torquatus*	Africa
Margay	*Felis wiedii*	Central &
		S. America
Markhor, Kabal	*Capra falconeri megaceros*	Asia
Markhor, st-horned	*Capra falconeri jerdoni*	Asia
Marmoset, buffheaded	*Callithrix flaviceps*	Brazil
Marmoset, b. tufted ear	*Callithrix jacchus aurita*	Brazil
Marmoset, cotton top	*Saguinus oedipus*	C. America
Marmoset, Goeldi's	*Callimico goeldi*	S. America
Marmot, Vancouver Isl.	*Marmota vancouverensis*	Canada
Marsupial, E. jerboa	*Antechinomys laniger*	Australia
Marsupial, mouse	*Sminthopsis psammophila*	Australia
Marsupial, mouse long-tailed	*Sminthopsis longicaudata*	Australia
Marten, Formosan	*Martes flavigula chrysospila*	Taiwan
Monkey, black colobus	*Colobus satanus*	Africa
Monkey, Diana	*Cercopithecus diana*	W. Africa
Monkey, howler	*Alouatta palliata*	C. and S. America
Monkey, L'hoest's	*Cercopithecus lhoesti*	Africa
Monkey, Preuss red	*Colobus badius preussi*	Cameroon
Monkey, proboscis	*Nasalis larvatus*	Borneo
Monkey, redbacked	*Saimiri oerstedii*	C. America
Monkey, redbellied	*Cercopithecus erythrogaster*	Nigeria
Monkey, redeared	*Cercopithecus erythrotis*	Africa
Monkey, spider	*Ateles geoffroyi frontatus* also subspecies *panamensis*	C. America
Monkey, Tana R. red	*Colobus rufomitratus*	Kenya
Monkey, wooly spider	*Brachyteles arachnoides*	Brazil
Monkey, y-tailed wooly	*Lagothrix flavicauda*	Peru
Monkey, Zanzibar red	*Colobus kirkii*	Tanzania
Mouse, Alabama beach	*Peromyscus polionotus ammobates*	Alabama
Mouse, Australian	*Zyzomys pedunculatus*	Australia
Mouse, Aust. native	*Notomys aquilo*	Australia
Mouse, Choctawhatchee	*Peromyscus p. allophrys*	Florida
Mouse, Field's	*Pseudomys fieldii*	Australia
Mouse, Gould's	*Pseudomys gouldii*	Australia

Mouse, Key Largo	*Peromyscus gossypinus allapaticola*	Florida
Mouse, New Holland	*Pseudomys novaehollandiae*	Australia
Mouse, Perdido Key	*Peromyscus p. trissyllepsis*	Florida
Mouse, salt marsh	*Reithrodontomys raviventris*	California
Mouse, Shark Bay	*Pseudomys praeconis*	Australia
Mouse, Shortridge's	*Pseudomys shortridgei*	Australia
Mouse, smoky	*Pseudomys fumeus*	Australia
Mouse, western	*Pseudomys occidentalis*	Australia
Muntjac, Fea's	*Muntiacus feae*	S.E. Asia
Native cat, Eastern	*Dasyurus viverrinus*	Australia
Numbat	*Myrmecobvius fasciatus*	Australia
Ocelot	*Felis paradalis*	USA and C. & S. America
Orangutan	*Pongo pygmaeus*	Borneo & Sumatra
Oryx, Arabian	*Oryx leucoryx*	Arabia
Otter, Cameroon	*Aonyx congida microdon*	Africa
Otter, giant	*Pteronura brasiliensis*	S. America
Otter, long-tailed	*Lutra longicaudus*	S. America
Otter, marine	*Lutra felina*	S. America
Otter, southern river	*Lutra provocax*	S. America
Panda, giant	*Ailuropoda melanoleuca*	China
Pangolin	*Manis temmincki*	Africa
Panther, Florida	*Felis concolor coryii*	Florida
Planigale, little	*Planigale ingrami subtillisima*	Australia
Planigale, southern	*Planigale tenuirostris*	Australia
Porcupine, thin spine	*Chaetomys subspinosus*	Brazil
Possum, Leadbetters	*Gymnobelideus leadbeateri*	Brazil
Possum, mtn. pygmy	*Burramys parvus*	Australia
Possum, scalytailed	*Wyulda squamicaudata*	Australia
Prairie dog, Mexican	*Cynomys mexicanus*	Mexico
Prairie dog, Utah	*Cynomys parvidens*	Utah
Pronghorn, peninsular	*Antilocapra a. peninsularis*	Mexico
Pronghorn, Sonoran	*Antilocapra a. sonorensis*	Mexico
Pudu	*Pudu pudu*	S. America
Puma, Costa Rican	*Felis c. costaricensis*	C. America
Quokka	*Setonix brachyurus*	Australia
Rabbit, Ryukyu	*Pentalagus furnessi*	Ryukyus
Rabbit, volcano	*Romerolagus diazi*	Mexico
Rat, false water	*Xeromys myoides*	Australia
Rat, Fresno kangaroo	*Dipodomys nitratoides exilis*	USA
Rat, giant kangaroo	*Dipodomys ingens*	USA
Rat, Morro Bay	*Dipodomys heermanni m.*	USA
Rat, Stephens kangaroo	*Dipodomys stephensi*	USA
Rat, stick nest	*Leporillus conditor*	Australia
Rat, Tipton kangaroo	*Dipodomys n. nitratoides*	California
Rat, brushtailed kangaroo	*Bettongia penicillata*	Australia
Rat, Gaimards kangaroo	*Bettongia gaimardi*	Australia
Rat, Lesuers kangaroo	*Bettongia lesuer*	Australia
Rat, plain kangaroo	*Caloprymnus campestris*	Australia
Rat, Queensland kangaroo	*Bettongia tropica*	Australia
Rhinoceros, black	*Diceros bicornis*	Africa
Rhinoceros, great Indian	*Rhinoceros unicornis*	Asian

Rhinoceros, Javan	*Rhinoceros sondaicus*	Asia & Indonesia
Rhinoceros, n. white	*Ceratotherium simum cottoni*	Africa
Rhinoceros, Sumatran	*Dicerorhinus sumatrensis*	SE Asia
Saiga, Mongolian	*Saiga tatarica mongolica*	Mongolia
Saki, southern bearded	*Chiropotes satanas satanas*	Brazil
Saki, whitenosed	*Chiropotes albanasus*	Brazil
Seal, Carib monk	*Monachus tropicalis*	Caribbean
Seal, Hawaiian monk	*Monachus schauinslandi*	Hawaii
Seal, Mediterranean monk	*Monachus monachus*	Mediterranean
Seledang (Gaur)	*Bos gaurus*	Asia
Serow	*Capricornis sumatraensis*	Asia, and Sumatra.
Serval, Barbary	*Felis serval constantina*	Algeria
Shapo	*Ovis vignei vignei*	Kashmir
Shou	*Cervus elaphus wallichi*	N. Asia
Siamang	*Symphalangus syndactylus*	Indonesia
Sifakas	*Propithecus spp.*	Malagasy
Sloth, Brazilian threetoed	*Bradypus torquatus*	Brazil
Solenodon, Cuban	*Solenodon cubanus*	Cuba
Solenodon, Haitian	*Solenodon paradoxus*	Haiti & Dominican
Squirrel, Carolina northern flying	*Galucomys sabrinus coloratus*	USA
Squirrel, Delmarva	*Sciurus niger cinereus*	USA
Squirrel, Mount Graham red	*Tamiasciurus hudsonicus grahamensis*	Arizona
Squirrel, Va. Northern flying	*Glaucomys sabrinus fuscus*	USA
Stag, Barbary	*Cervus elaphus barbarus*	N. Africa
Stag, Kashmir	*Cervus elaphus hanglu*	Kashmir
Suni, Zanzibar	*Neotragus moschatus m.*	Zanzibar
Tahr, Arabian	*Hemitragus jayakari*	Oman
Tamaraw	*Bubalus mindorensis*	Philippines
Tamarin, gold rumped	*Leonpithecus spp.*	Brazil
Tamarin, pied	*Saguinus bicolor*	Brazil
Tapir, Asian	*Tapirus indicus*	SE Asia
Tapir, Central American	*Tapirus bairdii*	C. America
Tapir, mountain	*Tapirus pinchaque*	S. America
Tiger	*Panthera tigris*	Asia
Tiger, Tasmanian	*Thylacinus cynocephalus*	Australia
Uakari	*Cacajao spp.*	S. America
Urial	*Ovis musimon ophion*	Cyprus
Vicuna	*Vicugna vicugna*	S. America
Vole, Amargosa	*Microtus californicus scirpensis*	USA
Vole, Hualapai	*Microtus mexicanus hualpaiensis*	USA
Wallaby, banded hare	*Lasgostrophus fasciatus*	Australia
Wallaby, brindled	*Onychigakea fraenata*	Australia
Wallaby, crescent	*Onychogalea lunata*	Australia
Wallaby, Parma	*Macropus parma*	Australia
Wallaby, west hare	*Lagorchestes hirsutus*	Australia
Wallaby, y.f.rock	*Petrogale xanthopus*	Australia
Whale, blue	*Balaenoptera musculus*	Oceanic
Whale, bowhead	*Balaena mysticetus*	Oceanic

Whale, finback	*Balaenoptera physalus*	Oceanic
Whale, gray	*Eschrichtius robustus*	Oceanic
Whale, humpback	*Megaptera novaeangliae*	Oceanic
Whale, right	*Balaena glacialis*	Oceanic
Whale, Sei	*Balaenoptera borealis*	Oceanic
Whale, sperm	*Physeter catodon*	Oceanic
Wolf, gray	*Canis lupus*	USA, except Alaska
Wolf, maned	*Chrysocyon brachyurus*	S. America
Wolf, red	*Canis rufus*	USA
Wombat, hairy-nosed	*Lasiorhinus krefftii*	Australia
Woodrat, Key Largo	*Neotoma floridana smalli*	Florida
Yak, wild	*Bos grunniens*	N.Asia
Zebra, mountain	*Equus zebra zebra*	S. Africa

Endangered Birds

Akepa, Hawaiian	*Loxops coccineus c.*	Hawaii
Akepa, Maui	*Loxops c. ochraceus*	Hawaii
Akialoa, Kauai	*Hemignathus procerus*	Hawaii
Akiapolaau	*Hemignathus munroi*	Hawaii
Albatross, short tailed	*Diomedea albatrus*	N.Pacific
Blackbird, yellowshoulder	*Agelaius xanthomus*	Puerto Rico
Bobwhite, masked	*Colinus v. ridgewayi*	US & Mexico
Booby, Abbots	*Sula abbotti*	Oceania
Bristlebird, western	*Dasyornis b. longirostris*	Australia
Bristlebird, w. rufous	*Dasyornis b. littoralis*	Australia
Broadbill, Guam	*Myiagra freycineti*	W. Pacific
Bulbul, Mauritius	*Hysipetes b. olivaceous*	Indian Ocean
Bullfinch, Sao Miguel	*Pyrrhula p. murina*	E. Atlantic
Bushwren, New Zealand	*Xenicus longipes*	New Zealand
Bustard, Great Indian	*Choriotis nigriceps*	Asia
Cahow	*Pterodroma cahow*	N. Atlantic
Condor, Andean	*Vultur gryphus*	S. America
Condor, California	*Gymnogyps californianus*	California
Coot, Hawaiian	*Fulica americana alai*	Hawaii
Cotinga, banded	*Cotinga maculata*	Brazil
Cotinga, white-winged	*Xipholena atropurpurea*	Brazil
Crane, black necked	*Grus nigricollis*	Tibet
Crane, Cuba sandhill	*Grus canadensis nesiotes*	Cuba
Crane, hooded	*Grus monacha*	Japan & USSR
Crane, Japanese	*Grus japonensis*	Asia
Crane, Mississippi sandhill	*Grus canadensis pula*	Mississippi
Crane, Siberian white	*Grus leucogeranus*	Asia
Crane, white-naped	*Grus vipio*	Mongolia
Crane, whooping	*Grus americana*	N. America
Creeper, Hawaiian	*Oreomystis mana*	Hawaii
Creeper, Molokai	*Parareomyza flammea*	Hawaii
Creeper, Oahu	*Parareomyza maculata*	Hawaii
Crow, Hawaiian	*Corvus havaiiensis*	Hawaii
Crow, Mariana	*Corvus kubaryi*	W. Pacific
Cuckoo-shrike, Mauritius	*Coquus typicus*	Ind. Ocean

Cuckoo-shrike Reunion	*Coquus newtoni*	Ind. Ocean
Curassow	*Mitu mitu mitu*	Brazil
Curassow, redbilled	*Crax blumenbachii*	Brazil
Curassow, Trinidad	*Pipile pipile p.*	W. Indies
Curlew, Eskimo	*Numenius borealis*	All Americas
Dove, cloven feathered	*Drepanoptila holosericea*	SW Pacific
Dove, Grenada g.f.	*Leptotila rufaxilla wellsi*	W. Indies
Duck, Hawaiian	*Anas wyvilliana*	Hawaii
Duck, Laysan	*Anas laysanensis*	Hawaii
Duck, pinkheaded	*Rhodonessa caryophyllacea*	India
Duck w. winged wood	*Cairina scutulata*	Asia
Eagle, Greenland	*Haliaeetus albicilla g.*	Greenland
Eagle, harpy	*Harpia harpyia*	C.S. America
Eagle, Philippine	*Pithecophaga jefferyi*	Philippines
Eagle, Spanish imperial	*Aquila heliaca adalberti*	Spain, N. Africa
Egret, Chinese	*Egretta eulophotes*	N. Asia
Falcon, A. peregrine	*Falco peregrinus anatum*	N.S. America
Falcon, Eurasian peregrine	*Falco peregrinus p.*	Worldwide
Falcon, northern aplomado	*Falco femoralis septentrionalis*	N. America
Falcon, peregrine	*Falco peregrinus*	Worldwide
Finch, Laysan	*Telespyza cantans*	Hawaii
Finch, Nihoa	*Telespyza ultima*	Hawaii
Flycatcher, Euler's	*Empidonax euleri johnstonei*	W. Indies
Flycatcher, Seychelles	*Terpsiphone corvina*	Indian Ocean
Flycatcher, Tahiti	*Pomarea nigra*	S. Pacific
Fody, Seychelles	*Foudia sechellarum*	Indian Ocean
Frigatebird, Andrews	*Frigata andrewsi*	Indian Ocean
Goose, Aleutian Canada	*Branta c. leucopareia*	N. America
Goose, Nene	*Branta sandvicensis*	Hawaii
Goshawk, Christmas Island	*Accipiter fasciatus natalis*	Ind. Ocean
Grackle, slender billed	*Quisicalus palustris*	Mexico
Grasswren, Eyrean	*Amytornis goyderi*	Australia
Grebe, Atitlan	*Podilymbus gigas*	Guatemala
Greenshank, Nordmann's	*Tringa guttifer*	Asia, Indonesia
Guan, horned	*Oreophasis derbianus*	C. America
Gull, Audouin's	*Lanus audouinii*	Mediterranean
Gull, relict	*Lanus relictus*	India, China
Hawk, Anjouan	*Accipiter francesii pusillus*	Indian Ocean
Hawk, Galapagos	*Buteo galapagoensis*	Galapagos
Hawk, Hawaiian (Io)	*Buteo solitarius*	Hawaii
Hermit, hookbilled	*laucis dohrnii*	Brazil
Honeycreeper, crested	*Palmeria dolei*	Hawaii
Honeyeater, helmeted	*Meliphaga cassidix*	Australia
Hornbill, helmeted	*Rhinoplax vigil*	Indochina
Ibis, Japanese crested	*Nipponia nippon*	Asia
Kagu	*Rhynochetos jubatus*	S. Pacific
Kakapo	*Strigops habroptilus*	New Zealand
Kestrel, Mauritius	*Falco punctatus*	Indian Ocean
Kestrel, Seychelles	*Falco araea*	Indian Ocean
Kingfisher, Guam	*Halcyon c. cinnamomina*	W. Pacific

Kite, Cuba hookbill	*Chondrohierax u. wilsonii*	W. Indies
Kite, Everglade snail	*Rostrhamus sociasbilis plumbeus*	Florida & Cuba
Kite, Granada hookbill	*Chondrohierax u. mirus*	W. Indies
Kokako	*Callaeas cinerea*	New Zealand
Macaw, glaucous	*Anodorhynchus glaucus*	S. America
Macaw, Indigo	*Anodorhynchus leari*	Brazil
Macaw, little blue	*Cyanopsitta spixii*	Brazil
Magpie robin, Seychelles	*Copsychus sechellarum*	Indian Ocean
Malhoka, redfaced	*Phaenicophaeus pyrrhocephalus*	Sri Lanka
Mallard, Mariana	*Anas oustaleti*	W. Pacific
Megapode, Maleo	*Macrocephalon maleo*	Celebes
Megapode, Micronesian	*Megapodius laperouse*	W. Pacific
Millerbird, Nihoa	*Acrocephalus familiaris kingi*	Hawaii
Moorhen, Hawaiian	*Gallinula chloropus sandvicensis*	Hawaii
Moorhen, Mariana	*Gallinula c. guami*	W. Pacific
Nightjar, Puerto Rican	*Caprimulgus noctitherus*	Puerto Rico
Nukupu'u	*Hemignathus lucidus*	Hawaii
'O'o, Kauai	*Moho braccatus*	Hawaii
Ostrich, Arabian	*Struthio camelus syriacus*	Arabia
Ostrich, West African	*Struthio camelus spatzi*	Sp. Sahara
'O'u	*Psittirostra psittacea*	Hawaii
Owl, Anjouan scops	*Otus rutilus capnodes*	Indian Ocean
Owl, giant scops	*Otus gurneyi*	Philippines
Owl, Seychelles	*Otus insularis*	Indian Ocean
Owlet, Morden's	*Otus ireneae*	Kenya
Palila	*Loxioides bailleui*	Hawaii
Parakeet, Forbes	*Cyanoramphus a. forbesi*	New Zealand
Parakeet, golden	*Aratinga guarouba*	Brazil
Parakeet, hooded	*Psephotus chrysopterygius*	Australia
Parakeet, Mauritius	*Psittacula echo*	Indian Ocean
Parakeet, ocher-marked	*Pyrrhura cruentata*	Brazil
Parakeet, orange bellied	*Neophema chrysogaster*	Australia
Parakeet, paradise	*Psephotus pulcherrimus*	Australia
Parakeet, splendid	*Neophema splendida*	Australia
Parakeet, turquoise	*Neophema pulchella*	Australia
Parrot, Australian	*Geopsittacus occidentalis*	Australia
Parrot, Bahamian	*Amazona leucocephala*	W. Indies
Parrot, ground	*Pezoporus wallicus*	Australia
Parrot, Imperial	*Amazona imperialis*	W. Indies
Parrot, Puerto Rican	*Amazona vittata*	Puerto Rico
Parrot, red-browed	*Amazona rhodocorytha*	Brazil
Parrot, red-capped	*Pinopsitta pileata*	Brazil
Parrot, red-necked	*Amazona arausiaca*	W. Indies
Parrot, red-spectacled	*Amazona petrei petrei*	S. America
Parrot, St. Lucia	*Amazona versicolor*	W. Indies
Parrot, St. Vincent	*Amazona guildingii*	W. Indies
Parrot, thickbilled	*Rhynchopsitta pachyrhyncha*	Mexico, USA
Parrot, vinaceous breasted	*Amazona vinacea*	Brazil
Parrotbill, Maui	*Pseudonester xanthophrys*	Hawaii
Pelican, brown	*Pelecanus occidentalis*	SE USA

Penguin, Galapagos	*Spheniscus mendiculus*	Galapagos
Petrel, Hawaii dark-rumped	*Pterodroma phaeopygia s.*	Hawaii
Pheasant, bar-tailed	*Syrmaticus humaie*	Asia
Pheasant, Blyth's	*Tragopan blythii*	Asia
Pheasant, brown-eared	*Crossoptilon mantchuricum*	China
Pheasant, Cabot's	*Tragopan cabotii*	China
Pheasant, Chinese monal	*Lophophorus lhuysii*	China
Pheasant, Edwards	*Lophura edwardsi*	Vietnam
Pheasant, Elliot's	*Syrmaticus ellioti*	China
Pheasant, imperial	*Lophura imperialis*	Vietnam
Pheasant, Mikado	*Syrmaticus mikado*	Taiwan
Pheasant, Palawan	*Polyplectron emphanum*	Philippines
Pheasant, Sciaters monal	*Lophophorus sciateri*	Asia
Pheasant, Swinhoe's	*Lophura swinhoii*	Taiwan
Pheasant, western tragopan	*Tragopan melanocephalus*	Asia
Pheasant, whiteeared	*Crossoptilon crossoptilon*	Asia
Pigeon, Azores wood	*Columba palumbus azorica*	E. Atlantic
Pigeon, Chatham Island	*Hemiphaga novaeseelandiae chathamensis*	N. Zealand
Pigeon, Mindoro	*Ducula mindorensis*	Philippines
Pigeon, Puerto Rican	*Columba inornata wetmorei*	Puerto Rico
Piping-guan	*Pipile jacutinga*	Argentina
Pitta, Koch's	*Pitta kochi*	Philippines
Plover, New Zealand	*Thinornis nmovaeseelandiae*	New Zealand
Plover, piping	*Charadrius melodus*	N. America
Po'ouli	*Melamprosops phaeosoma*	Hawaii
Prairie chicken, Attwaters	*Tympanuchus cupido attwaterii*	Texas
Quail, Montezuma	*Cyrtonyx monrtezumae mearriami*	Mexico
Quetzal, resplendent	*Pharomachrus mocinno*	C. America
Rail, Auckland Island	*Rallus pectoralis muelleri*	N. Zealand
Rail, California clapper	*Rallus longirostris obsoletus*	California
Rail, Guam	*Rallus owstoni*	W. Pacific
Rail, lightfooted	*Rallus l. levipes*	USA, Mexico
Rail, Lord Howe	*Tricholimnas sylvestris*	Australia
Rail, Yuma clapper	*Rallus l. yumanensis*	USA, Mexico
Rhea, Darwin's	*Pterocnemia pennata*	S. America
Robin, Chatham's Island	*Petroica traversi*	New Zealand
Robin, Scarlet-breasted	*Petroica multicolor m.*	Australia
Rockfowl, grey-necked	*Picathartes oreas*	Africa
Rockfowl, white-necked	*Picathartes gymnocephalus*	Africa
Roller, long-tailed	*Uratelornis chimaera*	Malagasy
Scrub-bird, noisy	*Atrichornis clamosus*	Australia
Shama, Cebu black	*Copsychus niger cebuensis*	Philippines
Shrike, San Clemente loggerhead	*Lanius ludovicianus mearnsi*	California
Siskin, red	*Carduelis cucullata*	S. America
Sparrow, Cape Sable	*Ammodramus maritimus mirabilis*	Florida

247

Sparrow, dusky seaside (now considered extinct)	*Ammodramus m. nigrescens*	Florida
Sparrow, Florida grasshopper	*Ammodramus s. floridanus*	Florida
Starling, Ponape Mtn.	*Aplonis petzerlni*	W. Pacific
Starling, Rothschild's	*Leucopsar rothschildii*	Indonesia
Stilt, Hawaiian	*Himantopus m. knudseni*	Hawaii
Stork, Oriental white	*Ciconia c. boyciana*	Eurasia
Stork, wood	*Mycteria americana*	N. & C. America
Swiftlet, Mariana	*Aerodramus v. bartschi*	W. Pacific
Teal, Campbell flightless	*Anas aucklandia nesiotis*	N. Zealand
Tern, California least	*Sterna antillarum browni*	N. America
Tern, least	*Sterna antillarum*	N&S. America
Tern, roseate	*Sterna dougalli d.*	USA-Africa
Thrasher, white-breasted	*Ramphocinclus brachyurus*	W. Indies
Thrush, large Kauai	*Myadestes myadestinus*	Hawaii
Thrush, Molokai	*Myadestes lanaiensis rutha*	Hawaii
Thrush, New Zealand	*Turnagra capensis*	N. Zealand
Thrush, small Kauai	*Myadestes palmeri*	Hawaii
Tinamou, solitary	*Tinamus solitariius*	S. America
Trembler, Martinique	*Cincocerthia ruficauda gutturalis*	W. Indies
Vireo, black-capped	*Vireo atricapillus*	USA
Vireo, least Bell's	*Vireo belli pusillus*	USA
Wanderer, plain	*Pedionomus torquatus*	Australia
Warbler, Bachman's	*Vermivora bachmanii*	USA, Cuba
Warbler, Barbados yellow	*Dendroica petechia p.*	W. Indies
Warbler, Kirtland's	*Dendroica kirtlandii*	Michigan
Warbler, nightingale reed	*Acrocephalus luscinia*	W. Pacific
Warbler, Rodriques	*Bebrornis rodericanus*	Mauritius
Warbler, Semper's	*Leucopeza semperi*	W. Indies
Warbler, Seychelles	*Bebrornis seychellensis*	Indian Ocean
Whipbird, western	*Psophodes nigrogularis*	Australia
White-eye, bridled	*Zosterops conspicillatus c.*	W. Pacific
White-eye, Norfolk	*Zosterops albogularis*	Indian Ocean
White-eye, Ponape	*Rukia longirostra*	W. Pacific
White-eye, Seychelles	*Zosterops modesta*	Seychelles
Woodpecker, imperial	*Campephilus imperialis*	Mexico
Woodpecker, ivory-billed	*Campephilus principalis*	USA & Cuba
Woodpecker, red-cockaded	*Picoides borealis*	SE USA
Woodpecker, Tristam's	*Dryocopus javensi richardsi*	Korea
Wren, Guadalupe house	*Troglodytes aedon guadaloupensis*	W. Indies
Wren, St. Lucia house	*Troglodytes aedon mesoleucus*	W. Indies

Endangered Amphibians

Frog, Israel painted	*Discoglossus nigriventer*	Israel
Frog, Panama golden	*Atelopus varius zeteki*	Panama
Frog, Stephen Island	*Leiopelma hamiltoni*	N. Zealand

Salamander, Chinese giant	*Andreas davidanus d.*	China
Salamander, desert slender	*Batrachoseps aridus*	California
Salamander, Jap. giant	*Andrias d. japonicus*	Japan
Salamander, Santa Cruz	*Ambystoma macrodactylum croceum*	California
Salamander, Texas blind	*Typhlomolge rathbuni*	Texas
Toad, African viviparous	*Nectophrynoides spp.*	Africa
Toad, Cameroon	*Bufo superciliaris*	Africa
Toad, Houston	*Bufo houstonensis*	Texas
Toad, Monte Verde	*Bufo periglenes*	Costa Rica
Toad, Wyoming	*Bufo hemiophrys baxteri*	Wyoming

Endangered Clams

Mussel, Curtus'	*Pleurobema curtum*	USA
Mussel, Judge Tait's	*Pleurobema taitanum*	USA
Mussel, Marshall's	*Pleurobema marshalli*	USA
Mussel, penitent	*Epioblasma penita*	USA
Pearlshell, Louisiana	*Margaritafera hembeli*	Louisiana
Pearly mussel, Alabama	*Lampsilis virescens*	USA
Pearly mussel, Appalachian	*Quadrula sparsa*	USA
Pearly mussel, birdwing	*Conradilla caelata*	USA
Pearly mussel, Cumberland	*Villosa trabalis*	USA
Pearly mussel, C. monkeyface	*Quadrula intermedia*	USA
Pearly mussel, Curtis	*Epioblasma f. curtisi*	Missouri
P. Mussel, dromedary	*Dromus dromas*	USA
P. mussel, green-blossom	*Epioblasma torulosa gubernaculum*	USA
P, mussel, Higgins eye	*Lampsillis higginsi*	USA
P. Mussel, little wing	*Pegias fabula*	USA
P. mussel, Nicklins	*Megalonaias nicklineana*	Mexico
P. mussel, orangefoot	*Plethobasus cooperianus*	USA
P. mussel, pale lilliput	Toxolasma cylindrellus	USA
P. mussel, pink mucket	*Lampsilis orbiculata*	USA
P. mussel, Tampico	*Cyrtonaias tampicoensis tecomatensis*	Mexico
P. Mussel, tubercled	*Epioblasma torulosa t.*	USA
P. mussel, turgid	*Epioblasma turgidula*	USA
P. mussel, cats paw	*E. sulcata delicata*	USA
P. mussel, wartyback	*Plethobasus cicatricosus*	USA
P. mussel, yellow-blossom	*Epioblasma florentina f.*	USA
Pigtoe, fine rayed	*Fusconaia cuneolus*	USA
Pigtoe, rough	*Pleurobema plenum*	USA
Pigtoe, shiny	*Fusconaia edgariana*	USA
Pocketbook, fat	*Potamilus capax*	USA
Rifle shell, tan	*Epioblasma walkeri*	USA

Spinymussel, James River	*Pleurobema collina*	USA
Spinymussel, Tar River	*Elliptio steinstansana*	USA
Stirrup shell	*Quadrula stapes*	USA

Endangered Crustaceans

Amphipod, Hays Springs	*Stygobromus hayi*	USA
Crayfish	*Cambarus zophonastes*	Arkansas
Crayfish, Nashville	*Orconectes shoupi*	Tennessee
Crayfish, Shasta	*Pacifastacus fortis*	California
Isopod, Socorro	*Thermosphaeroma thermophilus*	New Mexico
Shrimp, Alabama cave	*Palaemonias alabamae*	Alabama
Shrimp, California freshwater	*Syncaris pacifica*	California
Shrimp, Kentucky cave	*Paleomonias ganteri*	Kentucky

Endangered Fishes

Ali Balik (trout)	*Salmo platycephalus*	Turkey
Ayumodoki (Loach)	*Hymenophysa curta*	Japan
Blindcat, Mexican	*Prietella phreatophila*	Mexico
Bonytongue, Asian	*Sclaropages formosus*	SE. Asia
Catfish	*Pangasius sanitwongsei*	Thailand
Catfish, giant	*Pangasianodon gigas*	Thailand
Cavefish, Alabama	*Speoplatyrhinus poulsoni*	Alabama
Chub, bonytail	*Gila elegans*	USA
Chub, Borax lake	*Gila boraxobius*	Oregon
Chub, humpback	*Gila cypha*	SW USA
Chub, Mojave tui	*Gila bicolor mohavensis*	California
Chub, Owens tui	*Gila bicolor snyderi*	California
Chub, Pahranagat	*Gila robusta jordani*	Nevada
Chub, Yaqui	*Gila purpurea*	US, Mexico
Cicek (minnow)	*Acanthorutilus handlirschi*	Turkey
Cui-ui	*Chasmistes cujus*	Nevada
Dace, Ash Meadow	*Rhinichthys osculus nevadensis*	Nevada
Dace, Kendall	*Rhinichthys osculus thermalis*	Wyoming
Dace, moapa	*Moapa coriacea*	Nevada
Darter, amber	*Percina antesella*	SE USA
Darter, Elk River	*Etheostoma spp.*	SE USA
Darter, fountain	*Etheostoma fonticola*	Texas
Darter, Maryland	*Etheostoma sellare*	Maryland
Darter, Okaloosa	*Etheostoma okaloosa*	Florida
Darter, watercress	*Etheostoma nuchale*	Alabama
Gambusia, Big Bend	*Gambusia gaigei*	Texas

Gambusia, Clear Creek	*Gambusia heterochir*	Texas
Gambusia, Pecos	*Gambusia nobilis*	NM & Texas
Gambusia, San Marcos	*Gambusia georgei*	Texas
Killifish, Pahrump	*Empetrichthys latos*	Nevada
Logperch, Conasauga	*Percina jenkinsi*	SE USA
Madtom, Scioto	*Noturus trautmani*	Ohio
Madtom, Smoky	*Noturus baileyi*	Tennessee
Minnow, loach	*Tiaroga cobitis*	USA & Mexico
Nekogigi (catfish)	*Coreobagrus ichikawai*	Japan
Pupfish, Ash Meadows	*Cyprinodon nevadensis mionectes*	Nevada
Pupfish, Comanche Springs	*Cyprinodon elegans*	Texas
Pupfish, desert	*Cyprinodon macularius*	US & Mexico
Pupfish, Devils Hole	*Cyprinodon diabolis*	Nevada
Pupfish, Owens	*Cyprinodon radiosis*	California
Shiner, Cape Fear	*Notropis mekistocholas*	N. Carolina
Spinedace, White River	*Lepidomeda albivallis*	Nevada
Springfish, Hiko W.	*Crenichthys baileyi grandis*	Nevada
Springfish, White River	*Crenichthys baileyi b.*	Nevada
Squawfish, Colorado	*Ptychocheilus lucius*	SW USA
Stickleback, 3 spine	*Gasterosteus aculeatus williamsoni*	California
Sturgeon, shortnose	*Acipenser brevirostrum*	North America
Sucker, June	*Chasmistes liorus*	Utah
Sucker, Lost River	*Deltistes luxatus*	W. USA
Sucker, Modoc	*Catostomus microps*	California
Sucker, shortnose	*Chasmistes brevirostris*	W. USA
Tango, Miyako	*Tanakia tanago*	Japan
Temolek, Ikan	*Probarbus jullieri*	SE Asia
Topminnow, Gila	*Poeciliopsis occidentalis*	USA, Mexico
Totoaba	*Cynoscion macdonaldi*	Mexico
Trout, Gila	*Salmo gilae*	AZ & NM
Woundfin	*Plagopterus argentissimus*	SW USA

Endangered Reptiles

Alligator, Chinese	*Alligator sinensis*	China
Anole, Culebra giant	*Anolis roosevelti*	Puerto Rico
Boa, Jamaican	*Epicrates subflavus*	Jamaica
Boa, Puerto Rico	*Epicrates inornatus*	Puerto Rico
Boa, Round Island	*Casarea dussumieri*	Indian Ocean
Boa, Round Island (2)	*Bolyeria multocarinata*	Indian Ocean
Boa, Virgin Islands tree	*Epicrates monensis granti*	Virgin Islands
Caiman, Apaporis River	*Caiman crocodilensis apaporiensis*	Colombia
Caiman, black	*Melanosuchus niger*	S. America
Caiman, broad-snouted	*Caiman latirostris*	S. America
Caiman, Yacare	*Caiman crocodilus yacare*	S. America
Chuckwalla, San Esteban	*Sauromalus varius*	Mexico

251

Crocodile, African dwarf	*Osteolaemus tetraspis t.*	W. Africa
Crocodile, slender-snouted	*Crocodylus cataphractus*	Africa
Crocodile, American	*Crocodylus acutus*	USA & Central America
Crocodile, Ceylon mugger	*Crocodylus palustris kimbula*	Sri Lanka
Crocodile, Congo dwarf	*Osteolaemus tetraspis osborni*	Africa
Crocodile, Cuban	*Crocodylus rhombifer*	Cuba
Crocodile, Morelet's	*Crocodylus moreletii*	C. America
Crocodile, mugger	*Crocodylus palustris p.*	Asia
Crocodile, Nile	*Crocodylus niloticus*	Africa
Crocodile, Orinoco	*Crocodylus intermedius*	S. America
Crocodile, Philippine	*Crocodylus n. mindorensis*	Philippines
Crocodile, saltwater	*Crocodylus porosus*	Australia & S.E. Asia & Islands
Crocodile, Siamese	*Crocodylus siamensis*	SE Asia
Gavial	*Gavialis gangeticus*	C. Asia
Gecko, day	*Phelsuma edwardnewtoni*	Indian Ocean
Gecko, Monito	*Sphaerodactylus micropithecus*	Puerto Rico
Gecko, Rd Island	*Phelsuma guentheri*	Indian Ocean
Iguana, Anegada ground	*Cyclura pinguis*	W. Indies
Iguana, Barrington	*Conolophus pallidus*	Galapagos
Iguana, Fiji banded	*Brachylophus fasciatus*	Pacific Island
Iguana, Fiji crested	*Brachylophus vitiensis*	Fiji, Tonga
Iguana, Grand Cayman	*Cyclura nubila lewisii*	W. Indies
Iguana, Jamaican	*Cyclura collei*	W. Indies
Iguana, Watling Island	*Cyclura rileyi r.*	W. Indies
Lizard, blunt-nosed	*Gambelia silus*	California
Lizard, Hierro giant	*Gallotia simonyi s.*	Canary Isl.
Lizard, St. Croix ground	*Ameiva polops*	Virgin Isl.
Monitor, Bengal	*Varanus bengalensis*	Asia
Monitor, desert	*Varanus griseus*	Africa, Asia
Monitor, Komodo	*Varanus komodoensis*	Indonesia
Monitor, yellow	*Varanus flavescens*	Asia
Python, Indian	*Python molorus m.*	India, Ceylon
Snake, S. Frisco garter	*Thamnophis sirtalis tetrataenia*	California
Tartaruga	*Podocnemis expansa*	S. America
Terrapin, river	*Batagur baska*	S.E. Asia
Tomistoma	*Tomistoma schlegelii*	Indonesia Malaysia
Tortoise, angulated	*Geochelone yniphora*	Malagasy
Tortoise, Bolson	*Gopherus flavomarginatus*	Mexico
Tortoise, Galapagos	*Geochelone elephantopus*	Galapagos
Tortoise, radiated	*Geochelone radiata*	Malagasy
Tracaja	*Podocnemis unifilis*	S. America
Tuatara	*Sphenodon punctatus*	N. Zealand
Turtle, Alabama red-bellied	*Pseudemys alabamensis*	Alabama
Turtle, aquatic box	*Terrapin coahuila*	Mexico
Turtle, black softshell	*Trionyx nigricans*	Bangladesh
Turtle, Burmese peacock	*Morenia ocellata*	Burma

Turtle, C. America river	*Dermatemys mawii*	C. America
Turtle, Cuatro Cienegas	*Trionyx ater*	Mexico
Turtle, geometric	*Psammobates geometrica*	S. Africa
Turtle, hawksbill sea	*Eretmochelys imbricata*	Tropic seas
Turtle, Indian sawback	*Kachuga tecta tecta*	India
Turtle, Indian softshell	*Trionyx gangeticus*	India
Turtle, Kemp's Ridley	*Lepidochelys kempii*	Tropic seas
Turtle, leatherback sea	*Dermochelys coriacea*	Tropic seas
Turtle, peacock softshell	*Trionyx hurum*	India
Turtle, Plymouth	*Pseudemys rubriventris bangsi*	USA
Turtle, shortnecked	*Pseudemydura umbrina*	Australia
Turtle, spotted pond	*Geoclemys hamiltonii*	India
Turtle, Asian 3-keeled	*Melanochelys tricarnata*	India
Viper, Lar Valley	*Vipera latifii*	Iran

Index